*Also by Erna Fergusson*

CHILE

DANCING GODS

FIESTA IN MEXICO

GUATEMALA

OUR HAWAII

OUR SOUTHWEST

VENEZUELA

*These are Borzoi Books, published by*

ALFRED A. KNOPF

# CUBA

# CUBÁ

BY

# ERNA FERGUSSON

*NEW YORK: ALFRED · A · KNOPF*

1946

# ACKNOWLEDGMENTS

THIS BOOK could not have been written without the aid and advice of many people. Most of those who helped me have been mentioned in the text. Others I wish to thank here.

The Cuban Tourist Commission was most generous with time, travel information, and especially its excellent collection of pictures, from which came many of the illustrations I have used.

The University of New Mexico Library gave me access to all the books I needed, wherever they were. I am grateful for personal interest and assistance to its librarian, Arthur M. McAnally, and Ruth Russell and Susan F. Horn, research librarians.

Certain chapters have been read and commented on by Hubert Herring of Claremont College; Dr. Miguel Jorrín of the University of New Mexico and his wife, Tessie Kent de Jorrín, both Cubans whose quick eyes and humorous response saved me from many a stupid blunder. Dr. Fernando Ortiz of the University of Havana gave me time to talk as well as to read my efforts, and Dr. Dorothy Woodward of the University of New Mexico checked my history.

I also thank Patricia Antoine for her steadiness, skill, and good humor in preparing the manuscript.

ERNA FERGUSSON

# CONTENTS

✿

*vii*

# CONTENTS

# ILLUSTRATIONS

*ix*

# CUBA

## I

# CUBA, THE KEY

WE OF THE UNITED STATES ARE LIKELY TO THINK WE know all about Cuba. We fought a war there; we remember the *Maine*, Hobson's exploit with the *Merrimac*, the message to García, and something about yellow fever. We know also that Cuba sends us sugar and its more convivial product, rum, Havana cigars, the conga, nightclub singers, at least one movie star — Cesar Romero — and several baseball stars. Moreover, hundreds of us have spent a day or several days in Havana.

Thousands of travelers know the wonder of slipping into Havana's close-mouthed harbor in the dawn, passing El Morro Castle which squats on the long peninsula, merging into La Cabana Fortress, and reminding them of the might of imperial Spain. Americans also recollect that there the *Maine* went down. The sea smell is fresh, but one gets too the sense of rich tropical earth from the thick-growing shade trees along the Prado, and behind and above the city's buildings are green and gracious hills where tall royal palms fly their feathery tops like the Caribbean's special wind-socks. As the steamer docks, the scent of sea salt yields to all the fascinating port smells — fish and tar, rotting fruits, aromatic tobacco, and coffee roasting or steaming in the pot. Port

noises in Havana are more deafening than anywhere else. Men
and boys yell, whistles shrill, cars honk, carts jingle their bells,
ells, *and* horns.
trength of arm
strangeness is
m. Sun so bright that it ca. ill iron-barred
buildings, ink-black on pale gray pavements, ets so narrow
that a car barely squeezes through, wide doorways into green
patios, and a chauffeur — always! — who insists upon taking
you away from all that and out to see the Country Club, the modern homes in El Vedado, and the fine new tourist hotels.

The one-day visitor can hardly expect to cope with the chauffeur. He understands or does not understand English as the case
demands. Either go afoot, poking into the narrowest streets, pause
where enterprising housewives have set dolls' cups on their win-
dowsills, and pay a penny to sip the pure essence of coffee;
stumble into patios of perfect proportions where balconies, stairways, and windows all float laundry, spill children, or resound to
the screams, roars, and bellows of ordinary Cuban communication; lunch in a restaurant open to the street where Cubans come
because the shell fish is good and cheap; attend a popular theater;
buy lottery tickets; and cross the bay in a launch for a nickel and
get a sense of the rest of Cuba — either that or go the tourist way
with the chauffeur.

Any chauffeur, having caught his tourist, will pass the Capitol,
which is much like ours, and drive the length of the Prado with a
turn around to show the President's Palace and the twelve-story
apartment house that President Batista built out of his savings.
He will take you the length of the beautiful Malecón, the embank-
ment that General Wood built against the tossing spray from the
blue-green Caribbean, past stately houses of the last century, and
out to the Vedado, where modern Cubans of wealth have taken to
the hills. Out there Havana is a typical modern tropical city with
wide avenues, gardens glowing with hibiscus (which the Cubans

*4*

call *mar pacífico*), scented with gardenias and roses, arbored with wisteria and bougainvillea. The visitor with cards will play tennis at the Country Club, swim at the Yacht Club, visit the women's smart Lyceum. All tourists will be regaled with a Bacardí cocktail in the ornate Maxfield Parrish Bacardí Building, where *daiquirís* are not mentioned. But *daiquirís* may be ordered at the equally hospitable fine old colonial building on the Cathedral Plaza, where Havana Rum is offered gratis.

The usual tourist day includes shopping. Cuba has no handicraft, but one can lay in a supply of rum and cigars, and there are curios in leather, tortoise-shell, or gourd. "Buy Cuban *matraca;* he will carve your name right on it." French lingerie, silks, and perfumes have been cheaper than at home, though shops on the Prado know New York prices. There are antiques from very good to very bad. One plays the races or plunges at El Casino after dining well and watching a nightclub adaptation of Afro-Cuban dances, and — inevitably — buys a drink at Sloppy Joe's. Many travelers have been able to boast, back home in Podunk, of meeting Spain's Don Alfonso there. "Perhaps the next king of Spain!" The Prince married a couple of Cuban girls — in turn, of course — and he was often found at Sloppy Joe's, graciously willing to accept presentations. If a commercial transaction was involved that was not mentioned in Podunk. So the vacationer, whatever his taste, finds plenty to do in Havana.

Even more traveled or longer lingerers are apt to accept Havana as just another Latin American capital. First impressions are so familiar. Not choosing the tourist hotels out the Malecón or the noisy ones full of refugees on the Plaza de Armas, I was luckily guided to the Hotel Packard. The proprietor was more interested in Packard cars and politics than in his hotel, but the Señora managed an excellent house where I was comfortable and at home. Little noise, as no buses or streetcars passed. A view across the Fortress, where Cuba's navy drilled in the early morning, and toward El Morro with its one-star Cuban flag by day, and by night the beacon that commands the Florida Straits. Until almost daybreak its flashes competed with motor headlights, for Havana never goes to bed. When the light died at dawn, the cold early day revealed the night's derelicts asleep on park benches or waiting shiveringly for the sun. They used to shelter against the monument that honors eight young students viciously assassinated in 1871 at the Spanish Governor's order, or against the cell where Cuba's idolized José Martí was imprisoned at the age of sixteen because he too dreamed of a free Cuba. Street noises began very early. Newsboys and bootblacks shouted and vendors with pushcarts or baskets on their heads cried their fish or flowers in chants as rhythmical as rhymed verse.

| | |
|---|---|
| *Galleticas de María* | Get your crackers! |
| *Medio paquete* | Half a package |
| *Medio paquete* | Half a package |
| *Son de María* | Mary made 'em |
| *Las galleticas!* | These fine crackers! |

| | |
|---|---|
| *Zapatero, zapatero* | Shoeman, shoeman |
| *Yo compongo sus zapatos.* | I fix shoes |
| *Me los llevo* | I take 'em |
| *Se los traigo* | I send 'em back |
| *Por poquísimo dinero* | For jus' a little cash |
| *Zapa — te — ro!* | Shoe — man! |

My hotel served no meals, but Pedro, the male chambermaid, brought orange juice, rolls, and coffee; and he and all the others guided and advised me. The elevator man spoke with a Castilian accent and was generally upstage about Cubans. "A boy is asking for you." The bellhop spoke Cuba's special dialect and taught me the most useful words and phrases, which appear in no dictionary. He fetched beer or Coca Cola to regale my guests on the flat roof where it was delightful to sit and watch the sunset spread out into one spectrum in the sky and another on the wavering sea. Below, in the laurels on the Prado, the *gorriones,* those fussy little black birds, kept up a noisy chatter until night shut them down.

All downtown Havana reminds one of other American cities where history has been caught in stone and some of the finest houses have descended in the social scale from palace to tenement. Balconied buildings opening into patios are closed at night with iron bars or shutters, and many have burst open into shop windows that display radios, sport goods, clothes, and food exposed to dust and flies. Beggars huddle in doorways, asking alms with "for the love of God" and whining their thanks with "may God repay you!" Those above begging sell lottery tickets, wearing big placards with numbers a foot high: no Cuban is too illiterate to read numbers. One could buy chances ten times within a block. Sidewalks, one to three feet wide, are jammed not only with vendors and walkers but with talkers who know no better place for long gesticulative discussions, impeding traffic but affable enough when petitioned for gangway.

Havana shows no trace of Indian blood. In respect to its Negro population it is very like Washington; the general effect seems about the same. Colored people are everywhere, and color varies from coal black to very white with certain African features that only a professional Southerner could — or would bother to — recognize. In both cities one sees many well-dressed, well-mannered professional or clerical colored people who occupy government posts, and many in private employ. There as here too many remain in the lower reaches, live in the worst slums, produce the most problem children. In Cuba, as in most parts of the United States, colored children attend the public schools and a few advance as far as the University, where they do very well. There is a color line in Cuba, but it follows social rather than political lines; it notably lacks the sadism that bitter economic struggle has caused in our South. Individuals are free to be seen with colored people in public places; restaurants and theaters do not refuse them admission unless they are pandering to Northern prejudice. In such cases they often operate as clubs. But I saw a beautiful *mulata* at a symphony concert in a group of white people; men and women of all shades of skin as well as opinion appear at political, civic, and cultural meetings. Altogether one finds in Cuba an attitude both kind and sensible in the face of an incontrovertible fact.

So many familiar incongruities lull one easily into the sense that this is all well-known. But don't set out expecting to stroll through another slow-motion Latin city! On any downtown street the unwary will surely be knocked about by quick-moving folk, for the Cubans are as fast-stepping as New Yorkers. Both men and women dress casually; men in tweeds, women in sports clothes, often hatless, gloveless, stockingless. Unlike other Latin American women, Cubans seldom wear mourning, so the streets are full of color as well as noise. People hail each other with informal friendliness; one seldom sees the *abrazo*, even the handshake is rare. And they talk faster, surely, than any people on earth. Conversation shoots out of them in an uninterrupted spate of words like the chatter of a machinegun. They interrupt each other, talk against each other, both going at once, rising to crescendos that sound like a very fury of anger, gesticulating until one expects them to knock each other's glasses off; leap aside for traffic without pause; dash, still vociferating, for streetcars or buses that clang by at fire-engine speed, daring the leaping passenger to make the step if he can.

Cubans not only talk fast; they have telescoped Spanish into a sort of shorthand speech with all the consonants left out, and they make it more difficult as well as more interesting by hundreds of slangy shortcuts that can be understood only in the light of the prevailing jokes. And Cuban jokes, above all, are too swift for most foreigners. No, in spite of the look of the city and the claims of the advertising folders, Cubans are not the soft-spoken, slow-moving Latins of our dreams. They are quick — quick of speech and step, quick of apprehension, quick to see or make or take a joke, quick to anger or resent, quick to make a deal.

Even the most incurious visitor might wonder how all this has come about. Why are these Cubans like us in so many ways? Why is their country so different from ours? What are they to us? And why?

First, geography. In physical position Cuba is closer to us than any other Latin neighbor, even Mexico. Cuba is just an hour by plane from Florida; New York and Havana are so near that Cubans run up for shopping or to summer in northern resorts; we dash over there for a warming winter cruise or to replenish the stock in the cellar. And Cuba is important to us. It always has been, since our colonial days; it is now; and so far as man's prophetic eye can see it always will be. Because of its position, Cuba commands the entrance to both the Caribbean and the Gulf of Mexico. That is why so many of us have spent a day ashore in Havana. Whenever you are going southward, east coast or west coast of South America, your ship will put in at Havana. It is arguable also that Cuba is one key at least to our relationships with other Latin American countries. Our dealings with Cuba are under the closest and not always the friendliest scrutiny. Little Cuba is like the smallest member of a family, who may be disregarded but who is underrated only at one's peril.

Cuba has been called — by Columbus — the fairest land ever seen by human eyes; by Spain, the "Pearl of the Antilles," and later, but mistakenly, the "Ever-Faithful Isle." Cubans like to call their country a *caimán*, and its shape does suggest an alligator with a long tail flipping impudently at Florida and forming both the Florida and Yucatán Channels. No shipping passes there without being sighted by Cuba's lighthouses. Who can count on friendly inspection is safe enough; no American country would risk those promontories in enemy hands. Eastward the alligator pokes a monstrous snout toward Haiti, and so dominates the Windward Passage, which was Spain's best approach to the Caribbean. Cuba's own sense of her strategic importance is plainly set forth on her coat of arms, which, with her royal palms, victory wreath, and liberty cap, shows a powerful key closing the approaches to the setting sun.

Not only her situation but her form has given Cuba key importance. Although the largest of the Caribbean islands, Cuba is only 750 miles long and never more than 125 miles wide; but her landlocked harbors (called *bolsa*, bag, by the Spaniards) have given her another title: "The island of a hundred harbors." Spain found them useful throughout her four hundred years in America; they serve the modern American states as well today, for many of them can take the largest ships afloat. Soon after the discovery, these harbors were busy outfitting expeditions for the west and south and repairing and revictualing the convoys laden with fabulous wealth for Spain. Cuba did not appeal to Spaniards as a place to stay: little gold and no Indians such as were found in the Aztec and Incan empires already enslaved and inured to work.

Cuba is the only Latin American country in which the North American is not reminded that we killed off all our Indians. All other Americans resolutely refuse to accept the fact that there are more than half as many Indians in the United States now as before the discovery, and that they are rapidly increasing. In Cuba the subject is never brought up because the natives Columbus described had disappeared within twenty-five years of his landing. The Cuban historian Herminio Portell-Vilá says that the fierce Caribs were about to conquer all the Antilles by their own system of island-hopping. If they had succeeded, Spain might have had to subdue an island empire as strong as those in Mexico and Peru. But the conquerors found Cuba's original Ciboneys and Tainos still free except for occasional Carib raids, living happily on fruits and fish, garbed in leaves, and blowing aromatic smoke through their nostrils. They were hospitable, but both firm and resourceful in their refusal to work. They hanged, drowned, or starved themselves; women cut their rapers' throats and their own; children were strangled at birth. In the 1500's, they were finally finished off by an epidemic.

So the Spaniards were on their way. Everything had worked together to make Cuba not an end but a means: a steppingstone to lands where wealth was easier to accumulate and where Indians could be handed Christianity and peonage in the same package. This makes Cuban history endlessly fascinating because we meet there so many figures important in the histories of other lands, including our own.

*Hernán Cortés,* the conqueror of Mexico, was mayor of Santiago, and there he wed and from there he sailed off for Mexico in defiance of Governor Velázquez's orders to stop. In Mexico he was to meet the peerless Indian maid, Malinche, who made him forget the wife in Cuba until she came posting after. In Cuba, Cortés enlisted Bernal Díaz del Castillo, who was to write the classic story of the conquest of Mexico. Like so many, Díaz left a comfortable home in Cuba to go soldiering.

*Bartolomé de las Casas,* the Dominican who made his fame and gave Spain's enemies their best propaganda against her colonial system, held an *encomienda* in Cuba. So he knew at first hand the evils of apportioning human beings to work for other human beings, even in exchange for religious instruction. Revolted by the system, Las Casas surrendered his lands and devoted the rest of his life to making inflammatory reports to the Council of the Indies. He was largely responsible for the benign Laws of the Indies and for the Papal Bull of 1512, which formally declared that Indians were human and had souls.

*Juan Ponce de León* was in Cuba in 1513 when its conqueror, Diego de Velázquez, was rapidly crossing the island, dividing the lands among Spaniards, and founding towns. Spain was insisting upon permanent settlements and Velázquez did his best; he established seven cities, *Las Siete Villas,* erecting a church and a government house and encouraging citizens to build stone houses instead of inflammable straw huts. But Cuba was full of rumors of wealth farther west, and men were restless. Ponce de León, hearing of Bimini, our Florida, got royal permission to discover and settle there. Any place might prove to be *El Dorado*, and Bimini had the added lure of a fountain that would cure anything, even old age. Instead of finding the Fountain of Youth, as we all learned in the eighth grade, Ponce de León was wounded by an arrow in Florida and returned to Cuba to die. But he had taken Florida for Spain, and that fact was to have great importance in United States history.

*Álvar Núñez Cabeza de Vaca*, more impressed with the possibilities than with the dangers, signed up in 1527 with Pánfilo de Narváez, who was recruiting an expedition to dominate those Indians in Florida, whether he found the Fountain of Youth or not. But his ships were wrecked in a Gulf storm and hundreds of his original six hundred were killed by Indians or disease. Finally only four were left; young Álvar Núñez, two other white men, and Estevanico, a black Moor who was probably the first Negro to see our country. He saw a good deal of it for he and Cabeza de Vaca crossed the continent in an epic walk from eastern Texas to the west coast of Mexico.

*Hernando de Soto*, explorer of the Mississippi, was buried beneath its muddy flood, but he gave Spain command of the Mississippi Delta; that fact colored our diplomacy for years. He was also a spectacular Spaniard and typical of Spain's sixteenth century. Born in Estremadura where they bred conquerors, De Soto had served in Darién and with Pizarro in Peru before he returned to Spain, famous and rich. There he married Isabel, daughter of a powerful courtier. When Cabeza de Vaca returned from Mexico with his tale of all that country just waiting to be conquered, De Soto begged royal permission to go and colonize. The King at once joined Cuba and Florida, appointed De Soto administrator of both, and sent him off with the royal blessing but at his own expense. The new governor of Cuba was received with extravagant splendor in Santiago, then still the capital city, and soon started westward, ostensibly to visit all the towns Velázquez had founded. But his heart was in Florida. He paused only long enough to enlist the richest and most important men, collect the best horses on the island, and set up headquarters in Havana. That town, founded in 1514 on the southern coast where Batabanó now is, had only recently moved to its present site when De Soto honored it in 1538, and was still rebuilding after a disastrous fire.

De Soto encouraged some functional building, and when he sailed for Florida in 1540 he left his wife, the Lady Isabel, in La Fuerza, which *habaneros* claim is the oldest occupied building in the Western Hemisphere. It now houses the National Library, and they say the ramparts one walks are the very ones where Isabel paced anxiously for three years until they finally brought her word that her beloved had died and been buried in a great river. Spain thus commanded the mouth of our great waterway from the center of the continent to the Gulf of Mexico. And Cuba was the key to "the two Floridas."

Spain was not alone in appreciating the strategic value of Cuba. During the frequent European wars, Spain's enemies coveted the island and used its facilities without permission or thanks. Pirates found many unfortified harbors where they could rest and replenish their food stocks with stolen cattle and native fruits, and from which they could harry the regular trade lanes. The Isle of Pines, that oysterish island with a rudimentary tail, which is Cuba's only considerable island, still flashes the first beacon raised by ships eastbound from Honduras, Yucatán, or Panama. The Spanish government paid little attention to the Isle of Pines, but pirates — and later smugglers — found its mangrove swamps and hidden coves highly useful. Robert Louis Stevenson described it so accurately in *Treasure Island* that explorers say they can locate every spot young Jim described; and modern yachtsmen still cruise along its shores with cryptic charts and faded letters. Sometimes they dig up an iron chest full of doubloons and pieces of eight.

Europe's interest in Cuba made the island interesting to the United States too. Long before our country's emergence as a nation, as early as 1630, there was a respectable colonial trade with Cuba. Grain, pork, fish, leather, corn, and lumber were exchanged for cotton, sugar, tobacco, indigo, and silver. A trade not so respectable soon developed, when the clipper ships began taking New England rum to Africa in exchange for manacled Negroes, whom they sold as slaves in the West Indies, where they bought sugar and molasses to take home for the manufacture of more rum. So they squared the circle. How they squared their New England consciences history does not relate, for the trade was not approved by either Spain or England, and its smooth operation required the greasing of many palms about the docks and in the customs.

In 1739 Admiral Vernon of the British Navy attacked the Spanish colonies; among his thirty-six hundred colonials was Lawrence Washington, who suggested that his brother George name his new estate on the Potomac for the British commander. Mt. Vernon it was, and is. In 1762 there were colonials in the British army that captured Havana and held it for a year. So when the United States came into being its nationals already knew the sea lane to Cuba.

As the vigorous young republic expanded westward, it opened up a new route to the south via the rivers that led into the Mississippi and so to the sea. Chester Lloyd Jones estimated that in 1801, 58.3 per cent of all United States exports went south, 19 per cent of them to the Spanish West Indies. But the mouth of the Mississippi was controlled by France and Spain, and Spain's two colonies of Florida and Cuba were too close for comfort. Thomas Jefferson, who believed that the United States would need the continent to grow in, bought Louisiana, which turned out to include Oregon, in 1803; and in 1819 the United States acquired the two Floridas; the peninsula and a 150-mile stretch of territory reaching as far west as the Mississippi.

At this time the United States developed the policy that was to color our diplomacy for the entire century. The Monroe Doctrine, formulated in 1823, assured that no Spanish colonies that had freed themselves would ever be retaken by Spain or captured by another foreign power. As to Cuba, in 1827 the United States minister in Spain said: "The island must in no event pass into the possession of or under the protection of any European power other than Spain." Spain was feeble then and failing fast; we had nothing to fear there. But we were taking no chances on having England, France, or Germany control an island that might become a gun pointed at our vitals rather than a key for our uses. England and France, both with possessions in the West Indies, were equally eager to see Spain keep Cuba; they distrusted us as we did them, and for the same reasons. Little Cuba was rather like a fragile heroine of legend, surrounded by brigands who were protecting her from each other. But the island remained a key too.

With the annexation of Texas, the Mexican War, and the acquisition of the whole Southwest, our frontier was pushing into Spain's empire. The gold rush made Panama and Nicaragua important routes to California as gold seekers crossed their mountain trails on horseback, in litters, or afoot. Many of them stepped ashore in Cuba; the idea of annexing that handily placed isle took root. So the key began to figure in our internal politics as well as in our diplomacy. Southern pro-slavery expansionists advocated the purchase of Cuba whose one-crop, slave economy made them hope for another slave state. Many Cubans, irked by Spanish rule and fearful of abolition by international agreement, liked the idea too. During the Civil War, Cuban planters generally favored the Confederacy. The North would have found it easier to maintain the blockade if Confederate ships had not found haven in Cuban ports. Control of Cuba was proved essential if the United States was to control its own coasts.

This created a delicate diplomatic situation for the last third of the nineteenth century. Nobody in power cared to contemplate the addition of any more territory with its twin headaches of post-slavery phobias and illiterate freedmen. So friendship with Spain became the official attitude, and the United Sates government enforced the neutrality laws that prevented shipment of arms and munitions to the rebels in Cuba. Meanwhile, Cubans maintained active revolutionary juntas in cities from New York to New Orleans, and many American hotheads enlisted in expeditionary forces while cooler persons made fortunes out of equipping ships and selling guns. The United States, classic example of a country that had won its freedom from European domination, appeared in the role of an unfeeling great power preventing a weaker neighbor from doing likewise.

The end of the nineteenth century saw the beginning of an era that gave a different importance to Cuba. As the United States, geographically rounded out, developed its industry and commerce, it began to export more manufactured than raw materials. This meant that we were importing from the other Americas more and more food stuffs and an important share of our raw materials. So we had a growing interest in the internal affairs of countries to the south. Business demanded stability, and many of our neighbors could not maintain the internal peace that made for stability. In this light, which I have seen in Chester Lloyd Jones's *Caribbean Interests of the United States*, the Spanish-American War was not a break with tradition, but a continuation of it. It is true that the yellow press stirred up popular opinion by lurid accounts of Spanish General Weyler's concentration camps in Cuba. But the maintenance of peace was a large part of our concern.

Cuba, the Spanish colony, had played a role in forming our policy toward Europe; Cuba, the Republic, was no less vital to us. Because of the Panama Canal and our expanding interests in all the Americas, an unfriendly nation in command of the entrance to the Caribbean was, and is, unthinkable. This was well understood by our peacemakers at the end of the Spanish-American War when the United States demanded from Cuba control of Guantánamo Bay. There we have some of our most important naval and air bases, which keep an eye on Caribbean shipping — and submarine — lanes.

In time we learned that all attacks would not come from the sea. Both Imperial Germany and the Nazi Reich found insidious and partially successful ways of attacking us through propaganda. In World War I, Cuba declared war against Germany the day after the United States did. There was no doubt that the Cuban government and most Cubans favored the Allies, but Germans in Cuba — as in most Latin American countries — enjoyed great prestige. Everywhere they quickly master the language, show appreciation of the culture, integrate themselves fully into the social and business life of the country. In Cuba, as elsewhere, certain important newspapers had supported the Central Powers; and business houses, diplomats, and individual Germans had great influence among their customers and relatives, for many Germans had married Cubans, many Cubans had been educated in Germany. The Cuban government quickly blacklisted firms suspected of favoring the Central Powers and interned their sympathizers. But the episode served as a sharp reminder that so near a neighbor in so strategic a position must harbor no enemies of the United States.

Nazi Germany offered another problem, for the Nazis worked through Spain to invoke the strong Spanish sympathies of the Catholic Church in Cuba. *Hispanidad* was the word. Franco's announced platform for the Americas was: "One race, one culture, one language, one religion." This policy, with its strong racial content, seems shortsighted for a continent so largely populated by dark-skinned people; but it had potent snob and religious appeal, and it played on the capitalists' fear of Communism. Many Spaniards resident in Cuba had large agricultural and industrial holdings in Spain; even the Church in Cuba owned tenements

*17*

and orange groves in the mother country. Such people saw no advantage in a Republican Spain that promised higher wages and an improved standard of living. And fascists in Latin America never fail to stir up the latent hatred and distrust of the United States; anti-imperialism could alternate with fear of "New Deal Communism."

According to Allan Chase's well-documented *Falange*, Cuba was the center of Franco's Falange Española Tradicionalista, which was organized throughout the Spanish-speaking world. Havana's oldest and most conservative newspaper, *Diario de la Marina*, was the Falange's organ in Cuba, as it had been spokesman for Spain and against the revolutionists from the date of its founding in 1832. It had committed the unforgivable sin of denouncing José Martí as a foolish dreamer, the two great Cuban generals, Máximo Gómez and Antonio Maceo, as bandits. In 1919 it impugned the motives of the United States in declaring war against Germany in an editorial, "Gold, Gold, Gold," which brought a sharp protest from our Department of State. During Mussolini's rise to power, *El Diario* supported him as a bulwark against Communism, and when Franco invaded Spain with his African troops José Rivero, the papers' owner and editor, came out for him in both print and speech.

"Pepín" Rivero was soon joined by other businessmen, Spanish nationals, clergymen, and devout Catholics who believed that Franco was favored by the Pope. In 1936 Havana's aristocratic group formed the Comité Nacionalista Española de Cuba, which celebrated *hispanidad* at sumptuous banquets where were displayed Nazi, fascist, and Falange flags, and raised hundreds of thousands of dollars to send to Franco's aid in Spain. Other organizations followed. Mr. Chase offers convincing proof that they were directed from the Spanish Legation, which controlled the spy network for all the Americas from Canada to Chile and Argentina, and that many of the thirty thousand *falangistas* in Cuba had enlisted in a secret army and were learning the manual of arms. Six thousand Nazis were also said to be under military orders in Cuba.

In 1939 Cuba followed Washington's lead in recognizing Franco, but at the same time the government cracked down on the most flagrant of the pro-Axis organizations, arrested many leaders, and forbade the publication of all shipping news that might be of value to the enemy. It is significant that the labor paper, *Hoy*, and the liberal and anti-Axis papers, *El Mundo* and *El País*, now have a larger circulation than the venerable and socially correct *Diario de la Marina*. Mr. Chase believes that the Falange has only gone underground to bide its time and offer secret masses for the restoration of King and Church. But it seems likely that Cuba in the future, as in the past, has too keen a sense of its Americanism, too urgent a need for independence to fall into any trap, even one so attractively baited with Spanish culture and the Catholic Church.

Now that Americanism has come to mean a union of all American nations and not a dominant state protecting weaker states from European aggression, Cuba has taken on a new significance as a key. What we do in Cuba, our nearest and in many ways our most dependent neighbor, is jealously watched by all other American nations. Granting that our activities in Cuba have been justified by the need to protect not only the United States but all America from Europe, the sad fact is that our country has too often dealt with Cuba in complete disregard of Cubans. If our policy takes any note of people, they are apt to be American investors.

Some students of international affairs make out a very good case for everything the United States has done in Cuba. But as is often the case in abstract discussions, they neglect entirely the effect of these so sensible and justifiable acts on the people concerned. To Cubans, the United States even — or perhaps most of all — in its most exalted moments of altruism is insufferably superior.

Neighborliness is inevitable; whether we face each other across that narrow strait as good or bad neighbors is largely up to us. Size, power, wealth, and prestige, which we cannot deny, which we perhaps do not deserve, give us the whip hand. Whatever we do, even when we do nothing, we are intervening in our neighbor's affairs. We cannot help doing that. How we do it depends in larger measure than many realize upon how we, as individuals, think and act toward other peoples.

It is too easy to speak scornfully of Cuba's many internal upsets, of her apparent inability to manage her affairs safely and sanely, of the dishonesty that has too often marked her officials, of certain backwardnesses. It is more difficult and much more important to try to understand why Cuba is as she is. This cannot be done in Havana alone; no country is only its capital; one must know the other cities, the country, the people — where and how they live.

# II

# THE INTERIOR

AVANA REFERS TO THE REST OF CUBA AS "THE INTERIOR," though many other cities are ports, several quite as important as the capital. In Havana they say, "Who would live anywhere else if he could live in Havana?" But citizens of other cities have just as much pride in their antiquity — Havana is younger than most of them — in their colonial buildings, their revolutionary heroes, their scholars and writers. A few of them, like Santiago and Cienfuegos, boast of modern developments, but Cubans tend generally to brood on the past. As in our South, every town's local heroes are the greatest, its houses the most beautiful, its poets the most musical, its families — above all its families — of the most distinguished lineage. Like our "old Southerners," these people live with slow graciousness, are waited upon by underpaid Negroes, and display a gift for disregarding the poverty of their crumbling mansions and the filth of the broken pavements under their aristocratic feet. No two towns are alike. Even short visits leave vivid impressions of their individual personalities.

Every Cuban city is worthy of a visit for its own charm or the beauty of its surroundings. The visitor remembers a town from its situation, its views, smells, and noises, but the mark it leaves indelibly is made by the people he meets. Perhaps all the places I saw would seem different on second visit, though my memories are confirmed by what others say about them. As Cuba comes of age, its towns are bound to be discovered, as those in Mexico have been, by artists — and finally, when screens and a few other amenities have been adopted, by tourists.

A look at Cuba from the air is recommended. Railroads connect the principal towns, and a highway runs the length of the island; it was well built and lacks only upkeep. To know the people and how they live one should travel as they do — in trains and buses. But for a view of the land, Cuba's excellent airline is the best way.

We think of Cuba and sugar together, and rightly so. The island's overall pattern, both physical and social, is conditioned by sugar; sugar and Negroes. The sixteenth-century *hacendados* were right: Negroes could and would work under conditions that Cuba's Indians refused. The importation of slaves began during the conquest, and continued until the last slave ship docked in 1871. By that time a good half of the population was colored. In spite of four hundred years, independence, and abolition of slavey, rural Cuba is still largely a land of Negroes working sugar.

From the air the land shows every shade and tone of green with the delicate ripple of cane predominating. The best land for sugar consists of the broken-down limestone which makes Cuba's typical color scheme, rosy red plaided on green and pointed up, always and everywhere, by the royal palm, which is Cuba's emblem. No Cuban scene is conceivable without royal palms in clusters or in files, singly or in dignified avenues, flaunting elegant green banners, bowing slender stems in the wind. The big purple smudges one sees are cloud shadows and the deep green cushions are ceiba trees, the only island flora that can withstand hurricanes. They say no ceiba has ever been uprooted even when its foliage is badly torn and every tree in its neighborhood lies prone.

The western end of the island, the tail that whips out toward Florida, is scaly with mountains — the Sierra de los Órganos and Sierra del Rosario — and boasts scenic peaks and canyons and strange monticules standing like islands in country almost all tobacco *vegas*. This is Pinar del Río Province, which produces the tobacco that has given Cuba its worldwide reputation for the best of all cigars. One gazes down from a plane on blue-green *vegas* varied with smaller fields where white cotton veils protect infant plants from the sun. The tall, slant-roofed buildings are tobacco barns where the leaves are dried, and the thatched huts are *bohíos* where Cubans live just as the native Indians did when Columbus found them. There are also fields of pineapple and of cane. Sugar is everywhere; no province fails to produce some sugar. Even the Isle of Pines, which many settlers thought would be United States territory, is tied to the main island by the color of sugar. But the Isle of Pines is distinctive in every way: its best product is grapefruit; it is rich underground with minerals: its mountains, many of them, are almost solid marble, and its population is largely American.

The provinces of La Habana, Matanzas, and Las Villas (Santa Clara) repeat the blue-green tones of tobacco, though their product is not the unparalleled aromatic leaf of La Vuelta Abajo in Pinar del Río. But beyond that the island takes on a different character.

Lying across the island's center in a great swatch is Cuba's wide rolling plain; agriculturists say that at least half the island is suitable for machine agriculture. Much of it is hilly or terraced and cut by streams that water their immediate environs but are too short to dam and thus to impound water for the dry season. Agriculturists disagree as to the feasibility of irrigation projects, but the climate with its long rainy season would permit much greater and more varied production than exists at present. From

May to November, rains can be counted on; there is no frost; and hurricanes are infrequent enough to figure only as one more hazard for the gambling Cubans.

The farsighted Columbus introduced the first domestic animals: sheep, mules, hogs, and cattle. They all, staggering from weeks at sea, soon accustomed themselves to the new grasses, spread widely, and reproduced enormously. In 1547, Oviedo credits the widow María de Arana with forty-two thousand head of cattle. Nowadays, herds of several thousand are not unusual, most of them in the province of Camagüey. Sugar is in evidence too, binding all Cuba together. Huge *centrales* send tall smoke spires into the sky. Cane fields run down to the sea and reach up into the Sierra Maestra, the island's highest and wildest mountains.

Altogether Cuba's scenery is not most notable for magnificence of mountain or variety of terrain — Cuba is one of the mildest parts of the Americas — but for the glory of its colors. The sea, the bays and estuaries, make its setting sparkle like jewels; sugar-green and earth-red run over the lower hills and up toward the peaks, where forests give them a deeper tone. But sugar has taken over many square miles of territory that used to be covered with hard woods — ebony, mahogany, and cedar, all irreplaceable now. During the "Dance of the Millions" in the 1920's, Yankee enterprise, aided and abetted by Cuban eagerness to emulate such good business practices, burned off that source of endless wealth just before the collapse in the price of sugar. Therein lies Cuba's tragedy.

The island's eastern tip is perhaps most like the island before man began his devastating upsets of nature's economy. There one sees traces of the primeval jungle with the noble domes of mango and ceiba interspersed by fluffy bamboo and palms of every species.

This is the Cuba the Spaniards first saw; and those first Spaniards were the officers and crew of the ships of Capitán Cristóbal

Colón, serving her Royal Majesty, Isabel of Castile, in the year 1492. So it is interesting to start one's personal exploration of Cuba with its oldest city, Baracoa.

## BARACOA

BARACOA, on Cuba's northern coast, is the first serviceable bay west of Cape Maisí on the tip of that eastward-reaching snout. Baracoans claim this was the spot which Columbus hailed as "the most beautiful land that human eyes have seen."

Baracoa's halcyon beauty more than justifies the discoverer's remark. It is impossible to imagine anything lovelier than those long beaches swept to gleaming cleanness by the foamy edges of the emerald and azure sea. Coming in by air, one looks down on a mass of green: the bamboo's delicate spires, deeper ceibas, and rounded mangoes frosted over with pink blossoms. Tall aristocratic palms bend with the wind, and sturdy pines on the hills refuse to be so gracious. Every tropical fruit gives there of its best; orange groves alternate with cocoa plantations, cocoanut palms and bananas shade coffee shrubs; and papayas cling awkwardly to the slender stems that seem too weak to support them. Great riches were produced here when sailing vessels carried cocoanuts and coffee to Boston and New York and the *hacendados'* iron chests were always full of gold coins for gambling. Now sea trade has gone elsewhere, and for lack of roads Baracoa has only air communication with the rest of Cuba. So it remains a lovely Eden bursting with potential wealth, but rich now only in its memories.

Of Baracoa's beauty and Baracoa's claim to be the first settlement there is no dispute. But two other powerful claimants contest her right to Columbus's first landfall on Cuban soil. Nipe Bay, farther west along the coast, is such an excellent harbor that it made out a good case; and Nuevitas Bay, backed by the powerful city of Camagüey, was once commemorated by a national stamp as the very spot. But unhappily for local pride the best claim seems to be that of an uninhabited beach near Bariay. This place has the endorsement of Samuel Eliot Morison, who followed Columbus's route with the Harvard Expedition in 1939–40, and whose book *Admiral of the Ocean Sea* is as exciting as any tale of adventure.

Professor Morison, a good navigator and the antithesis of a cloistered professor, decided that too many books about Columbus had "stopped at the water's edge." So the Harvard Expedition set out from Spain in three sailing vessels of about the size and speed of the discoverer's own, and faithfully followed his log, day by day, mile by mile, identifying every place he described. Reading Professor Morison's book, one has no doubt that he was precisely right in his conclusion that Columbus approached Cuba not from the east, as Baracoans claim, but from the Bahamas. He wrote Queen Isabel that he was going to "a much larger island which I believe must be Japan according to the description of these Indians whom I carry, and which they call *Colba*." Entering a river, he described there a hill topped by a smaller hill, shaped like a mosque, and he mentioned several native huts on the shore. That was October 28, 1492.

Columbus thought he had found the land of the Great Khan and he sent inland as the one most likely to be able to communicate a Jew who could speak Arabic. But they found no oriental splendors; only "many people who were going to their villages, women and men, with a firebrand in the hand and herbs to drink the smoke thereof, as they are accustomed." White men had had their first whiff of tobacco.

Morison's findings were verified in October 1941 by the Humboldt Group, the "Investigation and Direct Study Section of the Society of Geography and History of Oriente, Santiago de Cuba." These men, refusing to take their history at secondhand, cruised along the shore, taking soundings, observing currents, inlets, and landmarks, and fully satisfied themselves that they had located every spot mentioned by Columbus. Moreover, they went ashore near Columbus's little mosque — which they named La Mezquita de Colón — and uncovered a kitchen midden just where Columbus said he saw native huts. That the huts dated from the discovery is held proved by some conch-shells found among the potsherds and drilled as the aborigines drilled them to extract the meat. Here pines tall enough for masts grow down to the beach, and Columbus wrote of cutting masts; and Cuba's small native jacaranda and lavender orchids might have been the flowers he mentioned. The Humboldt Group is proud that its achievement has been recognized by the First and Second National Congresses of History held in Havana in 1942 and 1943.

After his landfall, Columbus, trailed 448 years later by the Harvard Expedition, cruised eastward, describing every landmark so accurately that Dr. Morison says his harbors can be identified even from the air. So the discoverer finally arrived at Baracoa. There he named El Yunque (The Anvil), a well-defined hill that can be seen for fifty miles. And there he landed on a point where his men raised a cross and traded brass rings, glass beads, and hawk's bells with natives who had seventy-foot canoes that could carry one hundred and fifty people.

I feel real regret that facts so stubbornly refuse Baracoa its claim! People were so nice to me there, and it means so much to them. As soon as word got around that a writer was in town they came with proof that here and only here could Columbus have landed on that October 28 of 1492. The editor of the weekly paper and his daughters thought El Yunque must have been the little mosque Columbus mentioned. The young man who picked me up in the soft-drink parlor and took me to call on the mayor was confident that the cross could not have been planted at Enseñada de Miel at any later date. The priest, too recent a comer to burn with local pride, was reticent but willing to show the cross, which he said was smaller now because so many bits had been chipped off for devout worshipers who were also influential. The mayor could not imagine any spot better fitting Columbus's description. But the most convincing advocate was Señor Francisco Marroto Scott, who came to my hotel the day I left, guided by the chamberman with his big black cigar. He cited the Spanish historian, López de Gómara, who quoted Columbus as saying: "I reached here coming from the east and turning back went to Santo Domingo." Señor Scott is writing a book to establish Baracoa's claim. He is so blind that he needed help to find the stairway's top step when he left. But his vision of what Columbus did is crystal clear.

Wherever that historic landfall may have been, Columbus was a practical man who recommended Baracoa's bay so strongly for "good water, good land, good surroundings, and much wood" that Diago Velázquez founded here the first of his seven *villas* in 1511. Of the fort he built there remain only heavy walls overrun with creeping plants and barefooted urchins who clamber down over the rocks and dive into the pellucid bay.

Velázquez was not concerned only with settlement. He was thirty-four, tall, blond, fattish, and a bachelor. And he fell in love with pretty María de Cuellar, daughter of one of his civil staff. María had come from Spain as lady in waiting to Doña María de Toledo, lady of Columbus's son Diego, Viceroy of La Hispaniola. No place Spain touched was too remote or primitive for regal pomp and splendor. So when little María went to Baracoa she had her *doncellas* too, and her wedding to the Captain General was celebrated with a whole week of jousting and feasting. But within that week the young bride died; the Spanish had no protection against the tropical fevers hidden in that Eden.

Veláquez then would have wooed one of María's maidens, Catalina Suárez, but she had been won, perhaps seduced, by Hernán Cortés. Cortés had left Spain in some haste, following his escape from a lady's bedroom window, and his historian, Bernal Díaz del Castillo, wrote that "as a young man in Hispaniola he was somewhat sportive about women." In Cuba, Velázquez insisted upon a marriage and then approved his sportive secretary's request for permission to explore and perhaps conquer a land farther west, reputed to be rich Cathay itself. So Cortés, who never took his eye off the main chance, promptly left Catalina to follow his westering star. Sober Bernal Díaz, who was little concerned with romance, mentioned that the marriage was for love, thus suggesting a scandal. Most historians do not even state where the luckless Catalina was abandoned, though the marriage was entered in the church record of Santiago.

Baracoa had a later period of grandeur, typified by the Marqués Victoriano de Lobato and his marquesa, Josefa Luisa Garrido, generally referred to as "Pepa Luisa." They owned two huge *fincas*, which produced cattle, coffee, and cocoanuts. And they lived in a vast mansion, now divided into many homes. The editor and his family graciously received me in a house with lofty carved ceilings, handsome tiled floors, and a patio that had been part of the Lobato *palacio*. It was all work of slaves, who carved the wood, laid the tiles, and worked the iron. Underneath was a cellar where unruly slaves were chained for punishment — for such a family owned many Negroes.

One of them, María de la O, shrivelled and tottery, was quite willing to talk about those old days. She and her family, black as shadows, received us in a very clean room, also a relic of the Marqués's palacio; the old slave was willing to talk and the younger women were hospitable, but the man of the family refused to, let María de la O pose for a photograph. Superstitious fears still rule in Baracoa. De la O had been one of the Marquesa's maids; she helped care for the clothes, carried chairs and cushions to church so the noble knees should not touch stone, parasols and red rugs to the beach when her mistress strolled there. Every Sunday, she said, they killed an ox for the many guests, and at night the gentlemen gambled around a big table with gold coins that the maids had scrubbed clean. "We were very rich then," she said again and again.

Baracoa must have been as splendid as any city in Cuba then.

On all the streets are fine houses — closed now — and along the waterfront they had laid a fine pavement, wide and protected from moisture, and at intervals they had set fountains and broad stone seats. Now the stonework has crumbled to let grass grow through, and instead of stately aristocrats little polychrome Cubans jump from curving seat to empty urn, and pitch baseballs, and shout and mingle all unaware that color makes any difference.

One evening I sat there. An evening direct from heaven it was, with a path of gold reaching straight into the pale green sky where rose and apricot clouds had parted to let the glory show. As I watched I realized that I had an old man for a neighbor. Leaning on a cane and gazing sourly at the children he began, without introduction, to talk. "Worthless brats. What are they learning? Nothing! What is better now than in the days of slavery?"

It was like meeting an unreconciled Confederate. His father's house and crops had been burned; the war of fifty years ago was so clear to him that he could see none of the gains since. A royalist in Cuba is rarer far than the unreconciled Confederate; it was worthwhile to meet him; one needs a few sad voices from the past to point up the solid gains of the present.

## SANTIAGO

VELÁZQUEZ's second capital is the first city a traveler must know if he is not to believe that Havana is Cuba. *Santiagueros* are fiercely proud of their long history, but free enough of the past to enjoy the present and forge ahead into the future. They are bitterly resentful of Havana's control of revenues, for they claim that their province of Oriente, the largest and richest, pays about a third of all national taxes and gets little in return. Santiago handles a huge export-import business through its harbor, which was roomy enough to shelter the whole Spanish fleet in 1898. Here young Hobson sank the *Merrimac*, but sea currents swept her in from the bay's bottleneck and Admiral Pascual Cervera, filled with Spanish pride, sailed gallantly out to meet certain defeat by a larger United States fleet. The bay's entrance is guarded by another Morro Castle, and there young Hobson and his mates were imprisoned until General Shafter's army landed on Daiquirí Beach eighteen miles away.

My personal memories of Santiago Harbor are colored by Bacardí rum. For it was a representative of that paternalistic company who arranged a launch trip down the bay with stops at Ciudad Mar, where society swims and rests on the way to country homes at Punta Gorda, facing El Morro. At every stop cocktails. The cocktail, by the way, should be called Bacardí. The name *daiquirí* is due to an error on the part of United States naval officers who in Daiquirí first tasted such a drink as they had never known before. Sweetness of sugar cane, but not too sweet; freshness of lime, not at all sour; and authority of Bacardí rum, always Bacardí.

Facundo Bacardí arrived in Cuba from Spain in 1862. He set up an import business, and after he had married a Cuban lady of French descent, returned to Spain, leaving his affairs in the hands of a manager. When the manager had ruined him, he returned to Cuba, retrieved what he could, and went into rum. Rum in those days, as you will remember from reading English novels, was the grog of the ordinary seaman, aship or ashore. From the day of Nelson until our own, the British Navy has issued rum to its sailors. But Don Facundo was not content with that. Through years of experimenting he gradually eliminated the impurities which remain in the crude rum produced by sugar planters everywhere. Don Facundo, European, sought something as smooth and fiery as a French brandy. In time he and his descendants, through a process so secret that it is known only to three men at a time, have achieved their aim, the best of all rums.

Nor is this only the opinion of the family. In 1876 Barcardí rum was awarded first prize at the World's Fair in Philadelphia. This was only the first blue ribbon. Others were awarded in Madrid in 1888, in Chicago in 1893, in Paris in 1901 and 1903, in Buffalo in 1901. Barcardí rum was then declared *hors de concours,* and other rums began to get prizes. The United States Navy declares that it was responsible for bringing Bacardí up out of the grog shops and onto elegant dinner tables. The Bacardí Company agrees and is suitably grateful, but they mention that there was a time when King Alfonso was ill and Bacardí was found soothing to the royal interior. Perhaps that point is not considered so important now. In any case Bacardí is big business, and interesting as one which has been developed by Cubans, in Cuba, and without outside capital.

Santiago is a busy town which seems to be enjoying endless leisure. The Parque Céspedes is filled all day and all the noisy night with sitters, talkers, speech-makers, and gesticulators. Two men soon attract a dozen, the dozen becomes a crowd, one mounts a bench, another challenges, words fly so fast and in such confusion that it seems impossible that anyone could follow. What are they talking about? Politics, I was told, the war, how much they hate Havana, how much they hate Yankee imperialism, politics, and the war. They are of all colors; Santiago with its Negro population of about 40% is comparable with Memphis, which has 41.5%. A pleasant Cuban, summing it up, said: *"Juntos, y no revueltos."* (Together, but not mixed.) Certainly they do not look any more mixed than our mulattoes, quadroons, and octoroons do. Cuba has names for them, too. *Negro,* very black; *mulato,* less so; *cuaterón,* quadroon; *pardo,* lightish. *Moreno* is a useful word; as it means dark and may mean brunet with no implication of Negro blood it is also useful in slipping across from Negro to white.

The Parque Céspedes has been denuded of its dark-foliage trees, *laureles.* This vandalism was committed in the name of progress — in this case, paving. It is harder to account for the row of shops that block off the Cathedral from the street. One enters the basilica from the side; the great front entrance is seldom used, and just below it is a sign: *Guinabeer, Bar Mirta.* The tourist agency is alongside, and curio shops and a barber shop fill out the block.

The man in the beauty shop said: "The Cathedral used to be on a hill, but they cut away the hill for the shops. Of course, the Bishop did not do that. He lives for religion and is above all that. I remember a story about throwing the money-changers out of the temple. Santiago has brought them back. Even lawyers are there." He repeated the point about the lawyers several times as though that were the ultimate indignity. He also deplored cutting down the laurel trees in the plaza. "It was easy then to take pictures of the Cathedral without showing the shops. They kept the mosquitoes away too, and people used to come for the leaves, which give a very good savor to food."

In the Cathedral close a *parda* woman directed me to the only unlocked door, where my hail was answered by a voice musical as an angel's. "Indeed, *señora*, it would be a pleasure to show you our Cathedral." A beautiful boy appeared. Immaculate white set off clear lightly bronzed skin, kinky hair, and large soft eyes, with lashes long beyond belief. Grandson, perhaps, of the woman outdoors, and two generations whiter. He could have posed for young David or Saint John. He glowed over everything, pattering his facts, though dates escaped him. An inlaid cross from India. A silver altar from Mexico. Copies of Murillo, Velázquez. Portraits of bishops and archbishops. One who died in Spain, so loving Cuba that he asked to have his body sent back here.

"Your country," he interpolated at one point, "is unfortunately a Protestant country." He seemed happy when I assured him that in fact mine is reputedly the largest Catholic country in the world.

In front of the marble altar from Italy stood a statue of Santiago in a long monastic habit instead of mounted and garbed like a warrior as usual. "There was a Santiago on a horse," the boy said, "but they took it to the Bacardí Museum. You should go there to see it."

I learned the story later. *Santiagueros* less devout than my little guide love to tell it. It seems that when Charles III of Spain fell, the governors of Santiago, both thrifty and politically wise, transformed the king's statue into one of the saint. Few changes were necessary, but when the reverent saw the new Santiago in the Cathedral they felt that something was still wrong. "It was," my informant said delicately, "a complete horse — you understand — and *las beatas* [the sanctified ladies of the congregation] considered such a display of virility unsuitable for a saint." So an operation was performed, and Santiago's charger, still rearing like the most rampageous stallion but with perhaps a startled look in the eye, carries a warlike saint wearing the upturned hat of Cuba's revolutionary heroes.

Cornerwise to the Cathedral is Santiago's great tourist hotel, the Casa Granda, and that is not a misspelling of *grande*, but the name of a family. Casa Granda's big time was when Grace Line steamers put in regularly, bringing North Americans to ride out to San Juan Hill where Teddy Roosevelt charged; El Caney, where the Rough Riders landed; Daiquirí, of mixed memories, and Santiago itself where our General William R. Shafter accepted the surrender of Spain's General Toral. *Santiagueros* will never forgive or forget that United States and not Cuban troops marched into the conquered city, that it was a Yank and not a Cuban who took the Spaniard's sword. Indeed the whole episode of surrender and occupation was marked by our national genius for doing things wrong. Our officers even neglected to invite Cuban generals to participate in the surrender ceremonies.

Following advice, I tried the Casa Granda. On a corner, the wide-open lobby caught everything that moved in Santiago. Dust from the dug-up plaza swirled through, carrying bits of paper and fluff, which on closer look turned out to be scurrying mice. In the dining room, open to the plaza, spotted table cloths surged and waved against the cruet stands, and spotted waiters were forever diving after flying napkins and newspapers. On the veranda a fleet of rocking chairs gallantly rode out the gale. Noises came in too, in waves of radio, plaza argument, motor horns, street cries, and church bells. Especially at dawn the Cathedral poured out its warning against lazy indifference. Rumors too must have flowed through the Casa Granda, for townsmen came there to read their papers and to meet friends from everywhere. Cuba's folk have replaced the Grace Line's tourists, but I soon gathered that the cagiest of them came to Casa Granda for gossip and lived more comfortably elsewhere.

It finally dawned on me that I was paying New York prices for a room with no clothes-closet, no desk, a rickety bureau, a bad bed draped in soiled mosquito-netting, and a shower bath over a dubious-looking cement basin. So I moved, following Cuba's wise business men, to the Hotel Imperial, where for four dollars a day I had a cleaner room and better food. Spurious elegance will sometimes go over as quaint in a backward country, but not at New York prices.

Santiago is a modern city, but the curious may still trace its past in its architecture. A few old streets have not changed much from colonial, perhaps even early colonial days. Between low plaster houses with overhanging eaves, small wooden-barred windows, and steep entrance steps, they pitch sharply down from hill to shore. One street is so picturesquely steep that it mounts on steps, and they say that in the rainy season it becomes a foaming torrent. Here Cortés led his swaggering conquistadors through the town, getting quickly away before the jealous Velázquez should change his mind about that order to sail west. On the shore cool stone warehouses still dispatch and receive the huge cargoes that Santiago sends and receives. And among them stand smaller houses with pink and yellow oleanders in their gardens and shower-of-gold vine draping the walls.

Soon after the conquest, as children of Spanish parentage were born, there apeared the *criollo* — the Spanish born in the colonies. Our word for it is Creole, but as that has come to imply Negro blood, the word *criollo* better expresses these proud white Cubans. Often they were rich, able to build themselves fine homes and furnish them with Europe's best. A French-Spanish lady received me in such a home one hot afternoon. A large double door opened into a tiled salon, beyond which one could see across another of equal size and on into the flowery patio. Cuba's ceilings are distinctive and beautiful. Very high, they are pitched above heavy hand-carved beams of native mahogany; it gives a sense of space and coolness that more economical modern construction finds it hard to better. The furniture too is native mahogany, much of it made by slaves, and instead of thick upholstery it has seats and backs of cool ventilating cane.

My hostess reminisced about her girlhood, when she lived on the family coffee *finca* in the Sierra Maestra. Everybody was happy then, she said. Planters' families lived on the richest food, rode in carriages or on horseback from estate to estate for parties that lasted days or weeks. Pilgrimages to Europe were almost annual; only a poor crop could keep the family at home. Many an *hacendado* chartered a ship for his family, always including a grandparent or two, leftover maiden aunts who had refused or been denied the veil, never less than a dozen children with a nurse or tutor apiece, and other servants as needed. Slaves, the old lady assured me, were well treated and very happy in their quarters. One had only to hear them singing at night, the deep, sad wailing of the Congo or the mad wild notes of war drums. Now and then, she remembered, disturbing things happened, but only when bad Negroes came over from Haiti, where black men had successfully rebelled against whites. There was always fear in Oriente that such ideas might leap the Windward Passage. But little girls and young ladies were naturally protected from such thoughts. She learned that later.

The *señora's* daughter then brought us delicate sugary cakes and an icy drink, also heavy with sugar. Cubans eat sugar as though it were their obligation to consume as much as possible of the national crop.

One such old house had gone completely modern as a combined British-American club for service men. Santiago is fairly bilingual; many of the pretty younger hostesses were daughters or granddaughters of the Rough Riders of '98 or of General Wood's administrators, who married pretty *santiagueras* and stayed on. Society is gay with country clubs, beach clubs, and monthly trips for girls to Guantánamo Bay for dances.

Other old houses, down under the hill, have degenerated into near-slums, occupied by Negroes. One night, drifting about the city, my host suddenly suggested our looking in on a *tumba francesa*. Even as we left our car we heard the thump of African drums, and saw the crowd pushing against open doors and windows. *Tumba francesa* is an importation from Haiti brought by the many immigrants shipped in legally when more cane workers were needed and by those who have entered illegally between times. It is found only in Oriente province. Many Cubans in western Cuba have never seen it.

As we peered over the shoulders of the crowding people, we could see the dancers. Many were old women wearing long ruffled skirts such as mistresses might have given to slave grandmothers and are now featured as the Cuban costume. Younger women wore up-to-date ten-cent store dresses and stood aloof, there but not taking part. Younger men, some of them, stayed apart too; but others danced eagerly with the old women, hugging them, making them whirl until the ruffles stood out, laughing when the ancient dames outdid them in speed, accuracy, or variety of step. The older men were not dancing; they spelled each other with the musical instruments, beating with fingers or heel of hand, shaking *matracas,* altering their tempo to try to catch the dancers off-guard. That they did not do. Some of them wore bits of uniform — old *mambises,* veterans of the wars of independence; some were wizened old men looking like witch doctors right out of Africa, which no doubt they were. One approached us with courtly mien to make us welcome and offer seats. My companions, a bit nervous and out of their element, showed no disposition to stay long. Then a young man attracted our attention.

For a long time he had stood near the doorway, dressed in his proper suit with white shirt and tie. *Trigueño,* wheat-colored, he was trying to keep his distance — a white man. But the beat of the music's rhythm was working on him, and he began to come in gradually as a swimmer enters cold water. He edged in, bit by bit, catching the rhythm in his shoulders, then in his arms, swinging hypnotically, finally with his feet. He danced alone awhile. Then a laughing old hag marked him for her own. She danced up to him, spinning her train out behind, shaking all over, snapping her fingers. He caught her in his arms and gave her a quick whirl before he drew back into civilization again, scorn in his face, but his whole body betraying him and yearning to go all the way. The old dame watched without forcing him, but she lured him with her glance, with her whole old body as she must have lured many a young man in her day. Finally he gave in. Off went the coat; the tie was torn off; he sloughed civilization with one eloquent shrug and plunged happily into the pulsating rhythms of the dance. I think we were all pleased, modern Cubans as well as unregenerate foreigner, to see civilization defeated again and another libido freed for its ancient expression.

Santiago's hospitality was for me unexpectedly expressed by the newly organized Business and Professional Women's Club, which, hearing that a writer was in town, invited me to its inaugural luncheon. There I felt, as I had in Havana, that Cuba's women are looking forward and providing much of the motive power for the country's social advance.

Bringing the invitation came Doctora Leida Zarábia de González, president of the club. She was small and very businesslike in a tailored costume of ivory-white, with a Latin touch in small earrings of fine diamonds. Her straight black hair was brushed shiningly into a heavy bun, and her dark skin was of Indian and not Negro brown. So confident did I become in that first interview that I ventured to say she was like Malinche, that highly intelligent Mexican-Aztec girl who made Cortés forget Catalina Suárez waiting for him here in Cuba. Leida liked the idea, and told me that her family did indeed have Cuban-Indian blood. Later, visiting a school in the village of Caney, she flew up and down the aisles until she could say: "Here, Erna, is a little Indian; see, he is of the same type I am." He was indeed, with clear brown skin, straight nose, fine features, and deep warm eyes.

Leida was a revolutionist in the student uprising against Machado in 1933. She laughs now about smuggling arms and munitions past the police, of receiving code messages from Havana, of hiding escaping students. She met her husband then, though they were too busy with their revolution for some months to indulge in much courting. Now she is an inspector of secondary schools for the Province of Oriente, and a very captious one with her sights set high and no illusions that Cuba has yet an adequate school system. Politically she is whatever she thinks most likely to advance the rights of little men. Her basic platform is more education, more food, more internal development for Cuba and less — much less — Uncle Sam. I found such women refreshingly free of nonsense. Leida and her numerous brothers and sisters are incorporated in a furniture factory that is trying to teach Cuba that it is smarter to "buy Cuban" than to import from the States.

The Business and Professional Women's Club of Santiago, at its luncheon in the airy dining room of the Hotel Imperial, dedicated itself to three immediate objectives, notable for their civic consciousness and lack of feministic propaganda. They proposed, first, suitable quarters for the detention of juvenile delinquents who had always been incarcerated along with adult criminals. Second, a special school for newsboys who were unable to attend regular sessions. And, third, the establishment of a municipal day nursery to help working mothers. Between the time of my visit and my writing of this item, word came that two of the objectives had already been attained. Cuban women accomplish what they set out to do!

The members of the club hospitably took charge and planned many pleasant affairs for me. The most elaborate was a program in the home of Cuba's lyric poet, José María de Herédia, whose poem *Niágara* we know in William Cullen Bryant's translation. The speakers, as always in Cuba, all mentioned José Martí or quoted his words. Martí was the soul and spirit of Cuba's revolution. He is invoked as "the American saint," or *El Apóstol*, and his words are quoted like Holy Writ.

The purpose of the affair in the patio of Herédia's home was a program of Cuban music — that I might hear how fine and varied it is, ranging from classical to jazz, from primitive Afro-Cuban to sophisticated modern. It was performed by the municipal band, uniformed, well-trained, and conducted by a fine-looking very dark man with strong Caucasian features. Pretty girls in long frilly frocks sang haunting ballads, and an alluring *mulata* recited *Trienta Kilo' Na' Ma'*, which stays with me as the best expression of Cuba's gay insouciance. The carefree Negro as contrasted with the sobersided *gallego*.

One day we visited El Cobre, the copper mine that is out of operation and best known for the miracles performed by the Virgin in its church. We drove up to see the view and entered the church compound without passing through the mining town. The church is new; its priest, Father Vayrennes, employs a French cabinetmaker who has for twenty years been carving and erecting new stalls, pews, confessionals, railings, and altars. Father Vayrennes seems proudest of the chests and armoires in which he keeps the miraculous Virgin's wardrobe and jewels. At least he showed us those himself. With what delicate pride he opened door and drawer, each lined and tufted in pink brocade like a Parisian jeweler's casket! It was a dream for a little girl who still loved dolls. Tiny silken garments, embroidered with gold and silver threads, incrusted with seed pearls, adorned with more precious jewels. And, of course, the usual quota of valuable tiaras made for the image, and of rings, bracelets, necklaces, and single gems presented by grateful women.

The tenderest tribute to the Virgin came from a ten-year-old girl. It was a braid of hair, curled into a common cardboard box. The legend read: "Because my Mother loved my long hair more than anything, I promised it to the Holy Virgin if she should return to me from prison. She has come home again, and I dedicate this in thanksgiving to Our Holy Mother and Benefactress."

The most unforgettable aspect of the visit was the talk in the car coming home. We descended rapidly from the elegant church on the hill into the forlornest of abandoned mining towns. Ill-clad children played in front of hideous shacks along rutted roads piled with refuse, blowing with dust. One store showed a few fly-specked articles in a dirty window. There was no school. In a jolting moment we had passed out onto the pleasant highway again. But the conversation had been jolted from girlish chatter about the exquisite Virgin's garments to what those socially aware women had seen. At times it profits a naturally loquacious person to deal in a foreign language. I listened.

"What a crime that nothing has been done for these people!" This from the officeworker who is an active union member. "When the mines closed, nobody thought of them; there they are starving."

She who had bowed and crossed herself at every altar: "I am not devout like my sister, but it seems to me that people who give jewels to the Virgin might do better to give something for the relief of this dreadful poverty."

"Yes, it would probably please the Virgin as well. . . . My sister is devout. When she had been married several years and had no child, she came here to pray and she left her diamond bracelet for the Holy Mother. Later a child was born, but she was very dark, *prieta*. The next time, my sister prayed to the whitest Virgin she could find."

But it was the plight of the abandoned town that held their interest. Was this talk an augury of a future Cuba whose women would clean up a town rather than adorn an image?

## BAYAMO

To KNOW a country's people, travel by bus. Trains are pretty good, but impersonal by comparison. The bus conductor is generally young, hard-faced, and wears wrinkled cotton and a visored cap on backward. In motion he jabbers companionably with his fares, shouts greetings and messages to people awaiting him along the road, and at every stop is out and into the bar for a coke and for more and louder talk with denizens of the town. When the driver climbs aboard he pays no attention; in fact not until the gears have meshed and the bus is grinding dryly on again does he catch a rail and swing agilely along the side, grinning through the windows and making it in the last split second. If the conductor's camaraderie is not enough to break down all barriers, the bus, aided by Cuban roads (which are made but never mended) may be counted on to cure any standoffishness. Lurching and jolting, rattling every window and every bolt and bar, the bus concedes nothing to the holes in the road. If you are not pitched into your neighbor's lap, he is sure to land in yours. Conversation then opens with mutual apologies, moves easily into jokes, and ends with personal histories.

On the trip from Santiago to Bayamo I think I saw every type of Cuban. Priests and beggars, ladies and toughs, school children, traveling men. The country was beautiful as the road rose by swinging curves to ever-wider vistas of the sea, away off there, gray at the horizon, enameled blue close in. Near at hand small prosperous farms with bottle palms in the dooryards and red and purple bougainvillea burying garden gates and verandas. We were crossing a spur of the Sierra Maestra and seeing easily the land that Cubans fought so hard to wrest from Spain. In all these canyons Cuba's revolutionary fighters, *mambises,* had lurked, to dash out and ravage Spain's regulars and disappear again into their sheltering hills.

The bus was crowded when we pulled away from Santiago's plaza; at every crossroads, people got out and others got on. City people disappeared into garden gates, *guajiros,* countrymen, joined us to ride a whistle- or honk-stop or two. At every halt, venders showed up, though there was not a hamlet nor even a *bohío* in sight. Screaming, pushing, laughing, they thrust their wares through the windows, crying food, fresh and hot, and the inevitable lottery numbers.

"Here is bread of Caracas! A kilo, no more! Fresh and good!"

"Turnovers, hot and spicy! Meat or jam! And hot! Sell at a nickel! Special! Yes, lady! Two. Special!"

"Puffs, puffs, puffs! My mother makes 'em! I sell 'em! You eat 'em! Puffs at a nickel! And paper to wrap 'em in!"

My seatmate, nickel in hand, was leaning across me, eyeing all of the offerings, appraising. Finally with a deep sigh of hard-won decision, she decided. "I'll buy from you. After all, you are all children of God."

Lottery sellers, not content with sales aground, got aboard at every stop and made sales as we lurched along. Once a man thin to emaciation staggered up the step and stood swaying, it seemed, as much from weakness as from the motion of the bus. In his arms was a child, pitifully limp, five or six years old. Holding

*43*

her as an exhibit the man began a tirade; nothing weak about his voice or his ideas. What sort of a country was this, he demanded, in which a sick child could have no help, in which a man could find no work, in which all these overfat Cubans he saw refused help? They gave him alms; he collected enough in a few moments to pay his fare, and at the next stop he left us.

We stopped for lunch. It was a large tiled eating place with a bar across the back, covered tables, and a few screens to form booths. I was served chicken and saffron-yellow rice, *chayote* with cheese, and the smooth delicate custard that no Latin American restaurant ever fails to offer. An urchin with a well-filled looking tummy protruding between shirt and pants, begged what was left of my roll with a professionally pitiful eye. A brisker one with a bootblack's box pushed him aside.

"On your way! No begging! Get yourself a box. Shine, lady, shine!"

Then we were in the valley where Bayamo sits and I remembered that this is a little city of great pride. Maybe it was the second of Velázquez's Seven, though even Irene Wright, who wrote her *Early History of Cuba* from the archive in Seville, is not sure of the order of their founding. Bayamo, like Baracoa, was the Indian name of a region which Velázquez partitioned out among his followers. Bartolomé de las Casas held a *repartimiento* here, and Bayamo claims to be the site of the first revolt against Spain. Again Miss Wright dissents, but *bayameses* show the very tree — and what better proof does legend need?

Hatuey, the leader of that first uprising, was not a native Cuban, but an Indian from Hispaniola, modern Haiti. There he had known Velázquez's dreadful civilizing methods: killing, raping, enslavement. His own people lost, Hatuey migrated to Cuba where he added many Cubans to his original followers. One day he sent out runners to invite all the people to a great concourse under a certain ceiba tree. They came in hordes because the stranger from the other island had promised to show them the god the Christians worshiped. Then, one can imagine with what a dramatic speech and gesture, he drew aside a woven mat and showed — a basketful of gold! This, he reminded them, was the deity for which the invaders had committed such horrors. Thus he aroused the gentle Cuban Indians against Velázquez. They put up a good fight, but somewhere — whether at Bayamo or not — the Spaniards caught Hatuey and sentenced him to burn at the stake. Before the execution he was given a chance to abjure his heathen beliefs, and embrace Christianity. Would that, the Indian inquired gravely, take him to the Christian heaven? Told that it would, he declined with steady mien. He did not wish to go where he would meet more Christians. So Hatuey died. Velázquez named the place San Salvador in thanksgiving to the Holy Saviour who had preserved them all from the vicious savage. There are a few statues to Hatuey; the Spanish like to honor their brave foes. But his name is most widely known through a beer that the Bacardí Company makes and from ices sold from pushcarts everywhere. A *choteo*-maker has said: "We honor our great Indian hero not with coldly distant statues, but with what we love best, young and old — beer and sweets!"

Suddenly we stopped at a gate. Nothing there except two women looking anxious. A young man, who had stood just over us, laxly riding the bucking bus, put a hand on my shoulder and leaned over.

"She died," he shouted. "This morning at five. They told me to tell you."

One woman burst into loud sobs; the other comforted her with an arm. The bus shook itself, groaned, and leaped, jerking us all back and down again. A quicker way than a telegram to convey the news to such a remote spot, no doubt, and no more cruel. My seatmate crossed herself and murmured a prayer, and for a moment the general volubility was stilled.

Soon houses began to appear, and we were at last approaching Bayamo. I went, as advised, to the Hotel Imperial on the main plaza. The hotel was modern; I had a room with a shower and the dining-room windows were screened with a wire mesh fine enough to keep out the larger birds, but no deterrent to flies. It opened directly onto the narrow *portal*, where guests sat in a row of rockers, gazing across the plaza at other *portales*. The park benches were filled with unemployed, as were the verandas, though one is more elegantly idle in a club. All the houses were old colonial residences, now converted to other uses. From one of them emanated two days of uninterrupted roaring, the amplification of a labor meeting. I had wondered if a woman might attend to hear the speeches; soon I was wondering where a woman might go to escape them.

Leida Zarábia had made an official visit to the Bayamo schools coincide with my stay there, so we rode together in an ancient victoria up and down ancient streets between ancient houses. The home of Tomás Estrada Palma, first president of the Republic of Cuba, was closed, his family out of town. We called on the editor of Bayamo's paper, but he was preoccupied that day because his wife was "giving light" to their sixth child and the two just older children were in his charge. From the belfry of the old church we got a commanding view of the wide and peaceful valley cut by the green line of the Cauto River.

Bayamo's greatest pride is that here, or hereabouts, the Ten Years' War began in 1868. That abortive attempt began with a shout, as all American revolutions had since Father Hidalgo in Mexico had cried aloud from his church in Dolores in 1811. *El Grito de Yara* must be shared by Bayamo and Manzanillo, for Carlos Manuel de Céspedes, who uttered it at his plantation, was a native of Bayamo, and in Manzanillo it was published to the world in a Declaration of Independence. Cuba celebrates October 10, 1868, as her independence day, though it was to be thirty long years before the island was really rid of Spain.

In '68, Spain acted promptly against the rebels. The Spanish governor, Count Valmaseda, took the field at once, calling on all residents of Cuba to fly a white flag as a sign that they wanted peace; otherwise he promised to shoot every man over fifteen who was found beyond his farm without good cause, and to burn every uninhabited hut. He advised women who were not in their homes to make for Bayamo or Jiguaní. The rebels meanwhile had won and lost several battles and had finally centered their few troops in Bayamo. When it became clear that Céspedes could not hold the town against Valmaseda's troops, he set fire to Bayamo and withdrew.

With all that past, Bayamo seemed a forlorn little town, dusty, run-down, spiritless. By Sunday morning, Leida had gone. I seemed to have exhausted the possibilities. I paid my bill and planned to leave for Manzanillo on the noon train. Meanwhile I sat rocking on the plaza, as what else could one do? From there I idly observed a flag flapping limply above the city hall. It was not the Cuban flag of five blue and white stripes, its single white star on a triangular red field. This one had two wide blue and white stripes and a star on a red field. I asked a lady rocking beside me. She did not know; nor did her husband or the other rockers. The conversation died.

Then the editor arrived, spruce and elegant and accompanied by a friend as perfectly groomed and as smiling. They had come, they explained, at the first possible moment in busy lives to give me "all the truth" about Bayamo. Agog, I am afraid for the political lowdown — what else would seem truth to an editor? — I accepted gladly their invitation to stroll about the town. But now I saw a different town. To those enthusiasts the true Bayamo was not this; it was the proud city of long ago.

When Céspedes with his pitiful handful of *mambises* took Bayamo in 1868, it could not be held. But it could be turned to brilliant account for the furthering of the revolution. Abandoning the city, Céspedes called upon all loyal freedom-loving Cubans to destroy it and leave the Spaniards only the shell. Every Bayamo family still treasures its own tradition. How great the flutter when grandfather came home from the meeting with the news. How grandmother instructed the servants — free now, but still serving — and gave orders for the selection, the packing of what little could be carried. Jewels and silver, the more precious portraits, altar services. How one grandmother decided to leave the old Spanish silver to take the new china from Philadelphia with its red roses, and how a frightened servant dropped and smashed it all. How the *volantes* were ordered out, those open carriages with two horses driven tandem by a man on the lead horse. How children were petted and reassured in their fright, and how one devoted servant risked his life to dash back into a house already burning to get a doll that alone could comfort his crying little mistress. The city burned. But its sacrifice had roused all of Oriente; Céspedes's handful of patriots began to grow into a national army.

Suddenly, seeing through the eyes and the patriotism of those two, I saw Bayamo truly. Not a dusty little town, too noisy and not clean enough. Now it was a symbol, a shrine, the city courageous. And the flag I had not understood is the flag Bayamo is privileged to display as a national recognition of that glorious past. National too is the *Himno Bayamés* which is sung by Cubans with as much fervor as Frenchmen ever put into *La Marseillaise*.

> *Al combate corred, bayameses,*
> *Que la patria os contempla orgullosa!*
> *No temáis una muerte gloriosa,*
> *Que morir por la patria es vivir!*
>
> *El vivir en cadenas es vivir*
> *En oprobio y afrenta sumido.*
> *Del clarín escuchad el sonido*
> *Y a las armas valientes corred!*

*48*

> Haste to the fight, Bayameses,
> Your country looks proudly upon you!
> Don't fear a glorious death,
> To die for your country is to live!
>
> To live in chains is to live
> In submission to shame and insult.
> Hark to the sound of the trumpet
> And haste to courageous arms!

Bayamo, however it looks to the unknowing, is Cuba's shrine to the two forces that made her independence possible: sacrifice and the spirit of human freedom. If freedom for all has not been quite fully achieved, just as surely the lamp lit in Bayamo has never quite gone out.

## MANZANILLO AND MEDIA LUNA

MANZANILLO is a little city dominated by a big business. It is also a literary center with more than the usual number of poets who support a club and publish a review, *El Orto* (The Rising Star). My visit coincided with a supper in honor of a Manzanillo poet, at home on a visit, Dr. Angel Cañete; and with typical Cuban hospitality, the host invited me to attend. We gathered in a large *sala*, open to the quiet street in front, where nothing moved after dark, and in the rear onto the patio where cicadas sang and flower-scents were stirred by the breeze. Men in white and women in flowered cottons surrounded a table adorned with long sheaves of flowers. As in most intellectual and civic affairs in Cuba, various racial mixtures were represented; intellectual life knows no color line. The program was typical too. Every Cuban can make a graceful or eloquent speech; many rose easily to compliment the guest, the hosts, *El Orto*, the town. Every speech contained a reference to José Martí and was interlarded with quotations from the Apostle's writings.

Manzanillo makes a special claim to Martí, for *El Orto*'s editor and president, Juan Francisco Sariol, is the inaugurator of the *Cena Martiana* (Supper of Martí), which is celebrated on the eve of the patriot's birth. Señor Sariol, a tall, serious gentleman with a touch of color, but lacking the fire and humor one hopes for from an African ancestor however remote, told how the idea had come to him, how ardently it had flamed through the republic, how many towns now make an annual holiday of the outdoor supper with appropriate speeches and music.

This was unexpected and charming. But Manzanillo lingers most in my memory because it led to Media Luna, where I was handed one of Cuba's best tales on the ways of North Americans.

Morning light showed Manzanillo's streets without movement, except for vendors with flat baskets on their heads and children with book-satchels on their backs. Business centers in a squat stone warehouse on the bay, where all is bustle and order. Ships from many countries moor at the little pier, busy clerks run back and forth with papers, and passengers jump aside from screeching handcars. This is the Beattie Shipping Company, founded in colonial days by Richard H. Beattie, an Englishman, and now operated by his son-in-law, Delio Núñez Mesa, senator today, perhaps president some day.

Señora María Beattie de Núñez had invited me to call at her apartment in the warehouse. Entering a door large enough for a monster truck, I picked my way among packing cases, following a gleam of light and an encouraging voice. Then a stairway and at the top an amazingly citified apartment. This is the Núñez family stopover between the luxurious home in Havana and the *hacienda* down the coast at Media Luna. There I met two of the four sons, all of whom are active in the many Beattie-Núñez interests.

I asked one of the sons if he were the family cattleman. "Oh, no," he answered, smiling ruefully, "I'm the rice man, and not very good. You see, Cuba can't really raise rice; it's too dry. But we've been experimenting, and I'm the victim. I have to be carried by the more successful brothers."

The next day I set out for Media Luna to see a Cuban-owned-and-operated sugar plantation and *central*, all unaware that I should find out there who really carried the message to García. It was a launch trip down the shore, so I became one of the passengers swarming down the wooden pier, leaping aside for loaded trucks, being helped aboard by a stronghanded sailor.

The launch was immaculately clean, loaded with boxes and bales; men who looked like government officers; salesmen; and families of every age, color, and condition. There Gonzalo Núñez, the family "sugar man," joined me and offered me coffee at a long table on the lower deck. Later we sat above and watched the shore slide by. It looked inaccessible with its miles of mangroves dropping their long-legged roots into the water, but I knew that there were many coves where pirates and patriots had slipped ashore in their different times. Now the coves are marked with smoke banners, waving in emulation of the royal palms and marking the many sugar *centrales*. Usually we stopped at piers much like the one at Manzanillo.

At one place I watched a tall, fine-looking *mulato* go ashore, and remarked on his appearance and easy manner. There was nothing that the most sadistic *bilbo* could call "uppity" except that he was well-dressed, clean, and self-respecting.

"Yes," replied Gonzalo, "it is a good sign that people of color are advancing. Unfortunately that man, like too many Cubans, has got a useless job and is making more out of government than he could at anything useful." I remembered that young Núñez is an employer of labor and naturally resentful of a government inspector. But I liked young Gonzalo very much indeed.

I liked his comradely manner with the Negro driver who met

us at the port of Media Luna with the family gasoline car. It was fitted with cushions and shades like a yacht, and it bore us quickly past barns, sheds, garages, and the *central* itself redolent of the sickish scent of grinding cane. The car deposited us at the garden gate and we walked along narrow paths between flowerbeds that struck me as typical of the British in the tropics. I remembered that Señora de Núñez's English father had sent her "home" to be educated. The entrance hall was wide enough for a ballroom; wide stairs led to a gallery; long parlors opened on both sides, and the dining-room was built for banquets. But a bay window was roomy enough to accommodate a small table where Gonzalo and I lunched cozily.

Afterward we drove through the town of Media Luna, where the workers lived. Not comparable with the fine towns of Hershey or Banes, which American capital has built, Media Luna has a pleasant plaza, a creditable school building, and livable houses. There is a hospital, but I was not invited to inspect it. "It is not as good as the one at Banes," Gonzalo admitted. Cubans are quick to state that the great wealth of the United States companies makes it possible for them to do better by Cubans than Cubans can do. But figures indicate that all sugar planters are doing very well in Cuba these days.

At dusk, Señorita Adolfina Cassío came to dine. As principal of the Media Luna school, she had seen much of the shocking condition of plantation and central workers between zafras.

"It is tragic," she said, "to see how the children decline. When wages stop, food gets less and less until finally they are living on *yuca* and *malanga*. They get thin and lanquid; there is nothing one can do; they can't learn, they catch all the diseases.

"During the Batista regime we were all docked to provide hot lunches at school during the dead season, but none of that money ever came back from Havana. Now it's different!" She brightened into boasting. "Now we are getting money regularly and we are serving hot lunches every day. It will make a difference, you

*Havana: the Capitol, much like ours*

*The Prado, with the Morro at the end*

Old city wall and modern police station, Havana

Side entrance to Cathedral, Havana

will see!" I thought she was speaking to Gonzalo rather than to me.

Señorita Cassío is a historian whose university thesis was a real contribution to the lore of this coast. That evening on the moonlit veranda she told many tales of how the men of this region left their luxurious homes to live like aborigines in the jungle while they fought well-armed Spaniards. She told of a little sloop that plied between Pilón, a hamlet farther down the coast, and the shores of friendly Jamaica. Many heartening and heartbreaking messages that little vessel carried to refugee women in Kingston, Miami, or New York, for it maintained regular communication between patriots fighting in Cuba and their compatriots raising money and shipping supplies from other lands. Mention of that little sloop brought her to Lieutenant Andrew Summers Rowan and the message to García. Perhaps we have not had the true story of how President McKinley's message was really carried to the General in Cuba. I urged the señorita on, and here is the true account as she helped me to get it.

Few preachments, even those by the Sage of Roycroft, have more succinctly expressed the North American principle of getting things done than Elbert Hubbard's *A Message to García*. "By the Eternal," Hubbard wrote of Lieutenant Rowan, "there is a man whose form should be cast in deathless bronze and the statue placed in every college in the land. It is not book-learning young men need . . . but a stiffening of the vertebra which will cause them to be loyal to a trust, to act promptly, concentrate their energies; do the thing — 'Carry a message to García.' "

President McKinley, wishing to inform the commander of Cuban forces in Oriente that the United States was sending aid, asked for a messenger. "There is a fellow named Rowan," Hubbard says the President was told, "who will find García for you if anybody can."

"How the fellow by the name of Rowan took the letter, sealed it up in an oilskin pouch, strapped it over his heart, in four days landed by night off the coast of Cuba from an open boat, disappeared into the jungle, and in three weeks came out on the other side of the island, having traversed a hostile country on foot and delivered his letter to García. . . ."

Hubbard's preachment is good — for high schools. Rowan was good. And the message was superlative, for the Cubans were at a low ebb and the news that men, munitions, and a fleet would soon be on the way was heartening indeed. But the bland assumption that the American lieutenant, alone and unaided, had made his way across seas and over mountains, through jungles and an inhospitable land, found his general, and delivered his message is the sort of Yankee assumption that least endears us to our neighbors. In Cuba, where they admire Rowan, the phrase "Message to García" always brings up a slightly cynical smile. Tracing that smile to its source, I uncovered this tale.

Rowan, given the message to García, did what any sensible man would have done; he went to Señor Tomás Estrada Palma, who was the New York representative of Cuba's revolutionary forces and in constant communication with them. Estrada Palma put Lieutenant Rowan on the first ship sailing for Kingston, Jamaica. From there it was easy enough to conduct the American officer to Montego Bay, whence there was a fairly regular though highly dangerous shuttle service by sailing sloop that carried letters, orders, and some supplies to the Cuban armies in the south. This was the "open boat" in which Lieutenant Rowan found himself approaching the coast of Cuba.

The sloop's master was Gervásio Sábio; he took the American aboard as part of his regular cargo, and he has not recorded his impression of the man. More talk has emanated from one Goyito, a common sailor who was until recently living at Media Luna. He remembered all about the sober middle-aged American in khaki whom he found not at all *simpático* and far too uncommunicative to be interesting.

Rowan, who doubtless had every other quality for getting into and across a hostile land, had only one word of Spanish: "García." Our national genius for picking representatives who cannot speak with the people they are sent to was at its best in the war in Cuba. So a speechless Rowan was put ashore at Pilón along with the rest of the cargo. Sábio, a Spaniard sympathetic with the Cuban cause, was not interested enough to accompany him to the Cubans' camp, and that task fell to Goyito who lugged the mail bags on his back to the camp hidden in the woods.

The officer in command of the tatterdemalion patriots guarding that shore was General Salvador Hernández Ríos; and he was thoroughly surprised when a foreign visitor appeared. The General had no English, but he offered what hospitality he could, confident that his youngest officer — just then out hunting deer to supply the commissary — would soon be in. Lieutenant Eugénio L. Fernández Barrot, recently returned from school in the States, spoke English as his native tongue and would know how to handle this silent Northerner.

The rest of the tale I got from Señor Fernández himself. Sitting in his living room in Havana, I found a twinkling gentleman in tweeds. He showed himself a gracious host, ready to share his recollections of the message to García. General Hernández, he said, ordered him to conduct the American to General García, wherever he might be, taking as many men as he needed. Lieutenant Fernández asked for only five. One *guajiro* was so fair that Rowan addressed him confidently in English. There was a Negro lieutenant named Dionisio who knew the mountains so well that he could travel at night. Lieutenant Fernández's orderly was a willing *mulato* named Alfredo. He does not remember who the others were; there were not more than six or eight men in the party. None of them knew where General García was; he might have been anywhere between Holguín and Bayamo. Young Fernández had chosen men who could get safely through the jungle, whose sharp sixth sense would scent any Spaniards before they could be heard, and who would somehow find food. They would locate the General in time, he hoped.

"Rowan certainly saw how we Cubans had been fighting," he smiled. "I often wonder, looking back on it, how we kept alive at all. Sometimes we killed meat or caught fish; often not. Sometimes the men would come across a sweet-potato field and feast on roasted yams; just as often not. That first night out of El Chino it was a case of not. But if I could not feed my guest I offered him the best I had, and I invited him to swim in the Río Yao while Lieutenant Dionisio made camp. We had ridden all night and all day then, and how welcome that bath was! Especially as Lieutenant Rowan shared with me the unheard-of luxuries of soap and a towel. When we got back to our camp Dionisio had put the place nice. He had built a shelter of *manaca* branches, which so impressed the Yankee that he said: 'My God, you have built a regular house for me!'

"But he did not say much on the whole trip; mostly we just rode silently along in single file, crossing open *sábana* when we had to, but staying as close as we could to the wooded brow of the Sierra Maestra. The men were funny about the tongue-tied solemn stranger. They knew, of course, that he wished to see General García; every Cuban was hoping that the United States would send help; they were burning with curiosity as to what message this emissary brought. They called him *el loro*, the parrot, because we understood that his message was verbal. So every once in a while, on the trail, one of the men would pass me and whisper: '*¿Habló el loro?*' ('Has the parrot spoken?') But the parrot did not speak; he was riding hard on little food; doubtless he was wondering if this odd crew would really find the General in this vast unpopulated country; he was naturally a silent man."

Once they almost ran into trouble. Near Bueycito they heard firearms, and Dionisio, sent ahead to scout, reported that the Spaniards had left Bayamo and were heading for Manzanillo.

García might then have entered Bayamo; women running along the trails were heading there, hoping for loot. So Lieutenant Fernández changed his route, swinging northward toward Bayamo. The young officer was more careful now. He was only twenty-one, and here he was in the midst of scattered enemy troops and responsible for a precious courier with tidings of the utmost importance for Cuba. He must now not only find García, who was possibly moving too; he must make sure — at whatever cost to himself or his men — that the American did not fall into Spanish hands.

So young Fernández deployed his forces to afford the American the greatest possible protection. Lieutenant Dionisio, who knew every inch of the terrain, he sent ahead, riding close behind himself. Lieutenant Rowan followed with the orderly, Alfredo, whom Fernández considered the most loyal and most likely to be resourceful in a pinch. The others brought up the rear. So they rode for hours. They had been two days and one night riding. Soon they would reach the outskirts of Bayamo, and they had only rumor to assure them that Cubans and not Spaniards held the city.

Suddenly there was a challenge. *"Alto! ¿Quién vá?"* shouted from the leafy top of a *guásima* tree.

"Cuba!"

"Halt, Cuba! Dismount. One forward to show your credentials!"

Lieutenant Fernández stated his case, and was relieved to know that the challenger, hidden up there among the branches, was an outpost of García, who really was in Bayamo. The party was readily passed along to an officer who, curious as all Cubans were about this officer from the United States, supplied a guide to conduct them to the General's headquarters.

At this point in his tale Señor Fernández's twinkle breaks into an outright chuckle. "I had known New York and other major cities of the Atlantic coast, but never in my life have I seen as brilliant and beautiful a city as Bayamo looked that day. And girls! There were girls everywhere, and they all looked beautiful to me. I don't know how we got to the house where the General was; I'm not even sure now whose house it was. I only remember that Colonel Tomás Collazo met us there and took Lieutenant Rowan in to see the General at once. I was so tired that I just leaned up against a pillar on the *portal* to wait.

"Later Lieutenant Rowan came out to thank me for bringing him through so well, and then the General came and insisted that we must stay for dinner and a dance that night. I had my men; I told him that I had to find food and places for them to sleep; that we had to return at once. But the General overruled that. He gave orders that the men should be cared for, given all they could eat. Then Collazo took me off for a bath and some fresh clothes. We *mambises*, Cuban rebels, had no uniforms; often we went half-naked, barefooted and bareheaded.

"That dinner was the first I had eaten in two years and a half at a table with a cloth, with dishes, glass tumblers, and properly served food. I'll never forget it. General García at the head of the table watched me eat. He looked like a real general, military in his immaculate dress and in his movements, but he knew what to do for a young officer from the wilderness. Rowan sat beside him and they talked. General García was able to speak to him in English. Later the General went to Washington as Cuba's representative to try to negotiate a loan so we could return our troops to their homes. It was sad that he caught pneumonia in New York and died there before he saw his country free. He had fought for that long and valiantly.

"Well, that was how the message really got to García. My mission was completed after I had flirted with the pretty Bayamo girls. . . . No, I was not at all tired. Then we rode back to our camp at El Chino. Later I heard that Lieutenant Rowan had been escorted to the north coast, and, in company with Colonel Charles Hernández and General Enrique Collazo, returned to the

United States via the Bahamas. It is an interesting footnote to this story that Lieutenant Rowan was never taken to the Cuban government. That would have been a sort of official recognition of Cuba by the United States; something that the United States was very careful not to do just then."

## CAMAGÜEY

"CAMAGÜEY," I was often told, "is our Virginia. People are proud of being *camagüeyanos* and they accept it as a proof of aristocracy, just as your Virginians do." José Martí married a *camagüeyana*, a fact mentioned as sufficient to explain that she was aristocratic and royalist. This is contradictory, as Camagüey has a record of noble achievement all through Cuba's long and heartbreaking struggle for independence. One of the earliest patriots was Camagüey's Ignacio Agramonte y Loynaz who was killed in battle in 1873. A tablet in the Hospital San Juan de Dios marks the spot where the Spaniards exposed his body, but when rioting threatened they cremated it — a shocking act to Catholics — and the ashes have never been found. The principal plaza is La Plaza Agramonte and there the great believer in human liberty rears his horse and waves his sword over his campaign hat.

In this plaza — another incongruity — white people promenade on the inner walk, people of color on the outer, a step lower. There is another plaza, and *camagüeyanos*, in truest Virginia style, assure you that Negroes really prefer to go there because they feel more comfortable among their own people. Discrimination goes all the way in Camagüey. There is a smart *mulato* club that takes no members darker than their norm. Girl members are permitted to work as maids, but not to go marketing, bundles and baskets being considered the outer and visible sign of servitude.

Camagüey's business streets are generally remodeled homes; Woolworth's familiar red-and-gold front is topped by a balcony with a delicate iron grille and riotous plants in pots. Streetcars, buses, automobiles, and criers make a deathless din, and the air is so full of dust that the typical gesture is a handkerchief to the nose. In quieter streets, huge mansions occupy as much as half a block with long shuttered windows and coach-and-four doors with garbage pails set out and heavy knockers to admit the lowliest menial as well as the most honored guest.

A delightful lady received me in one such house. The outer door gave directly into a spacious *sala* with ceiling high enough to lure the heat up among the carved beams and leave the marble-patterned floor to the cool breeze from the sprinkled patio beyond. My hostess's slender waving hands, her sprigged white dress, the very look of her skin pallid from a lifetime indoors, the quiet pride with which she pointed out French consoles, mirrors from Austria, inlaid Cuban wood made by slaves, pictures framed in hair, carved and gilded images of saints, a collection of Chinese porcelain, a priceless chess set — all might have been in Richmond as well as in Camagüey. Virginia-like too were the other ladies rocking with their fine handiwork on the *portal*, beyond which the patio glowed with brilliant flowers against the green of vine-draped walls and grass.

Such homes extend themselves into the churches, where one sees ladies in black arranging flowers, dressing the images, adorning the altars. Camagüey's churches are neither as old nor as sumptuous as those of other countries. Here one sees clearly how little money Spain and the Church chose to spend in the wayside island. La Merced is the most ornate with its Holy Sepulcher of solid silver made in 1762 by an artisan from Mexico. Its weight of 2300 melted pesos is so great that it takes ten men to carry it in the Holy Week procession.

Many such items were told by the young lady who was showing me Camagüey. Her talk was sprinkled with *maravillosísimo* and *antiquísimo* (most marvelous and most ancient), and she was visibly distressed when a more modern young woman injected some scornful remarks about the worth of living elegantly on "all but slave labor among filthy streets and up against vicious and abominable neighborhoods." Camagüey's future is beginning to stir. But the church's *señoritas* are doing something too. One took me to a night school for illiterates in a room generously donated by the Bishop, who charges nothing for the lights either.

Out of an enrollment of thirty, fifteen were in attendance the night I visited. Two were Negroes; there used to be more, but an order of Negro nuns had recently opened a night school, and most of the colored preferred to go there. These pupils were servants or girls from the small factories; they were clean, polite, and trying very hard to learn. Teaching was by rote; over and over they repeated that two and two made four, that such and such symbols meant such a word. Some had gone as far as the fifth grade, the teacher told me.

Two young women, both teachers who had worked all day, were conducting classes simultaneously. They and their pupils addressed each other with the familiar *tu* and *chica* (little one) which is as usual as "Honey" is in our South. This work is carried on by volunteer members of *Las Hijas de María* (Daughters of Mary), and has produced quite a few readers.

Afterward my *señorita* took me to see the Plaza de San Juan de Dios, center of old Camagüey. On a moonlight night the aura of the past was so strong that it seemed no later than the early eighteenth century. Cobblestones underfoot, the irregular line of low roofs with only one two-story house with grilled balcony, a few narrow doors and windows softly lighted, the sounds of wrangling voices, the plunk of a guitar, and the huge shadowy bulk of the Hospital of San Juan de Dios. Built in 1728, it was the gift of a rich man and his wife who contributed $25,000 and the labor of slaves. Its opening was a gala day, when noble gentlemen carried the patients on their beds and ladies marched alongside holding ribbons and flower wreaths. During the years, the hospital was abandoned and the old building allowed to run down into shocking neglect. Only now it is being repaired to serve as a hospital again.

Next day I called upon Señorita Julieta Arango, the moving spirit in the new hospital. She has a noble head and face and eloquent hands, and she told the story simply, making no mention of the hours and months of her personal effort.

"The teachers of Camagüey, who know how much misery there is, have long maintained a place to care for sick children. But it was only one room in a hospital; we could receive only children under twelve — it was too little. So we banded together all the teachers' organizations and asked the city for help. All the clubs joined us, doctors and druggists promised help, and finally we were made a *patronato*. So we get an income from the National Lottery."

She gave me a statement of 1940. In a year they had cared for 1,227 children suffering from parasitism (that scourge of the tropics), fractures, appendicitis, adenoids and tonsillitis, and tetanus. They had maintained three servants, a washerwoman, a night servant, and had supplied them with medicine, clothes and food. Doctors and pharmacists had assisted generously; no trained nurses were included in any list. As Señorita Arango was interested also in saving the old building, that was selected as the site.

"It was full of *'llega y pon,'* " she said, laughing. *Llegar* (to come) and *poner* (to put) add up certainly to squatters in our lingo. Easy to picture how the place must have looked swarming with families cooking over charcoal braziers in the cloisters, children crawling underfoot among dogs and chickens in the courts, their wrangling, singing, trading, and gossiping everywhere. Now its cool cleanness is silent while its sponsors await opening day. Ladies have solicited so actively that nobody in Camagüey can have been overlooked. The Lions have equipped a dental clinic, the *camagüeyanos* living in Havana sent $10,000. The Comité Feminino has undertaken an obstetrical ward. Crudely I asked how many doctors and nurses would be needed to man the place. "That," she said, "we have not arrived at yet, though nine doctors have offered their services as volunteers on part time."

Well, in Cuba one counts on the Fates to fill any vacuum represented by a large building fully or partly equipped for some worthy purpose; such considerations as to how to staff, maintain, and operate it are left to the future. Is this religious faith or the result of centuries of colonialism, when help had always to come from above or afar?

A more practical service — at least in the modern, American sense — is Acción Cívica. I called upon its president in his bare, business-like office which is Lions headquarters too.

"Acción Cívica," he told me, "is different from similar organizations in other parts of Cuba because our membership is not individuals, but organizations. I think we've got them all; all are ashamed not to join. Bootblack clubs, the Tennis Club, churches, Masons, Knights of Columbus, church clubs — anything you can mention. Members are assessed according to ability to pay; the bootblack usually comes across readily with his twenty cents; some prominent citizens demur. But we get it at last." The gentleman himself and the efficient-looking file he flipped open to show me his careful lists convinced me that payments would probably come in.

"This began with a need everybody recognized. Our water supply has for years been hopelessly antiquated. In 1942 it failed altogether. Here we sat with our only reservoir all cleaned out and waiting for the October rains, and then no rains came. Disaster faced us. We appealed to the government and the so-called 'General' Batista promised to order pumps to make necessary repairs and to reorganize the whole system. Nothing was done. The water supply was getting lower and more dangerous.

The city brought suit against the officers responsible. The cases were thrown out of court. You understand that we are dependent upon the central government for all these things. Our taxes go to Havana, we wait upon Havana to return what we need — no, what they decide we need. Camagüey is a rich province, we pay between eight and twelve million dollars a year into the national treasury, and what comes back? [Hands rose with the Cuban's typical shrug of despair.] Nothing, a pittance comes back. [Hands dropped in a hopeless gesture.] So we raised money, fixed up our reservoir, formed a permanent organization."

So are democracy and the modern state coming to birth in Cuba.

Camagüey's wealth comes not only from sugar and cattle ranches all round, but from a variety of industries; they make furniture and carve wood, work leather, produce butter and cheese; they still supply all rural Cuba with the huge pottery jars known as *tinajones*. But Camagüey is Cuba's railroad center, the point where the British-owned United Railway of Havana meets the United States-owned Consolidated Railroads of Cuba. Its yards employ hundreds of men. And air travel is making Camagüey an all-American center of travel now. Cuba's own air line has been awarded the international prize for safety.

I learned that from Sr. Grossman, a young Cuban educated in the United States and the representative of Pan American Airways as well as proprietor of the Plaza Hotel. Without reference to the hotel where I lodged, he told me that the Plaza has its own artesian wells, hot water at all hours, inner-spring mattresses, screens everywhere, and a constant procession of distinguished customers, from diplomats to movie stars.

Over by the railroad track is the old cavalry barracks that the earliest tourists knew as the Hotel Camagüey, and which is now being remodeled for a museum, library, and civic center to be named for Ignacio Agramonte. It is a wonderful great place with huge apartments, groined ceilings, deepset windows, patios that are now full of tangled growth but will lend themselves to inspired gardening. This spot is claimed by *camagüeyanos* as that whereon Columbus raised the cross in founding Santa María del Puerto Principe, and where he collected the first batch of Indians to ship to Her Most Catholic Majesty as samples of the Orientals he had captured.

We returned from a tour of the city in time for my engagement at the Tennis Club. The smartest club in town, it is dominated by young unmarried women. Only they are full members and may serve on the governing board, though married women and men are received as sustaining members. We were received by the president; Doctora Shuri Hernández, graduate pharmacist, and the vice-president, Doctora Georgina Quevedo, lawyer. Neither practices her profession. They were pleased to be called modern Amazons and admitted that they enjoyed the company of the male associates who pay thirty dollars initiation fee and five dollars monthly. At five in the afternoon the wide verandas were filled, the tennis courts all occupied, and in the bar bobby-sock members were perched on red-topped stools taking ice cream sodas. Besides tennis, the club features archery and dancing. They plan a swimming pool, but are waiting until they have the cash in hand; this club in its twenty-six years has never gone into debt.

The province of Camagüey, besides being Virginia, is Texas and the center of Cuba's considerable cattle business. Cuba now produces all the animal products the country uses and some for export. On the streets one sees the cowboy in high boots, wide hat, and the South American *vaquero*'s *guayabera*, that cotton blouse tied in front. In hotels and banks appear the cattlemen, equally typical: heavy-set, sunburned men with farseeing eyes and a look of no nonsense.

I was lucky enough to hear one of these men talk at easy length one day, when Señor José Morel drove me out to visit his *fincas*. A mile or so out of town we had left the pavement and were

jouncing over rutted tracks, dusty in February but due to become
impassable mires with the rains. Cattle grazed all over the rolling
lands and we and they were separated not by barbed wire, but
by fences of flowering saplings.

"Yes," Sr. Morel replied to my enthusiasm, "it makes a pretty
fence. We call it *piñón amoroso* or *piñón cubano*. We just stick
a post in the ground, it takes root and flowers. Cuba is friendly
like that. But that shrub over there, you see, that mass of bram-
bles and thorns? That's the pest of Cuba and we owe it to a dear
old lady who visited Venezuela a century ago and brought back
a pretty plant she thought might do well here. It did well, all
right; it has all but run Cubans out of Cuba. Its name is *marabú;*
we call it 'Weyler' after the Spanish General who was such a
pest in the nineties. Well, we won the war and General Weyler
died and went, I hope, where he belonged, but the old lady's plant
is still the curse of the island. One cannot burn it off, dig it out,
or defeat it. You can plant another plant, like cane, for ten years,
and *marubú* will come back. It has thorns, so cattle cannot push
through; they cannot eat it; nothing can be done against it except
the very slow and expensive process of putting kerosene on every
single plant. And that's no good unless all your neighbors, the
whole province, all Cuba is doing likewise." Sr. Morel sighed
and rubbed his head in frustration. Then he went on.

"This province has a dreadful history. You see, Camagüey
was exactly in the track of the revolution. Everybody that passed
here slaughtered or drove off the stock, abused if they did not
burn the houses, fired the cane, stole the slaves. And that was all
true of patriot as well as Spaniard. You will see when we get to
my ranch.

"I call it *Las Tres Hermanas* for my three daughters. My
father owned it many years ago, and I have recently been able to
buy it back. It's typical, I think, of the smaller ranches. It's eight
*caballerías,* about 265 acres. We run about 1500 head of cattle
depending upon weather conditions, and also upon whether or

not we are fattening. We figure that for breeding stock one *caballería* — thirty-three and one third acres — will support ten to fifteen cows with calves. Our cows give about three liters a day. That's not much milk, and it has little cream. No, we don't feed. Camagüey, for instance, has one show dairy that is modeled on what they do in the States, and it's good. But generally we just let nature take its course. We figure that transportation being what it is, it just doesn't pay to feed. Nor do we breed to produce better meat. A few ranchers have experimented with zebu, that humped East Indian animal which does well in the tropics, and some have imported good American bulls. We'll see a show place later. Generally, our cattle produce ungraded meat at six cents a pound.

"Look, you just keep your eyes open today and you'll understand a lot that's the matter with Cuba. This *finca* of mine is fifteen kilometers from town — a city of sixty thousand people — and we don't consider that it pays to produce good milk and ship it that ten miles. Can you imagine a situation like that in your country? Of course, the road is bad. But it should be good. We send Havana enough in taxes to make this a modern state. And we get nothing — no roads, no hospitals, few schools, nothing! We in this family — and we are very American — we produce just enough milk for our own family and a few friends. Men milk at three to drive in over that bad road and get it there for breakfast." He sighed long rueful sighs, rubbing his head. Then he brightened. "My son-in-law, who is from Wisconsin, says that if I'll turn this *finca* over to him, he'll make it pay. And he will, too. . . .

"Cubans are not like Americans. Your people will invest a few thousand dollars in something and work hard for ten years without expecting any return. No Cuban would do that. If he invests he wants big interest and double his money back next year. It's still the gold-seeking Spaniard. And I'll tell you another thing. What is being done in the way of slow steady development of Cuba is done not by Cubans but by recent immigrants, *gallegos, canarios,* or Chinese and Americans. Yes, you're right; there is the beginning of a change in some young men's clubs here and there, and in labor unions. It'll certainly be a joke on us if it turns out that labor unions, who scare us so, are going to solve the problem of our own laziness." He rubbed his head again with that gesture of puzzlement. And went on to disprove his derogatory statement about Cubans by telling his own story.

By that time, we were seated on the veranda at *Las Tres Hermanas* watching the palm-leaf shadows waver across the lawn, hearing the croak of guinea fowl, smelling mimosa, sipping coolness. Two tall *tinajones* stood by the steps: "These have a history that bears on my own story. You see, once when my parents were very young, some army came by looting as usual, and my mother, who was alone in the house, got her servants to pack all her valuables into these *tinajones* and bury them under the flower beds. So we've got some old silver and we cherish the *tinajones.*

"Well, when I inherited the *finca* I was the typical young Cuban. I'd been educated in the States, but I hadn't yet learned the most important thing your country has got to teach us — that a man has to work for what he gets. So I thought I had to live in Havana. I left the place to a renter while I lived high on the rent. That was during the 'Dance of the Millions,' the twenties; and your people were more than a little responsible for that. Well, the bottom dropped out, and I was left flat. A wife and children, no income, and no sense about making one. But just then an American company, which had lost heavily, offered me a chance to pull them out, and I agreed.

"I began by firing the American who was pulling down $6000 a year for doing nothing. The assistant manager at $4000 was doing a little, but not enough to keep the place out of the red, so I fired him too. I worked for two years without pay; my wife stood by, we lived here, and our daughters grew well on milk and country products. Well, no sense in going into the details. The company finally only dropped about $2000 in Cuba, and they were satisfied to get out so well. Then I bought this place for $10,000. It's easily worth double now. I've been offered $100,-000 for *Las Catalinas,* but I'm not selling that either."

After our rest, we drove on to his *finca* of *Las Catalinas,* approaching it over broken country where *algaroba* trees provided lacy shade for cattle. Here too the verandaed house stood on a hill, but this one was occupied by the caretaker's family and lacked the charm of the family home.

In the corral, two cowboys were handling a couple of zebu cows. One man was tall, sunburned and blue-eyed, the other's color was indeterminate; they were not such good ropers, but they finally got the cow down and applied medicine to her side which had been torn on barbed wire. The blue-eyed cowboy then rode ahead of us, opening Texas gates from the saddle, leading the way across dry grass that was still edible, though he pointed sadly to many dried-out water holes and shook his head over this unprecedented drought. We were calling on a renter family that Señor Morel had not seen for six years.

The house was the typical *guajiro bohío,* with a dog in the doorway and a hen and chicks scratching under the bananas. Beyond, we could see a grove of oranges, lemons, and plums; and a patch where beans climbed the corn stalks and *yuca* and *malanga* raised their huge leaves. There were potatoes, too, to complete the Cuban's atrocious diet of starch-with-a-bit-of-meat. Nothing looked cleaned up, like a good farm. But I remembered that this was a one-man-with-a-hoe place.

A woman came to greet us and to present her children to "Don Pepe." The whole family looked plump and well-fed and definitely white. She invited us in, shooed flies, set chairs. The floor was packed earth, the windows were unglazed, but the woman had pinned up a few chromos of saints and a newspaper picture of President Grau San Martín, and on the sewing machine was a piece of coarse crochet. As always in such places, it hurt to see how hard an ignorant woman tries to make things as nice as she can.

Don Pepe, whom I had admired so much, said: "This is not a very good house, but people like this don't really care for anything better."

One third of this farm's output goes to the owner. His family uses what they can. The rest? "Well, these people eat it or it rots; there is no market, you see; no way to ship. . . . Yes, there is a school to which the children go. Three grades, I think. I suppose they go afoot or on horseback. These people don't really care about education, you know. It's altogether a forlorn situation. Look. This man works all week on his place. Then what can he do on Sunday? He takes a bath. Eats. Lies in the sun. Sometimes he goes to the nearest canteen and gets drunk — if it isn't too far away. And if he can, he gets to a cockfight. You'll see."

Driving home we passed a cantina. Far away we could hear the radio spreading abroad the conga's swing. Horses were tied to a hitching rail and men sat on the wide porch of a *bohío*. All were bronzed, some with sun, some with Africa; they looked like sturdy worthwhile countrymen.

"We have few real Negroes. In Camagüey they provide a problem. The trouble is they gather in the towns and insist upon going to school, bettering themselves, trying to be as good as whites." Was this Virginia? No, this was Latin America, where they boast of complete freedom from racial prejudice.

Don Pepe left me and returned, bringing iced beer. The thatched *bohío* cantina had electricity for ice and a juke box. At another stop we watched the backs of men sitting in the basket-like inclosure, called a *balla,* in which cockfights are held. Women, Don Pepe assured me, do not attend in Cuba. As I had witnessed the bloody horror in other countries, I was quite content to follow the custom. Into these cockfights and into the lottery goes whatever cash the *guajiro* can get his hands on. And why not? One buys what there is to buy, works to live, lives as conditions impose, takes a long chance on a stroke of luck, sings, and dances.

Nothing has really reached the *guajiro* yet — neither labor unions, civic organizations, nor, to any extent, schools. He remains the unrealized asset.

## *SANCTI SPIRITUS*

VELÁZQUEZ founded the *villa* in 1513 in that rapid sweep of his. Founding, for Velázquez, meant setting up a cross, perhaps erecting a *bohío* as a church, establishing a garrison, and marching on to the next. His job was dividing up the lands into the circular plots that have caused unending litigation, "commending" the Indians thereon to Spaniards, and declaring that all were now Christians. But it was more than a century before the stone church was built at Sancti Spiritus; the oldest entry in the dusty books records a wedding in 1652.

Two young men typify the town for me — the one who showed me the church and its dusty records, and the one who showed me the overcrowded tenement districts and talked of the Lions Club plans and the future.

The young man of the past came first. Spruce in white linen, he had left his work in a business house to devote the day to me. Talking steadily, he led me around the piles of rubble in the plaza, which was being paved, and first to the Centro Español. It would be hard to imagine a statelier edifice; from its magnificence one would judge it to belong to a city of a million inhabitants instead of to one of thirty thousand: marble halls and stairways with wrought iron and polished mahogany, and a huge bust of Martí, one of the costliest in the republic, billiard and gaming rooms, a mirrored ballroom, daintily finished rooms for ladies, reading and writing rooms — nothing is lacking for the most exacting clientele.

"Most of the members," my guide informed me, "are members of our oldest families. It would be a good detail for you to put in your book that many families in cities of the interior are descendants of the founders. . . ." He was aglow with pride in the antiquity and aristocracy of his city. "I am an *espirituano;* I want more than anything to be a good *espirituano.* I am collecting data on all the old families; who married whom, what children were born, whom they married, all the way back to the founders."

We arrived at the church. Its most notable feature is a circular altar ceiling made of heavy hand-carved cedar, as are the heavy beams throughout. The baptistry has a legend. Once, they say, two pilgrims arrived and asked to be given sanctuary there. They hung a curtain between baptistry and church, and there they stayed for three days. Food was brought, but nobody saw them. On the third day a dreadful storm, one of the worst hurricanes of all time, laid the entire city flat, but the church was unharmed. After the inhabitants had recovered they sought the pilgrims, but the two had disappeared.

The priest was courteous, but not too interested in showing the church records. In a breezy loft where open windows invited dust, bats, and birds, were piles of volumes and magazines of every date from old colonial publications to — actually — a recent copy of *Newsweek.* Perhaps the *padre* of Sancti Spiritus is more aware of the modern world than of ancient family trees. Among the publications stood or tottered several retired images sans noses, arms, or clothing. The attic of a church, I found, is not unlike anybody's attic.

We visited, too, the house of the Del Valle family. The city's oldest mansion, it is still owned by the family that built it in 1767. Its owner now divides his time between Havana and other capitals, but he has been interested to restore the large thick-walled rooms and the several patios, and to fill them with splendid furniture, most of it nineteenth-century.

This was all my aristocratic guide had to show of his town, though he mentioned several reasons for its being the best place to live in Cuba. House rent of twenty dollars a month, and three servants for as much more; pleasant country houses to visit; and good business. Sancti Spiritus is the center of a rich territory. Two mills grind sugar cane, tobacco is fine, and cattle produce not only meat, but cheese, butter, and condensed milk, which are processed right here. Hard woods are exported to the United States, and bricks, tiles and sewer pipes to all the island.

The young man of the future is a teacher. To show me his town he began with the oldest section, where narrow cobbled or muddy streets were just wide enough for our victoria. There were children, but not rambunctious, playing, shouting children: quiet, scrawny brats sitting listlessly on stone steps, wrangling querulously over homemade toys. The houses, tinted interestingly in many colors, were low, close-packed, with few and crowded patios. Slovenly women, as listless as the children, sat in grilled windows where scant cotton curtains hid little of the poorly furnished interiors, or moved about with the languor that bespeaks undernourishment. There were few traces of Negro, as is generally true in country that produces less sugar. Blacks belong to sugarcane.

"Yes, they might get jobs," the teacher said, " and they could come to school, but too many of them are malarial or suffer from other diseases that make slow starvation easier than hard physical labor, and nobody is interested in schooling. Look, the matter of health goes back to our water supply. The aqueduct, which supplies all our water, belongs to a few of our most distinguished families, who acquired it as a royal grant in colonial days. Under its terms the owners are obligated only to provide water for washing; nothing is said about drinking. So you ought to see what comes out of the pipes when the rains begin! Such an assortment of wild life! Those who can, naturally buy bottled water, but too many cannot afford it, and too many people have typhoid. We have tried to reorganize or to take over the aqueduct, but so far the owners have been too powerful."

We had come out of a narrow lane, just then, onto a wider, quieter street. Sauntering there was a stately gentleman — white linen, white hair, fine Panama, malacca stick, and the mien of an emperor. "He," chuckled my companion, "is the patriot who sells us water."

Speaking of schooling, I got again such comment as I had heard many times on the regime of Fulgencio Batista. "He did a good job in education. The *guajiro* has no appreciation of education; he would never bother to send his child even if there was a school near by. But when Batista put the schools in charge of sergeants — and remember that many school teachers were made sergeants for the purpose — *guajiros* sent their children right along. Anybody has respect for a uniform."

This young man of the future agreed with the young man of the past that Sancti Spiritus is a good town to live in, though his emphasis was different. "There is so much to be done here, and such splendid opportunity. The people are intelligent; they are only underfed. We need co-operatives in agriculture and marketing. We must clean up the water situation. We must see that children stay in school longer, that they have enough to eat to study. [This young man seemed to be thinking always of food, but food for others.] Too many people still sleep in doorways. We have tried to establish a refuge for the homeless, but so far they prefer the doorways.

"The best social force," he said, "is the Lions Club. We have opened a venereal clinic, manned by four doctors, Lions, which is reaching a few people; they back the *Prosaneamiento* (for health), which is trying to clean up the water situation, police the streets in the army sense, meet the most insistent needs of decent living."

Sancti Spiritus promises to have a future as well as a past.

## *TRINIDAD*

TRINIDAD is Cuba's colonial jewel, the untouched city of palaces, one of Velázquez's seven, and monument to hundreds of years of wealth. To date, a farsighted providence has spared it the sort of commercialism that so blights picturesque antiquity. Trinidad seems to be the wealth of the past preserved for the future in a cellophane wrapping of poverty. And that future is referred to as *el futuro turístico*. The touristic future is embodied at the moment in a young man with a truly Yankee disposition to go ahead, nicely balanced by a real appreciation of the old, and a blessed gift for consulting people of wide experience and artistic gifts.

Manolo Béquer is the direct descendant of Baker, a shipmaster and trader from Philadelphia who made Trinidad regularly, and there contracted matrimony with a personable *mulata* whom he took with him to Philadelphia. His dusky family still exists, according to reports, in the north. Later he married a white Cuban lady, whose great-great-grandson is Manolo. Captain Baker, in acquiring a wife and wealth in a Spanish colony, found it expedient to alter the spelling of his name — so Baker became Béquer, which leaves the pronunciation.

Béquer built one of Trinidad's most elegant homes. Wishing to outdo all rivals, he proposed to pave his *sala* with silver coins, but as he would then be walking over the portrait of the King, which would never do, the newly faithful subject of His Most Catholic Majesty imported instead an Italian craftsman to lay an elaborate mosaic floor. Legend has it that Béquer's palace — in Trinidad one refers only to palaces — was the most costly and imposing of all. Of two stories and several patios, its wrought iron, carved mahogany, marble stairs and floors, sculptured fountains, frescoed walls, crystal chandeliers, massive furniture, gold-framed mirrors, and services of finest gold and silver plate and Chinese porcelain were unequalled. Unhappily all this is gone, disappeared into tradition, leaving only legend and scattered bits of Béquer possessions. Almost everybody has a piece of wood, metal, or china that bears the Béquer crest. But only Manolo, a handsome, vigorous young man of the modern world, bears the enterprise that made his ancestor notable; he promises to put his town on the map again in the *futuro turístico*.

Trinidad's big season is Holy Week. Cubans gather from all the republic to witness the four splendid processions in which the most sacred images are carried around the city and every *trinitario* walks devoutly for miles and opens his home to all comers. Reservations are made months in advance, people sleep four or six to a room. I decided to visit Trinidad the week before Holy Week. After all, religious processions are more or less alike except in countries where Indians have added their distinction to the Spanish and Catholic formalism. It was a wise decision; I had a quiet week with a lovely family in a typical colonial home; I saw the quaint little city at its natural best; I made friends I shall always cherish.

The family that so hospitably received me consisted of a *señorita* and a married sister with her husband and two little girls. The *señorita*, with keys at her belt, ran the house, managed the four servants, was always busy, sweetly smiling, and tirelessly accommodating. Early every morning I saw her slipping quietly off to early Mass, her trim figure and tiny feet and hands in black. Aside from that she never went out. Indoors she wore white with black, but never colors, for she was in mourning for her fiancé who had died seven years before. They had been engaged for three years while he studied in the United States. After his return, in the midst of wedding plans, he died suddenly of a heart attack, leaving his fiancée to a widow's life. Her joy was in her older niece, whom she sewed for, cuddled in her arms, and sang to sleep every night. The *señora* said: "I have given her to my sister to alleviate her loneliness."

The *señora* was busy too, mostly with the year-old daughter.

She never went out either, living in uncomplaining resignation to years of baby-tending. And baby-tending in Cuba means constant attendance. The moment the baby opened her eyes in the morning, her mother picked her up and held her until the arrival of little black Cuca with her pretty shy smile. Cuca's job was to carry the baby all day long. Sitting, rocking, walking back and forth, hour after hour, that baby was in somebody's arms. Here surely is the beginning of that Latin American dread of being alone. The baby was well, seemed vigorous, and was pitifully eager to begin to walk. The mother, holding her, patting her, would say: "Yes, she wants to walk, but I'm not going to let her yet; it's so much easier to care for her in the arms."

My big front room, with its tall grilled window and blowing muslin curtain, put me on terms of complete intimacy with the street urchins who peered and commented openly. And I was privy to all that went on indoors. Everything passed through the great front door. All morning the maids came slap-slapping their sandals across the marble floor to open for the milkman, who poured our supply from his big tin can, to dicker with vendors, or to admit visitors who rocked and chatted for an hour with our two ladies cuddling their babies.

Meals were typical of old Cuba, though the *señorita* was worried about my appetite and tried to modify the diet to suit my tastes. It was not my taste but my capacity that was limited. Breakfast I could cope with: coffee and rolls with orange juice and often papaya. But lunch was another matter: soup, heavy with grease and packed with vegetables, including potatoes, chickpeas, *yuca*, beans, and corn. Then fish or meat, followed by meat or fowl, both cooked with potatoes, *yuca*, beans, chickpeas, corn, or *malanga*. Occasionally I found a stray sliver of onion or carrot lurking among the starches, but green vegetables were never served apart. Salad appeared frequently, always tomatoes with lettuce. Desserts were sweet, sweet, sweet. There is no word in English adequately to convey how sweet Cuban desserts are.

Happily an alternate, always available, is the delicate white Cuban cheese served with guava, preserved or in a stiff and tasteful jelly. Dinner was similar. Coffee ended both meals.

I ate alone, with the *señorita* or the *señora* rocking one of the children near by to keep me company, and a maid standing at my shoulder offering me dish after dish and murmuring complaints because I was not eating enough.

One evening I invited the *señorita* to go to the movies with me; we both, I thought, needed diversion. But she was gently shocked. I must remember that she did not go out; she was in mourning. That fiancé, I recalled, who died seven years ago! But the *señorita* would not disappoint me; her sister would accompany me. I was delighted to spend an evening with the charming sister, so we went. She was as pretty as a rose with light make-up, carefully done hair, a dainty, frilled dress, and slim high-heeled shoes. We walked two blocks through the quiet empty streets to the old mansion whose *sala* had been turned into a theater lobby. Inside, seated in the dark, I was only half-conscious that my guest was talking with someone on her other side. Only as we came out did I realize that her husband had quietly joined us. Naturally no *trinitario* would allow the women of his household to roam the streets at night unaccompanied. So he squired us correctly home, two blocks away. There we found the faithful *señorita* sitting up for us. But as she could not have spent an evening alone, one of the maids had stayed with her, and — as a good *mulata* could not walk home alone — the maid had brought her sister to accompany her home. My little expedition to the movies had upset the evening for *señorita, señora,* husband, and two maids. Such is colonial living in Cuba!

Outside of home, Trinidad is much the same. Fortunately for the touristic future the railroad has come in a mile or so away from the Plaza Martí, the religious center with the church and a nuns' school. So the business men's hotel, the bus station, and most commercial houses are together, leaving the old cobbled streets empty of traffic and noise. Old ladies and gentlemen drift about, chat through open windows; servants pass with baskets, and now and then a panniered burro clips by. A perfect setting for the development of Trinidad into a center of the arts and crafts that could rival Taxco, Chichicastenango, or any other dream-town. Trinidad has special charms to exploit; its languorous climate, its deep-sea fishing and fine beaches, its nearby mountains. Trinidad and Manolo Béquer add up to one of Cuba's greatest assets if only it is not ruined by overbuilding. Cubans do love the grandiose; the typical plan would certainly be the most formidable possible hotel in the most conspicious spot.

*Formidable* is a favorite Cuban word. Pronounce it with a Spanish accent, giving every vowel full value and you get the flavor not only of the word but of the state of mind that prevails in Cuba. Vastness, greatness, magnificence; everything must be so. Trinidad is the shell of all that. Its palaces are gone now, like the Béquer mansion, or remain filled with relics of former grandeur and inhabited by those members of the families who were never willing or able to leave. Most of them have relatives living in New York, in Havana, formerly in Paris or Rome. One enters through great doors wide enough for a coach and four into patios with balconies high above the *entresol*, which housed slaves in the old days. The lower floor was occupied by storerooms, wine-cellars, kitchens, master's offices. Nowadays they are often rented out to shops or stores.

One day my *señorita* took me to call at the Palacio Iznaga. The daughter of the house greeted us at the head of the grand staircase and led us past the potted palms and flowering plants into the *sala*, where her mother received us. The furnishings reflected the family's history with its eighteenth-century pier glasses, marbles and mosaics, nineteenth-century overworked splendor, twentieth-century gramophones and radios. The *señora*, who has lived in many capitals, now prefers the view from her balconies across the rooftops and the palms to Casilda on the sea. She told us the story of María del Consuelo y Clemens.

Consuelo was a beauty, slender and willowy, with sparkling eyes, an exquisite mouth, and the gayety that young ladies then knew how to reconcile with gentle voices and tender ways. Her suitors were many, but she was hard to please. Once a yacht from New York anchored at Casilda and its owner was invited to the Palacio Iznaga. There he fell in love with the capricious Consuelo. Several times he came, courting assiduously and as extravagantly as only a Vanderbilt could. But Consuelo would have none of him. Later, in London, she was won by a grander suitor, George Drogo Montagu, Duke of Manchester. Years later a visitor from New York reported that young Vanderbilt had grieved for years over his Cuban love; when he married at last he named his first daughter Consuelo — and so that Spanish name came into the New York Dutch family.

The same Iznaga family was responsible for the most formidable monument to extravagance until Fulgencio Batista in our own day outdid them all. In the old days when every Trinidad planter was a rich man with hundreds of slaves and there were a hundred plantations feeding half as many sugar mills, the problem was how to spend the money that came rolling in with every *zafra*. One could build a palace, and everybody did. But palaces are so durable that one cannot build a new one every year. One could charter a ship and sail for Europe with a large family, and everybody did. But having educated one family in Europe, or even two, what then? *Zafras* kept right on rolling in.

My *señorita* told me that her grandmother related that after every *zafra* the gentlemen used to meet and lay bets as to who could think up the most impressive expenditure. One year the two Iznaga brothers outdid them all. Teodoro dug a well, the deepest well ever known. And the other, Alejo María del Cármen, not to be outdone, erected a tower taller than the well was deep, such a tower as had never been seen before. Seven stories high! This was, remember, in the year 1833, and in Trinidad. In any case the Torre Iznaga was then and still is one of the great sights of Trinidad. It stands on a hill near the old house of the *Finca los Bocos,* and still gives all *trinitarios* enough satisfaction, perhaps, to justify the original expenditure.

Trinidad's other claim to the most formidable of all extravagances is that dream of the ex-sergeant, later President Fulgencio Batista, who used the president's extraordinary and emergency powers to realize his vision. Everyone who mentions Trinidad speaks of the *Tope de Collantes,* which might be translated Crest of the Hills. It was designed as a sanitarium for the tuberculous, one of the largest and best in the world. Not yet finished. One must see. I longed to see, but there are no buses and private cars are rare, not too reliable, and very expensive. Then a chance came. Manolo Béquer sent a boy running. The bus was making a special trip; they would await me in the plaza.

Thirty miles out of town, up over a hairpin road made for this purpose alone, stands Fulgencio's monument. A building designed to house 1500 patients sits there aloft, unfinished, unfinanced, unloved — apparently — by the present administration. These facts did not impress my companions, who, as true Cubans, gloried in the formidable, questioned not the practical aspects of it. I should have been saddened by the sight if they had not talked so sensibly when they got on their own topic; they were officers of the powerful union of Electrical Workers. And there is something truly *formidable* for Cuba's future.

The sharpest criticism I heard of *Tope de Collantes* came from an Englishman whose Cuban wife had asked me to tea. His criticism was so Anglo-practical, so annoyed with the wastefulness of the whole project that I found it quite out of keeping with Trinidad. I liked better the *señora's* talk, for she, deploring Trinidad's lacks, sighed: "This town has never been so clean or so well policed as when the Americans were here." Pleasant words! I had heard many of different import about the Occupation. But my hostess's mind was running back to her girlhood and the blue-coats. Then she added: "Of course, we had the Tennesseans, and everyone was a gentleman from Captain Hull on down."

"Cordell Hull?"

"And who else?" she smiled. "Perhaps his pan-americanism began right here."

Later I verified the facts. Young Captain Hull missed the war, but afterward he was put in command of Trinidad with orders to maintain peace and to make "recommendations looking to a wise, honest, and economical administration."

Captain Hull evidently carried out orders to the letter, with one exception. When his detachment moved out it was reported that the company dog, Nig, had been left behind. Nig was an important member of the company; he had even been a great help in English classes some of the officers had conducted; everybody liked to talk about Nig. So Captain Hull, disregarding the Colonel's explicit orders that nobody should return to Trinidad for any reason whatsoever, ordered Lieutenant Smith and two men to go fetch the dog. Unhappily just inside town they met the Colonel. But that gentleman, hearing what was afoot, added another order. The lieutenant and his detail were by no means to leave Trinidad without the dog. So Tennessee's Company H left Trinidad with a good reputation and Nig.


## CIENFUEGOS


DUE to the insistence of the most loquacious of my companions on that trip from Trinidad to the *Tope de Collantes*, I went to Cienfuegos. He had said: "But you must know Cienfuegos! It is the modern city of Cuba! You will see — not like Trinidad stuck in the past, but modern like a city in the good old U. S. A." Obviously he had been educated in the United States. I learned later that he had married there, too, and brought home a wife from Georgia.

I found Cienfuegos, if not quite all its advocate had claimed, indeed another Cuba from the colonial I had been seeing. Like many others, it is a port on a deep landlocked bay. One rides out in a launch past scores of wealthy homes representing every bad style of architecture for seventy-five years. There is a yacht club, of course, beach clubs, and pavilions for dining and dancing. The Prado has its quota of rich clubs, and it is sharply divided between the section where whites walk and that permitted to Negroes, one of the few places in Cuba where such open discrimination exists. Otherwise Cienfuegos is unlike most of Cuba. Its broad avenues, busy plaza, clean streets, and well-kept, freshly painted stores and soft drink places are like Florida or California. It is a brisk, busy town, not worrying about the rest of the country or the world.

Cienfuegos has differed all its life, for instead of having a sixteenth-century Spanish founding, it dates from 1819, when a Frenchman from New Orleans, Louis de Clouet, tried colonizing in Cuba with Frenchmen fleeing the United States, which had just bought their city. Velázquez, it is true, had paused on the Bay of Sagua, and the Spanish erected a fort there against the British in the eighteenth century. But modern Cienfuegos, named for the then Captain General, Don José Cienfuegos, still bears many French names and more than most of French and American influence.

It was my good luck to know the cosmopolitan circle of a Cuban *señorita* who is managing her own *finca* like a northern business woman; the Protestant missionary and his family; and the Unión Electrica. A good cross-section of the city's thoughtful citizens.

Señorita Margarita Iznaga I met through her family in Trinidad. One could not imagine a sharper contrast. They, in their palace among old things and old memories, gazing over the crests of palms to the Torre Iznaga and the glories of the past. She, living in the Hotel San Carlos and arising twice a week to catch the 4 a.m. train for her *finca*. There she changes into riding clothes, mounts her horse, and spends the day doing a thoroughly efficient managerial job. Her talk, when she could be lured to talk of labor problems, the price of sugar, or the rising middle class, was as remote from the union man's talk as though they were denizens of different planets. Mostly Margarita prefers another sort of conversation. Her tales of life on her *finca* and of how it is to live in Cuba like a modern woman instead of like an upper-class *cubana* seem stories told by a foreigner, but a foreigner with more background than any foreigner is apt to have.

With an easy cordiality more like the outside world than interior Cuba, she invited some friends to drop in after dinner. They were young men, residing and even working in Cuba, but living the intellectual life of several countries — preferably France, Spain, and the United States. Among them was a wide-eyed, gentle Cuban girl standing, but not with reluctant feet, where conventional and modern Cuba meet. She lives at home with an old-fashioned family; she yearns for the day she can muster enough strength to be another Margarita Iznaga. It is still not easy in Cuba.

We went out to see Cienfuegos. First an hour in the apartment of a French-Cuban near-expatriate. Passing through a door like all the heavy doors in flat stone walls, we entered a small salon full of fine furniture, good paintings, brocades, and tapestries: what a cultivated man acquires. Beyond, a narrow patio ran the length of other rooms, the moon made white blotches on green-leaf plants and vines, and the air was saturated with the fragrance of jasmine. Our host served us liqueurs, played a new recording of a modern Cuban musician. It was the cosmopolitan world of pleasant, comfortable people.

Señorita Iznaga bemoaned the fact that my visit was not coinciding with Christmas, a wedding, or some equally important

Las Jardineras *flouncing short, flowered skirts*

*Spain built splendidly: City Hall, Havana*

day, so that I could see the typical country feast, *el guateque*. An old Indian word has been applied to the Spanish countryman's *fiesta*, which is not unlike the peasant's entertainment back in Spain. *Lechón asado*, roast pig, is the main dish. Cooked in a pit heated by fires of guava-wood, covered with flavorsome leaves, and basted with a sauce of bitter orange and garlic, the little pig is roasted to a crisp perfection that brings tears to the eyes of any true Cuban. With it are served white rice, fluffy and dry, fried green *plátanos*, fried cakes made of *yuca*, turnovers also fried, perhaps some vegetables, and sweets of sugar and seeds. There are always jugs of wine made of grapefruit or papaya. The large green plantains are so much a part of the Cuban diet that they say of a stranger that he is *"bién platanado,"* if he has taken on truly Cuban ways. A *guateque* is served outdoors, of course; *bohíos* have no dining-salons. Rude tables are covered with palm-leaves and flowers, the moon or the stars give light as the fires fade, and the entertainment is old songs, *puntos cubanos*, accompanied by the plunk of the three-stringed *criollo* guitar. Often, if the company includes guests clever enough, impromptu songs are sung, celebrating the beauty of a girl, the night, or *Cuba libre*, or daring another singer to do better. Too bad that nobody was getting married just then. But every journey must leave some place beyond, not quite reached, some unrealized possibility for the next visit. For me this *guajiro's* feast in some fragrant wood or on some moonlit beach is for another visit to Cuba.

The next morning I presented my letter to the Reverend Dr. Miguel Soto, a Spaniard and a Methodist minister. Confident that Cuba will forge ahead and make a democratic nation, Dr. Soto is realistically aware of the handicaps she labors under. He spoke of the hopeless situation of the *guajiro* — "a worthy countryman in any country" — who has no roads to take his produce to market, little help in producing salable stuff, and no marketplace in the town. Like thoughtful Cubans everywhere, Dr. Soto hoped that the idealism of President Grau San Martín would triumph over the machinations of the horde of politicians who could even then be seen settling like so many buzzards on the public works. "Cuba has not outgrown her primitive ways," he mourned. "If only this man can be given his chance!"

He related the experience of a town that still depended upon the old political ways of meeting local needs. The *ayuntamiento* decided that the cement walks in and around the plaza should be mended. "Remember this," the doctor smiled, "the next time you wonder why Cubans don't keep their walks in repair." They ascertained what it would cost: $500 or so. A committee was appointed to travel to Havana and wait upon the President: the judge, two councilmen, and two other prominent citizens. One could hardly call upon His Excellency with less. The train trip, going and coming, came to $180. As the President was a very busy man, he could not see them promptly and they waited ten days at twenty dollars a day hotel bill for the group. Naturally they ran up a few other expenses seeing the right people, entertaining congressmen at lunch — any politician will know how that was. That added $150 to the outlay. Total: $530. One can only hope that the committee enjoyed the junket.

Dr. Soto is not one to repine. He thought that was funny, but something to better as well as to laugh about. Slim and energetic, a Protestant who believes in plenty of works along with faith, he is an active member of every go-ahead organization in the town. And he believes that a long step forward is being taken by the civic organizations that are called by various names in different parts of Cuba. In Cienfuegos it is La Acción Cívica through which citizens tax themselves for public works. They began with the aqueduct, which was old, Spanish, and very bad. They have bought land for an airport. Supporters are the Rotary and Lions Clubs, the Chamber of Commerce, and — naturally, in Cienfuegos — the labor unions. Besides every private citizen of right ideas, every business, including bootblacks, contributes as it can.

La Acción is managed with the most open and unquestioned honesty; every penny it handles does a job.

With Dr. Soto I discussed Cuba's regional societies. As a Spaniard he expressed pride in the good they do at such low cost for so many people. Such associations as Los Asturianos, Los Gallegos, and many others whose names indicate the Spanish province from which their founders came, are old. A century ago, when many Spaniards were coming to Cuba to work for other Spaniards, they were a lot of lonely young men. Clerks in stores or in plantation offices, they slept under the counter, worked from dawn till long past dark, made less than a living wage, and had few hours for fun. For those few hours and to maintain their sense of separateness from *criollos*, they formed little clubs. Probably first they met for chess or dominoes or to walk around the plaza together. In time, they found that several young men pooling their pennies could have a room, later a house. Pooling pennies became a habit that yielded richly. They bought or hired what they needed as a group: space, skills, education, and training. Now they represent, through their regional clubs, one of the most far-reaching and influential social developments in the island; incidentally one the United States might do well to copy. If not socialized medicine, it is group medicine, and apparently at its best. Few people say a word against it, though now and then a complainer may say that the one who most needs the benefits has the greatest difficulty in getting them.

This is how it works. If you join a society — and you may join almost any one of them without any possible connection with the region it names — you pay about two dollars a month; the fee varies, but not much. This allows the individual all privileges of the club. He may go there to play games or take classes, to attend meetings, to buy a drink for a friend. If he is ill he may enter one of the hospitals, most of which are as good or better than government or other private institutions: they are staffed with trained or partly trained nurses and attended by the best physicians in

Cuba. Doctors, in Cuba as in the States, fear any system that tends toward socialization, but they like the societies' good and regular pay. Many foreigners, not even Spanish, belong to one or another of the associations in order to be sure of the best doctors.

The hospital I visited was set in a large palm-shaded garden where one-storied pavilions housed everything a modern hospital needs — except perhaps screens. The Northerner becomes a bit too aware of flies crawling on food and babies. In the case of babies, any member woman may come to have her child. She generally brings with her a relative to assist the nurse; in fact to take all but the most highly trained professional care. The relative has a cot in the corner, the baby lies in a bassinet near by, and ambulant mothers stroll the corridors and sit on the verandas with babies almost ready to go home. The baby, soon after or even before delivery, becomes a member in his own right.

Another organization in Cienfuegos, which also covers Cuba. Surely no other country in the world, not excepting our own, is so well organized. Another point of view. The young labor leader I had met in Trinidad came to introduce his pretty wife from Georgia and to show me his Cienfuegos.

We walked along the Prado, where racial discrimination persists, but they were quick to assure me that no such thing is tolerated in the union. He launched then into the history of the Federación Sindical de Las Plantas Eléctricas y de Agua. Its beginnings coincided with the popular uprisings against the tyrant Machado in 1933; he referred me proudly to the Foreign Policy report, *Problems of the New Cuba,* as the fairest statement of the union's forming and its achievements. His phrases were not only contemporaneous, but of a world to come. "We know that what we do has wide implications in the economic of life of Cuba." This was before Walter Reuther said it. "We work with management, of course; we are all in the job together, but we demand fair treatment. . . Several times we have been able to assist management. Once, just to show you, the people in a certain district were afraid that they were being overcharged for current. It looked bad for a while. You know, a public sit-down strike can cause a lot of misery. But we took space in the newspapers and we told the people the facts. They knew that we knew. We were the men in the offices, the linemen, the men who read the meters. They had confidence in the union, and we ended that trouble. . . . Once we were able to lend money to tide the company over a bad spot. That too we were happy to do. Just now we are having a little trouble. My associate here will probably have to go to Havana to confer with the managers. They are trying to put over an American on us, a man brought down here to take the job, but the law distinctly calls for one who has risen through the grades in Cuba. They think they can fool us by calling this man something else. But he's not going to get that *botella*! You know what *botella* means? Bottle, like a nursing bottle that feeds pap to people who do nothing to earn it. None of that in Cuban Electric!"

Our stroll took us to union headquarters, where I was shown a file of members with personal and family data that a Tammany politician might have envied. In a large, bare room where tense silence reigned, the final bout of a checkers tournament was being played off. There were posters and pictures on the walls, magazines on the tables, the air of a quiet and very self-respecting club. Several of the members came on invitation to talk with us. It was impressive to see their quiet self-confidence and sense of being part of a better world in the making. Here was no fear of Yankee imperialism, either of government or business; here were young working Cubans believing that their class, being right and bright, could let foreign capital operate in their country, but believing too that they could control it to good ends. I agreed that Cienfuegos was of the future.

## MATANZAS

DOCTORA ADA LÓPEZ FLAMAND invited me to join her class in Social Service for two visits: to a rural school and to La Colonia Infantil in Matanzas. The trip promised riches. I should meet a group of university students, see Cuban country folk at first hand, observe an interesting experiment in child betterment, and know the lovely and famous city of Matanzas.

We were to cross the bay by launch, and take the Matanzas train at Casa Blanca. Our station was Jibacoa, just beyond Hershey's huge sugar *central*. From there, they warned me, we should have a walk of perhaps eight kilometers. Wear stout shoes.

The little water-edge platform where we took the launch was lovely in the early morning. The salt-sweet smelling water lapped softly against mossy stone and gave back deep reflections of spars and walls and somehow all the antiquity of Havana. I looked over the group. Fourteen young women, including Doctora López, a graduate of Columbia University, looking no older than the others; and one young man. Him I placed at once as a compatriot of mine, and addressed in English. *"Pardón,"* he replied, "I speak no English." One of those sandy Cubans, tall, sturdy, and gray-eyed like a Scotsman. Unmistakably Cuban — I thought — was a girl who was taking up all his attention, and well worth it. Tall, with dark waving hair, large dark eyes, and curving red lips. She, to my amazement, was Dutch, spending the war with her family at one of Havana's best hotels and improving her time at the University. After that I made no guesses as to nationality; just enjoyed myself talking with all of them, for their gentle courtesy made sure that I was never unattended, that I had an opportunity to ask questions of students of varied backgrounds. One was a lawyer, a pretty girl who is going to devote her life to legislation for women and children. One a gradu-

ate of a Protestant school; one a divorcee, courageously building up her shattered life by learning new techniques of doing
good. Another came from one of the old-fashioned families where
she had found her intelligence and her desire to serve being
stifled among her pious relatives. Charity no longer seemed to
her the adequate answer to Cuba's problems.

Leaving the bay, we ran between truck gardens attended by
Chinese in big hats. How Chinese they looked! They must have
been children and grandchildren of the contract labor that was
brought to Cuba after the importation of Africans was stopped.
Very Cuban they are, too, with a proud record as *mambises* and
as worthy law-abiding citizens since. Vegetables make a lovely
pattern of many greens varied by reddish beet tops and purplish
eggplant and underlaid by Cuba's coral soil. On every garden's
edge, the *bohío*, and beyond on every side, gray-white crested
palms.

Soon we came to Jibacoa. Eastward the hills rolled off to a
horizon fringed with palms; westward we could see how our road
slipped gently downhill toward the town with its church towers.
On the platform stood a smiling young man and a boy. It was
the boy, not the man, who stepped forward, hat in hand. With
perfect aplomb, he introduced himself: "Ramiro Álvarez, President of the Student Body." His speech of welcome was perfect
and not too much. He introduced the professor, Nicolás García,
and in a moment we were strung out along the road toward the
village. Señor García took us to his mother's home, where several
of the girls changed city garb for walking shoes, slacks, and ker-
chiefs around their heads. Señora García was a delight to know,
the small-town aristocrat who makes every country place pleasant. Her daughters were there, and two daughters of the family
that owns the surrounding sugar plantation. Then the walk.

Gray dust marked with shadows of flowering fenceposts; now
and then a dip into a damp spot or a jump across a tiny, drying
stream; a rise to another hilltop; a fence to be ducked under

*91*

while somebody parted the barbed wire; a magnificent ceiba making deep shade that one could settle in for life; or a mango heavy with the russet blossoms that promise such golden largesse of fruit later. The road, varied, beautiful, interesting, made full of fun by the girls afoot and on horseback, racing, playing. The road went on and on. Eight kilometers, I decided, must be fifteen miles and not five. Maestro García was reassuring; there really was a school, he said. *"Tras lomita, tras lomita."* Just over the hill. And I was not suffering as much as I let on.

This country teacher interested me. His manner with Ramiro Álvarez, President of the Student Body, was not what one often finds in Latin American educators — stiff, disciplinary, teaching by rote and demanding respect. He would have done credit to a progressive school. As would Ramiro. The boy, the teacher told me, had had a record at the age of twelve as an incorrigible. He hated school, used to play hooky, lying to mother at home and teacher at school. In school he was a constant nuisance, show-off, disrupter. But, elected President by his mates, he was as I saw him; full of importance, surely, but a quiet responsible importance. Maestro García said he had learned how to deal with Ramiro from books lent him by Doctora López, but my impression of the man was that he was so basically sound and fine that he would have worked out a good scheme without a book.

We passed occasional *bohíos,* set on hills, sometimes with fruit trees and gardens, generally not. Maestro García easily told stories of the families whose homes we passed; accurate and unsentimental case histories showing that here was a teacher who followed his pupils home. His ambition, he confided, was to save enough to take a degree, to rise to a city school, maybe a secondary school. What a pity that would be. For he works now at the very heart of Cuba.

At last Ramiro could come running back from the head of the procession to announce that the school was no longer *tras lomita,* but there in sight, on this very hill. A *bohío,* it was, like the others, but with a wide playing-field beyond, a few horses tethered under a ceiba tree, a Cuban flag flying, and children scrambling to get into line. By the time we got there they were in comfortable ranks, not stiff, but orderly and ready to greet the visitors with a formal salute. Breaking ranks they mingled with us easily, helping the young ladies to dismount, caring for the horses.

It had been a hot walk, but we were offered no water. Water is bad when one is heated from the sun. They gave us instead sugar-cane to chew, letting the juice slip down the throat, as refreshing as a soft drink, and later cocoanut milk.

These were Cuba's *guajiro* children. Handsome, most of them, looking sufficiently nourished, certainly of self-respecting people, a country school-full, which, given a fair chance could quickly put Cuba on a level with the best. But Maestro García told me sadly that his school offers only three grades. He has carried a few students on just because he could not bear to see them lost. But there is no more time in his crowded schedule. No money from Havana for more teachers. Nor for books or supplies or for making the future citizens Cuba needs so badly.

We heard a program of songs and speeches and were served an excellent lunch by the neighboring women and older girls in crisp embroidered aprons. The class from the University had brought gifts: a baseball bat, colored crayons, some books.

Among the grown-ups attending I noticed two especially, an old man and a very young one. The young one was so fair and so beautiful, and so at ease even cramped into a low school seat that I took him for some wealthy *hacendado* come calling on the young ladies. But no; he was a graduate of the school's third grade; the son of a *guajiro* who had not been able to go farther. Lost to Cuba at the third grade.

The old man wanted to talk. This school, he told me, as we sat under the ceiba tree, was his life's work. This building was the third. The first was carried away in toto by a hurricane twenty years or more ago. He got the neighbors together and they built another, trying to anchor its posts more securely. But the hurricane of 1940 lifted it, posts and all, and deposited it, so far as anybody knew, in the Caribbean. This, the third, was pretty badly shaken in the fall of '44: its roof sailed away and landed in somebody's tobacco field. But here it is again. "We'll have a school here," he boasted, "as long as I live, and I think longer, because I have made the neighbors know how important a school is." A moment's silence and then he added, quietly: "I never learned to read, but all my children can, and my grandchildren are here."

In Matanzas, still guided by Ada López, I was required to visit first La Colonia Infantil. Cuba has five of these wholesome refuges for sick and indigent children. They are conducted by a *patronato*, a government foundation directed by devoted men and women serving without pay. The one at Matanzas is set on a hill and overlooks the lovely bay with the city beside it. There we were received by the *directora* and several of her staff and shown the entire plant, house and gardens, playgrounds, vegetable patches, and quiet spots where shy children not yet very strong played alone or in small groups.

The breezy entrance hall was furnished with wicker furniture, a small piano and bright pictures. Flanking it were dormitories for fifty girls and fifty boys, all between six and twelve years of age. Each child had a small bed, a tiny chest of drawers, fresh and dainty spreads. There were bathrooms with shower, low basins, hooks for toothbrushes. Everywhere young men and women were working with the children, quietly, pleasantly. Nothing suggested a correctional institution; it was like a well-run sanitarium. We saw children, bright and happy, sitting in the garden for the morning milk, singing in chorus, resting after lunch, and bouncing up for outdoor games. Hard to remember that they all came here suffering from undernourishment and endemic diseases, especially from hookworm, that direst enemy of barefooted children in filthy places. It is estimated that fifty per cent of Cuba's children suffer from it; that it lowers the national efficiency some forty per cent. Sad to think that these blooming youngsters must go back to such living.

Some effort is made to follow them home and to instruct their mothers. Cuba's understaffed but intelligent health department has conducted several workshops for teachers, physicians, and social workers. They have reached thousands of homes; many mothers take pride in their healthy children, confess that vegetables are, after all, good to eat.

As afternoon was turning toward evening, we drove across to the hill of Monserrate for another view of Matanzas; another view, indeed, of everything. From there one gets the serenest vista of the reedy Yumurí, which has cut a wide valley through the hills and flows quietly into Matanzas Bay, joining there the only less poetic vale of the San Juan. Against the glowing sky, under the soft light, it seemed that a pageant of eighteenth-century poets should come to recreate the glory of the days when Matanzas was the Athens of Cuba. No pageant came; only the caretaker, a man of Monserrate whose vocation it is to make this new world shrine as much as possible like its prototype.

He had pruned the laurel trees in front of the church into disciplined precision. The grass was trimmed, the gravel raked, the stone seats brushed, the whole so tended that one could not imagine a bird so daring or a leaf so errant as to light.

The church, which houses the wonder-working statue of Our Lady of Monserrate, is as cozy as a parlor, with rugs on the floor, and on the walls hundreds of little paintings depicting the miracles caused by Her gracious intercession. One comes close to people's lives by reading about their miracles. The lady whose breast was cancerous and cured. The daughter whose mother fled with a lover, but returned. The automobile, shown consumed in flames on a cliffside, but also as saved in glory by the Virgin's hand thrust through a cloud.

Matanzas, the name of that haven of peace and memories,

means "slaughter." Its application here is attributed to a whole-sale killing of Indians. Another legend describes the victims as Spaniards. Twenty-six survivors of Ojeda's settlement on the Gulf of Darien in Panama had been wrecked on Cape San Antonio, Cuba's westernmost point. From there they made their painful way to a beautiful bay which has been identified as Matanzas. There the Indians set upon and killed them all except two women and a man. The women were grateful to be rescued, some time later, by Pánfilo Narváez, who was exploring the island for Velázquez. Spanish life had lost its charm for the man who chose to stay with his Indian family.

After this sixteenth-century appearance, Matanzas was neglected. Cuba had so many bays that the conquerors did not fortify the *bohío* village there until the British menaced it in the days of pirates. After that the city had a rich colonial life until railroads linked it with Havana and let the capital absorb its trade. Especially during the nineteenth century, rich *hacendados* lived in the stately mansions that still line its streets, and those families and much simpler ones competed in producing the artists and poets who gave the city its preeminence.

Among the most lyrical of Matanzas's poets was Diego Gabriel de la Concepción Váldez, who wrote under the name of Plácido. Not of the privileged group, the boy had no legal claim to his resounding polysyllabic name. He was the illegitimate son of a Spanish dancer, who abandoned him to an orphanage, and a Cuban who rescued him and left him with his own mother, a free Negro woman of character and wisdom. She could not, wise as she was, give the sensitive lad immunity from his duel handicap. He was free, but illegitimate; he was always of the despised race. As romantic poets must, Plácido lost his first love — in a cholera epidemic — so his earlier poems were mournful plaints or occasional pieces. He was apprenticed to a worker in tortoise-shell, and he traveled much as a comb-maker. He soon became involved in the underground independence movement and was one of the first to speak out boldly for Free Cuba. In spite of the pseudonym, Plácido, there was no concealing the authorship of such sentiments as he expressed in *El Juramento* (The Oath), which I quote in Ben Frederic Carruthers's translation:

> To be the tyrant's restless foe
> To stain my hands with poisoned gore,
> Spill all of it, yes, blow by blow.
>
> Then I can face the rifles, freed
> From bondage to his deadly breed!

He did face the rifles. Arrested once in Santa Clara and again in Trinidad, where he had gone for Holy Week, Plácido was finally taken in Matanzas as ringleader in the Stairway Conspiracy, so-called because the suspects were chained head down on a staircase and flogged to extract confessions. Plácido, with twenty-eight others, was found guilty. Clanking with chains, they were marched to execution through the Matanzas streets, crowded that day with twenty thousand silent spectators who had gathered from all parts of the island, a still voiceless but potent force for future independence. Plácido's revolutionary verse still stirs the soul of Free Cuba; his best lyrics rank with the best in Spanish literature.

Matanzas is a city of many memories, heroic and sad. In spite of many organizations pushing programs of betterment and bustling business men stirring up the promising murmur of trade and commerce, it remains a lovely provincial town. The shaded streets, with fragrant blossoms dangling over high exclusive walls, maintain a meditative calm too deep to be disturbed by the arrival of a bus. After all, there is disturbance only while a bus is actually there with its flurried passengers and urchins yelling their ices and sweets. Then the bus goes, taking the noisy modern world with it, and Matanzas relaxes into its quietude.

Cuba's intellectual life now centers in Havana, but the gentle ways of Matanzas's inhabitants and the exquisite views of the valley and the bay leave the visitor content to gaze upon poets' statues and read their verse without missing either commercial or intellectual stir.

One should wind up a day in Matanzas in a refreshment bar open to the street, sipping fruit juices, looking. There, in the late afternoon, which reflects long shafts of colored light from the sky and tinges high clouds pink and gold, one may see the whole town go by. Matanzas, except for the nameless revelations of the ex-votos in Monserrate church, is a city of reserved and exclusive families. Many are wealthy, living much abroad or keeping houses in Havana as well as in the ancestral town. More, perhaps, live on in the family mansion keeping to the old ways. Such Cubans of the interior are hospitable, but not at home. They proffer everything, lend books, write letters of introduction, take strangers to drive or to lunch at hotel or club. But, except in Havana which apes United States ways, they do not easily say: "Come on home to dinner." This is often because of the fact that family living is complicated. A household may consist of seventeen people of three generations dominated by a grandmother who has little use for foreigners or foreign ways. If one is asked to such a home for dinner, it is because of real friendship, old acquaintance, or because one's hosts have lived abroad. Younger people emerging into modern life literally come out of the house to do it.

Sitting on Matanzas plaza I watched for them. In spite of a few old ladies in conservative black and a rare old gentleman in white linen or black alpaca, Cubans generally make themselves comfortable. Women go without hats, gloves, or stockings. Sports clothes are as common as on a California street, and at the resorts and beach clubs they reveal pulchritude of Hollywood standard. Men in the provinces go about their business with shirt tails out and collars unbuttoned. This is not as casual as it sounds because of the national garment, the *guayabera*. Worn by the *guajiro* it may be a shirt open at the neck and billowing in the breeze, but on the business man in town it is a well-tailored garment with turn-back collar, belts and pleats and buttons. Whether Hollywood has copied Cuba or Cuba Hollywood, one sees many young men sporting color schemes of turquoise shirts with beige trousers, gray with green or even pink or lavender. In a tropical town, gay with flowers, this looks both right and cool. And when business hours end — as they do most reasonably early in Matanzas — one is correctly garbed for the beach.

Altogether, Matanzas is one of the few places on a senseless planet where one seems able to meet the modern world half way and still live with some of the easy grace of a time when ladies carried parasols and greeted their mounted gallants from *volantas* as they circled the plaza on just such a cool rose-and-gold afternoon. One could spend months in Matanzas. It should be saved for lazy folk who like to see an Athens dreaming into a quiet old age.


## PINAR DEL RÍO


My guardian angel in Cuba, who watched over me, saw that I missed no chance to go places and see things that would help me to know and to understand her country, called me on the phone one morning.

"Here is something you must not miss. We celebrate the birthday of our hero José Martí in ways that are very Cuban, I think very charming. You will probably get a better feeling for it in a smaller place than in Havana where everything is so official. So, if you would like, I shall arrange for you to go to Pinar del Río, where the mayor is a friend of mine and you will be well attended."

I never failed to accept any suggestion of Elena Mederos de

González for they were always good. She liked to show me what was good about her beloved Cuba, but she often said: "This is not what we are most proud of, but to get the complete picture you must see our shadows as well as our sunny spots."

What a woman is this Elena! I had seen her first at meetings of the Women's Inter-American Commission in Washington. With her clear-cut face, bright eyes, smart tailored costumes, and way of striking right to the heart of a matter, she stood out there even in a group of intelligent and thoughtful women. I remember well a report of women's rights in which several delegates outlined their countries' laws for women. They sounded wonderful. Then Elena Mederos remarked dryly that laws were different from performance. "We have still," she said, "to cover all the long way between nice words on paper and actual protection of women in industry." That cleared the atmosphere at the Pan American Union in Washington and made the rest of the discussion more factual and sensible. In her own country she works tirelessly to shorten that long way between words and works. She works within the frame of her tradition. I visited her home, where a charming husband talked intelligently of tobacco, which is his business, politics, which are his worry, or the intellectual life of Cuba, which is his interest. There is a darling daughter of about ten, who bubbles with enthusiasms, but keeps her voice low and her manners sweet without repression. And a not-very-well mother, whom Elena attends as a daughter without a single outside interest. Her orbit includes the Lyceum, where she goes every day.

Elena Mederos is one of those typically Latin women who keep that look of exclusiveness and feminine charm while they do a lot of social thinking and sapient political work. She would deny most of this; there are people in Havana who distrust her. On the right because she seems so leftish. On the left because her social position is so impeccable. But she is valuable. She is also one of the important links between the United States and Cuba.

Educated in our country, Elena has all our swinging, free-seem-
ing ways, a perfect command of our idiom, the personal independence of an Eleanor Roosevelt. But she is in the Latin tradition of a lady, who is the perfect wife, mother, and daughter.

Well, Elena thought I ought to go to Pinar del Río for the *Cena
Martiana* (Supper Martiana). That was understanding and kind.
She saw to it that I should be properly accompanied; that was
kind and very, very Cuban.

The train carried us quickly through Havana's typical environs, where Chinese raise vegetables for the city market and
cane fields ripple delicately up to stern stone bastions and
smokestacks belching heavy black clouds to remind us that life
is earnest and the sugar business is its goal. But yellow-green
cane was soon interspersed with and finally replaced by the blue-
green of tobacco *vegas* and, on the hillsides, serried rows of gray
spines on red earth, which mean pineapples. Over all, of course,
towered the bannered royal palms, flying Cuba's wind-tossed
banner above all the man-made plantings.

Tobacco is almost as truly Cuban as the palms. It too is indige-
nous, and modern science has learned little if anything to improve on the Indian's way of cultivating, curing, and enjoying
that gift of the gods. Thanks to the general imperialistic inroads
of the Machado era, much of the tobacco business has moved to
the United States, but many independent Cuban operators still
make a good living out of tobacco and enjoy the prestige of con-
tributing to luxurious and tasteful living. There is something
gratifying about tobacco all the way through. One may follow the
aromatic leaf from the carefully tended plant in its sheltered
plots, where every leaf is selected and plucked by an expert,
through its curing and into the factories where people work with
high skill in airy lofts, while a reader regales them with works
of their own choice — from classical Spanish poetry, novels, and
even philosophy, to the daily paper, modern thought, and murder
mysteries. The whole course of tobacco from tender baby plant

to the fragrant aroma of a fine *habanero* or even the comforting drag on a two-cent cigarette is as intimately human as such a pleasant indulgence should be. There have been strikes in the tobacco industry; but generally it has gone a pleasant, Cuban, and altogether human way. It was the tobacco workers who welcomed Martí in Florida and voluntarily taxed their wages to support the Cuban revolution; it is the tobacco workers who carry on many a lovely old tradition in spite of modern American pressure.

The province of Pinar del Río is *vuelta abajo*, the "turning down" from Havana rather than up, *vuelta arriba*, toward the mountains of Oriente. *Vuelta abajo* produces the finest tobacco in the world, and this is admitted by all tobacco-raisers everywhere.

Elena was right, as usual, about giving me a companion. She was María Augustina, one of the social-service class, a Protestant, a woman of unusual experience. She was dressed for the journey in a lacy black dress with a hat riding above a blonde pompadour, and wore strapped and heel-less slippers. She talked quietly as we rode along, giving me items of information about the houses, the towns, the plants, but always with an appreciation of the human equation. This is a money-maker, a profitable investment, or a growing town, yes. But here there is a small effort to make better living for underpaid workers, here citizens are combining for a good end, that town has neglected all health measures and suffers recurrent attacks of malaria. All the way we saw the terrific effects of a recent hurricane. Topped palms were just beginning to put out fresh leaves; many had fallen and lay with their long white trunks looking humanly dead with dry leaves like matted hair. Where the devastation had been worst we saw *bohíos* crumpled under their thatches or keeled-over walls where the roof had blown away. In some — but not enough — of these places, new houses were building, with signs stating that this was government provision for the damaged. Here the

Spanish word is much more expressive than any English equivalent. The storms victims were known as *los damnificados*. And what could sound more damned than that? Altogether María Augustina showed herself a woman of the twentieth century in her sense of human values, of the basic need for the full use and development of people if a country is to get ahead. From such people I heard least complaint of imperialism; they put more trust in national betterment and in themselves.

Pinar del Río the town is a pretty one with a back country that offers endless opportunities for exploring, either roughing it or in comfort. From a high cliff one looks down upon Los Mogotes de Viñáles, set in a valley that demands to be called a vale, so idyllic is it. *Mogotes* are tall needles of rock, not so very high perhaps, but adding great beauty to the softly cultivated fields below. They give a fine sense of a paleontological past, for they are outcroppings of the oldest rock base. Pinar del Río has other survivals of a long antiquity. Los Órganos Mountains, pine-clad only on the tops now, show vestiges of heavy forestation below, and mahogany still hides away in remote valleys. Out toward the westernmost tip, El Cabo San Antonio, one finds human survivals too. The Spaniards, as the native Cubans died off, used to catch Indians in Yucatán and ship them to this end of Cuba. Herminio Portell-Vilá says their features are obvious among the natives men hire as guides when they go out there to hunt birds and deer, to catch big fish, and to forget their worries. For the lazy there are hot springs. One day friends took me out to San Vicente, one of Cuba's undeveloped spas, which have been recommended even by European doctors as better than their most famous. At San Luis there is a charming hotel of the inn type where one who planned to write could find endless opportunities not to on wide sunny terraces, in fragrant woods, or splashing in the pool.

In town we were accommodated in the all-white Ricardo Hotel. Open on three sides, it was tropically cool, with ceilings almost too high to see, wide marble stairways, cavernous upstairs halls, and bedrooms with French doors opening onto balconies, mosquito-netting caught back for the day, and friendly chambermaids. Outside of touristy Havana most chambermaids are men with rolled-up shirt-sleeves, water-logged hands, long black cigars, and a willingness to serve — when they get around to it. There we met the Ichasa family, who had been told to look out for us and to introduce us to Mayor Barrera and his family. The Ichasas are one of those Cuban families that make you wonder whether you are in Cuba or the United States. Both mother and daughter were educated in the States; daughter was at home on vacation. With me their talk and manner was altogether Yankee; in a Cuban group their very voices and manner changed into the staccato fire of Cuban vowels and redundant phrases with shrugs and gestures such as English cannot sustain. Of course, they spoke both languages with an impeccable accent.

The Barrera home was an extensive apartment upstairs, where the tiled living room caught the mountain breeze blowing in across lower roofs, and where modernistic furniture seemed quite at home. As Cuban meals are, lunch there was a feast of many courses. A rich bean soup served with fluffy rice. Then came the inevitable starchy *yuca* with piquant croquettes, followed by cold sliced meat and salad with a rich mayonnaise. No, that was not all. There followed that Spanish dish which has taken on a distinct flavor in every American land — *arroz con pollo,* rice with chicken. A delicate white wine helped, and the dessert was Cuba's exquisite white cheese with guava jelly. Coffee, of course.

In the afternoon we sat on the balcony to watch parades of school children marching under their bright banners and led by their own bands with majorettes in shorts, high-heeled top-boots, and shakos on fly-away curls. They twirled and cavorted, the bands did their tuneful but not always accurate best, marshals dashed back and forth trying to keep inexperienced marchers proceeding evenly, and parents beamed all along the line. The children, I was told, would all assist at the *Cena Martiana*; they had been learning Martí's sayings, and many schools had prepared layettes in honor of the baby José. The *Cena Martiana*, like Christmas, adores the newborn babe; the emphasis is heightened by the custom known as *las canastillas*, the little baskets to be presented to children born at or near the hour when Leonor Pérez de Martí gave birth to her son José on January 28, 1853. The baskets are displayed in store windows with cards announcing that this gift is presented in honor of the "Apostle of our independence, José Martí." Most of the offerings are marked for hospitals that care for the poor, and the gifts are sumptuous. Not only all the clothes an infant could possibly need, but bed and bath equipment, baby carriages, canned milk for the baby, and strengthening food for the mother. Such "little baskets" would require a truck to haul them to wherever the newborn José might be found, and they would bring much-needed help to many poor homes. The man they honored would have liked that, probably more than many of the monuments raised to his memory.

The *Cena* itself was in the plaza, an elongated triangle in the center of town where tables and chairs had been provided for twelve hundred people, each with a place card inscribed with a saying of Martí. Mine said: *"Ver en calma un crimen es cometerlo"* (To witness a crime calmly is to commit it). My neighbor's: *"Los pueblos viven de la levadura heróica"* (Peoples live from heroic leaven). The speakers' table was marked by a huge Cuban flag made of flowers and there were three loud-speakers, a bevy of camera men, and one very busy young factotum who did the announcing with such meticulous attention to his stopwatch that he made nothing of cutting in on a speaker's most florid periods. (The radio promises to bring Latin America onto schedule.) Below the central park on which the tables stood, the streets and sidewalks were filled with school children who paid not too much attention to the proceedings. It was a fresh lovely night under a blue velvet sky luminous with stardust, and the planets hung very close.

The program began with "Judgment of Martí" read by its author, a thirteen-year-old girl in a middy blouse and blue ribbons. Three men speakers followed, but nobody paid any attention, as the photographers were very busy and most of the audience preferred their show to the oratory gathering momentum above. The supper, neatly boxed, consisted of excellent sandwiches and turnovers, chicken croquettes, slices of guava jelly, and soft drinks that passed along from hand to hand. Some women had put in many busy hours; it was an excellent meal and well managed.

The speaking went on. A child of twelve or so, but with a voice that carried, gave us his considered opinion of Martí as a politician. All opinions, both adult and juvenile were to the same end: Martí was above criticism. The teacher who sat near me whispered: "I wish we did not make a saint of him. It would do us more good to study him as a man." The photographers demanded that everybody at the speakers' table should face about.

Another speaker. Luckily no speaker was more disturbed by the photographers than they were by him. By this time there was confusion involving many yards of wire and penetrating whispers from man to man. This speaker was saying that Martí was greatest as a teacher, and referring to Martí's teacher, Rafael de Mendive. But he was outdone by the electricians who finally got connected up and flooded the lovely night with such incandescence that the velvet sky, the milky way, and the planets retired.

By this time the speaker of the evening was due: Señor Ichasa, a newspaperman, member of Congress, speaker noted throughout the land. His talk was an oration, delivered with all the skill of experience. In excellent voice, calm and commanding presence, he began simply, mounted gradually, and came to a grand and thunderous climax. Now everybody listened. Even the most officious man with electricity to apply stood to hear. Martí, we heard, in a variety of tones and illustrative incidents, was not only Cuba's but America's greatest contribution to the ages. A man without blemish, a brilliant mind comparable to the clearest of all time, a lofty spirit unexcelled anywhere, a patriot who labored that his country might be free, who foresaw its future, who died finally as a martyr to its cause. None could deny that in him were found all virtues and all excellences: as teacher, liberator, journalist, poet, politician, statesman, economist, orator, José Martí had all a people need to save them. In him were incarnated the greatest aspirations of the human being.

The audience was vociferous in its applause. A young girl near the speaker burst into tears and had to be helped down. The band burst into *La Bayamesa*, Cuba's stirring hymn to freedom, and the *Cena Martiana* was over.

Here I realized, were legend and tradition in the making. This celebration was only the third since Juan Soriol and friends of his had conceived the idea in Manzanillo. Since then it had run like a cane-fire the length and breadth of the island; every town, every school, every organization must now celebrate the birth of Martí with a supper and with ceremonies whose fervor takes on a religious tone. I wondered if I should not, as the teacher suggested, prefer to study the man than the saint.

## ISLE OF PINES

THE ISLE OF PINES is one of those places which make one hope that they will never change. Compared with its lovely quietude any sort of development — even that which might produce better eating, better housing, and more education for the people — seems just needless disturbance. This seems particularly true because the Isle of Pines is chock-full of potentialities. Its waters teem with fish, its hills are almost solid marble, its lands are fertile, its grapefruit is unchallenged for excellence; healing springs, both hot and cold, bubble out of its rocks, and its rocky coves and mangrove swamps are positively sown thick with pirates' treasure. How much better just to keep on dreaming, as it now does, of future wealth than to go in for progress. Think of the dreadful noise of machines grinding up rocks to make roads, tearing mountains into dust storms to dig out marble, and transforming all the peaceful porch-sitters and plaza-loafers into timed workers, producing and rowing over wages — which they now have none of — and hours — which now they do not count. It would be hard to imagine any actual rewards better than the golden dreams that are now everybody's equal portion. And this blessed isle has, if one should tire of contemplating a brilliant future, a very exciting past for reminiscences. And, lest the clime's perfection should pall, Nature has provided periodic drama in the form of a good rousing hurricane about every four or six years.

One way to go from Havana to the Isle of Pines is by train or bus to Batabanó and then across in a little steamer that hauls freight and lets second-class passengers roost atop the cargo or on benches alongside. There is an elegant outdoor salon for the first class. That way does, of course, give one the acquaintance of more entertaining Cubans. But I went by air, and I am glad I did; the little Cuban-owned plane seemed so casual and lightly put together, as though it were a boy's job of reassembling. It was, as a matter of fact, a hand-me-down from the States, but kept in apple-pie order and manned by well-trained and careful young pilots. Cuba has laws governing such matters and an enviable record of almost no accidents on any line. And it was so friendly. We were late in starting, of course, and by that time the traveling man, the government inspector, and the lady going home after shopping in Havana had made me feel as though I were part of an intimate week-end party. We flew slowly and that was an advantage. One should approach that calm island without haste, and the slow movement seemed an almost aimless drifting with time to enjoy the scene to the full.

Outside of Havana, of course, the country repeats the familiar red-and-green pattern with leafy canyons, ruffled-top palms, houses looking so tiny, and roads running straight for awhile and then dodging senselessly into the hills and getting lost forever. Then one is over water, but water so shallow that every little rock of every little key stands clear and all but waves at the passing plane. In fact the illusion of waving becomes almost certainty as the plane's own shadow drags across the ripples and changes the colors. The water itself looks like liquid jade, but the sand below is bluish, the rocks deeper green with purple shadows, and darting fish could be made of any jewel you care to mention. *Isleños* — the Isle of Pine dwellers choose to forget that all Cuba is an island and refer to themselves alone as "the islanders" — like to talk about building a causeway across the keys and making their trips to Havana in no time at all. This is another dream that is really too alluring to spoil by doing anything about it.

The very word key, as applied to drowned reefs and islets, is Cuban, *Taino*. The Indian word is *cayo*. Mr. Webster says that it came into English as the "key instrument," and that key was pronounced *kā* in those days. *Cayos* were important to all who cruise the Caribbean islands, and there can be few better ways to see how they are than by flying from Havana to Júcaro.

Another way to go to the Isle of Pines and to know its *cayos* intimately is strongly recommended for the young and adventurous. Charter a boat with a talkative *isleño* for pilot and cruise the length of the southern shore from Cayo Francés to Punta Brava, and then out among the coral reefs to Punto Largo and beyond. Anywhere along there, where the mangroves stick their branches into the swamps or where tall dry trees or pointed hills make unmistakable landmarks, you might — in fact you should — find treasure. Oh, yes, an essential part of the equipment is an old, yellowed, crumbling map with a few cryptic words and figures in the margin. But that is easy enough to secure. The attic in almost any old Southern mansion on our own pirate-infested coast should yield one. In fact the hotel-keeper at Nueva Gerona counts on treasure hunters as part of his regular clientele, and he is now keeping a heavy iron chest for the last one. That was a very affluent seeker for gold who traveled in his own yacht and with a crew and with such a good map that when he dug he actually turned up this chest, which is certainly heavy enough to contain millions in doubloons and who knows what jewels. Nobody knows, as a matter of fact, because the incurious owner went off in a hurry to the war and left the box without opening it. The hotel proprietor has been too honorable ever since to do more than let curious guests try to lift it. I could not, but two men can. When its secret is revealed I hope I shall know of it, although perhaps this is another way of keeping the island's untouched potentialities inviolate and one should never wish to learn the treasure chest's secret.

The honorable hotel proprietor, Señor Amable Ordóñez, was off on his honeymoon when I visited his inn, the Santa Rita Springs Hotel at Santa Fe. So I did not meet him, but his staff paid me every courtesy, including detailing an old gentleman, full of tales, to escort me into and around the village of Santa Fe, showing me the springs on the way. The springs are marvelous. They cure everything. Hot ones bubble out just beside cold ones. Some taste and smell foul, others yield water as sweetly fresh and cool as a mountain glade. Most of them now work their own way out among the roots of ceibas and palms, pushing aside leaves and other débris. One is inclosed into a stone house fitted with dressing rooms and presided over by a Negro with a very smooth voice and slow motion who has been becalmed on that porch for a lifetime. His certainty that his water is the best and most curative in the world works wonders even before you enter your private pool to splash as long as you will in a perfect temperature.

The town was sadder, for the most recent hurricane — that of 1944 — had left its harsh mark on trees with roots sticking up and houses without roofs. Happily the Isle of Pines climate is such that a family left without a house can live quite comfortably under a tree or in a palmleaf shelter until a new house appears. New houses were building, thanks to the government's indemnification program. *Isleños* complain that Cuba forgets all about them for generations at a time. But I saw new houses and a very good-looking schoolhouse. Not feeling social-minded that day, I did not go inside. I sat instead in the general store, where soft drinks were served, and talked with the oldest American resident, who remembered Abraham Lincoln. Then I called on my guide's wife and daughter and felt the gentle atmosphere of an island home, white and open on all sides. Chickens were scratching and clucking under the palms, bougainvillea running in utter unrestraint, and a parrot and dog let us sit for awhile on their porch, such a porch as one sees everywhere in the States.

The hotel porch was equally conducive to doing nothing and caring nothing. It is a wonderful hotel, just then recovering from having housed scores of North American aviators. Its kind can be found anywhere modern architects have not put their heavy modern feet. It has wide verandas all around, a circular entrance hall, a large enough lounge with a fireplace, and a dining room with no pretensions whatever, but very good food. On the porch we rocked and talked to the chirp of birds and the occasional passing of an ox-team, a horse loaded with fodder, or a kid kicking the dust. A nice family from Havana charted a cart and rode off in style with father driving the sleepy horse with his son's aid and mother and daughter sheltered by a flowered parasol. It will be a sad day when they make this all over for the taste of moderns from Havana and the States.

I could not spend my entire visit lazing away the sunny days around the Santa Rita Hotel. I had to be out seeing the island, which could not have been better done than with the friendly guidance of Dr. Waldo Medina, judge of the Nueva Gerona court. It was a delightful day, for Dr. Medina knows his island well and is a *martiano,* a student of Martí.

We drove along an excellent road that carried very little traffic and wound around gentle hills and topped gentle rises from which I could get the lay of the land. It is generally broken country, golden tawny at the end of the dry season, but refreshed with green trees here and there and waving royal palms everywhere. Geologically the Isle of Pines is older than the main island, and so has had time to compress its formation into the marbles that line its hills. Dr. Medina says there is inexhaustible wealth of fine marble there. It is of many colors, but mostly gray; much of it has been used in the Capitol and other government buildings in Havana.

As the Isle of Pines has an area of only twelve hundred square miles, including the mangrove swamps that merge into the sea, we were soon in Nueva Gerona, the capital and largest town. It is not very large at that. A wide street with cars parked down the middle, horse- and ox-drawn vehicles among them, low buildings, and people in no hurry at all. As the population of the whole island is only about eight thousand, it cannot spare many to make a big capital. About fifteen hundred of them are British, a good many of them very dark British from the other islands. There is a scattering of Germans, Scandinavians, perhaps four hundred Japanese with their families, who are very old residents, and fifty or sixty Chinese with no families or wives at all. The Japanese were farmers and fishermen, and Dr. Medina does not believe that they were disguised officers spying for the Japanese navy. There are some Cubans on the Isle of Pines, I gathered, few of them colored. But the style and tone of the island is North American and its business is controlled by immigrants from the States.

This came about because the Treaty of Paris, which ended the Spanish-American War, specifically stated that the question of ownership or the Isle of Pines should "be omitted from the proposed constitutional boundaries of Cuba, the title thereto being left to future adjustments by treaty."

Promoters in the States assumed that the Isle of Pines would be United States territory, and they at once set about advertising it, recruiting colonists to settle it, and selling its land — that which was above water and some which was below. It was a time of splendid prospects on paper, and it brought many good farmers and many less solid investors. As a rule the investors grew disgruntled because the island was not turned over to the States, and went home. The farmers, finding rewarding land and being used to working for results, stayed on, and are there yet. They live in small or large houses in the midst of citrus groves. Each house has a driveway that curves in around a bottle palm and a small lawn, and flaunts rain-of-gold and bougainvillea vines over open pergolas. California or Florida to the life!

The dispute as to who owned the Isle of Pines rocked along for a generation and was settled only in 1925, when the Coolidge administration finally accepted the fact that the island had always been a part of Cuba, having been so administered throughout the long colonial history, and that the only equitable solution was for it to remain so.

The Yankees have stayed and have established a school so good that all the leading Cuban families send their children there. This has made *isleños* even more bilingual than *habaneros,* and in Havana they boast of their command of English. This Central School, opened in 1926 with an endowment of eighteen thousand American dollars, was supported by a contribution of half a cent on each crate of grapefruit shipped out, and by tuition. But as the American colony lessened in numbers and in wealth, the school began to run behind, until in 1945 it showed a debt of $13,200 and all its buildings were in disrepair. The American colony in Havana then took a hand. Three men went over to investigate, decided that $3,000 was needed at once for repairs, got assistance through the Office of the Coordinator of Inter-American Affairs and raised enough among themselves to clear the debt. The school was now on a sound basis and a credit to the American colony, with the too frequent corollary that certain Cubans were left with hurt feelings because they were neither consulted nor asked to contribute.

The people one meets show no sign of anything but the best state of international amity. Dr. Medina, who was named Waldo for his father's closest friend, a Yankee, introduced me to several of his Yankee friends in Nueva Gerona. We chatted about buried treasure, the way the Smoot-Hawley Tariff had ruined the grapefruit business, and how the island, where anything you plant will flourish to new perfections, could easily support between three and four hundred thousand people. They offered to take me to see Cuba's great penal institution a few miles away, but I preferred to visit the Sarda farm where young José Martí had been given refuge after those fearful months as a prisoner of Spain in Havana. But there was no hurry.

We had time to while away another hour in the Tropical Gardens Café, where one sees hunters' and fishers' trophies on the walls, and where we saw bits of the handiwork *isleños* make for tourists. I came away with a mahogany candlestick; a mahogany paper knife, inlaid with my initials and the island's name in silver, followed me home.

If the drive out had been delightful, the return was unforgettable. Dr. Medina pointed out the two hills that swung into line for the benefit of Long John Silver and his piratical crew in Stevenson's *Treasure Island*. Somebody who knew the island well had given that description to the author writing away in California. Then we turned into a large gate and drove up a road bordered by plowed fields to the Sarda house.

Any Cuban takes on a reverential tone when he speaks of the great José Martí. Dr. Medina did too. But his talk was as intimately personal as though he had known that seventeen-year-old youth whose legs were still sore from the gyves, and who walked this road and the terrace in front of the house for so many wordless hours. Dr. Medina has dedicated his term of office in the Isle of Pines to collecting all available material on this period in the hero's life. In his talk he makes the young man come alive, for his deep appreciation of a noble character has given him insight into its youthful forming. Nothing the Isle of Pines may do will ever seem more useful, at least to Dr. Medina and to me, than giving refuge to the Apostle of Cuba's liberty when he most needed it.

# III

# THE COLONIAL COMPLEX

Ramón Grau San Martín, elected president of Cuba in 1944, took office in a heady atmosphere compounded of two surprising facts. The election was honest and the man was honest. President Fulgencio Batista, a colonel, and immensely popular with the army, had amazed everybody by permitting balloting without military or police interference and free of pressure from above. His own candidate lost and his opponent was sworn into office without disturbance. Moreover, Grau San Martín was an idol of the people and a symbol of the disinterested patriotism that Cuban politics has too often lacked. His election was a true uprising of the little people who remembered him as an opponent of the vicious tyrant, Gerado Machado, in 1933, and one who had suffered imprisonment and exile at that time. Grau had served as president for a precarious three months or so in 1933–4 and had given enough proof of his disinterestedness and integrity to offset in some degree the Cuban's ingrained cynicism.

Common talk in Cuba, as President Grau struggled to bring some sort of decency out of years of peculation and misgovernment, was revealing. Most Cubans, distrustful of government, cynically critical, were saying, "Of course the man is honest, but

*The quiet, empty streets. Trinidad*

*Business is in balconied, colonial houses. Camagüey*

*Santiago Harbor sheltered the whole Spanish fleet in 1898*

look at the mistakes he makes!" Americans placed the emphasis differently. We, of course, put up with plenty of graft at home, but with limitations as to amount and as to the grade of office in which it is tolerated. Honesty is generally expected and considered an asset. In any case, our observers in Cuba were saying, "Of course Grau makes mistakes. But the man is honest!"

Many farsighted Cubans take the same tone. A lawyer, summing up the political situation, said, "Certainly he makes mistakes. Perhaps he is not a very good judge of men. He has a big cleanup job to do and an angel from heaven couldn't do it without making enemies. But his honesty offsets everything. If we could have one honest administration and the honest election that would inevitably follow it, Cuba might then come of age. We might even begin to trust our own government. But if we again childishly refuse to give an honest man a fair chance, we shall slip back into the hopeless mess we have been in ever since our first administration."

This attitude, unhappily, is not the prevailing one. Most Cubans easily shrug off dishonesty in office. "Well," they say, "what can you expect? With the Spanish tradition of dishonesty in public office and then the training your Magoon gave us in some finer points, we've got more kinds of governmental dishonesty than any country in the world."

Magoon and the complaint against the United States come properly into another place. But that excuse, like the blame of Spain, seems to reveal a deep underlying mental habit. Cubans seldom express the sturdy, often brash attitude toward their government that says in effect, "This is our government and if we don't like it we'll get rid of it, come next election, and put in a better one." Cubans generally disapprove of government all right; but they do not threaten change through the orderly process of the ballot. Their method is refusal to vote or even revolution.

Salvador de Madariaga, in his *Hernán Cortés*, makes much of what he calls the Spaniard's basic democracy. He quotes from Calderón de la Barca's *La Vida es Sueño*:

> *En lo que no es justa ley*
> *No ha de obedecer al rey*

> In unjust laws
> One need not obey the King.

In similar vein is an old Spanish saying: *"Bajo la capa, mato al rey"* (Under my cape, I kill the king). Another, common in the colonial era when royal laws were more flouted than obeyed, says with an almost audible sneer, *"Acato, pero no cumplo"* (I obey, but I do not fulfill).

To a Spaniard, long dominated by kings whom he could neither control nor get rid of, these unconscious reactions and pithy sayings seem to express a basic democracy. To people experienced in self-government they seem to leave out the only dependable basis for real democracy: respect for law, willingness to observe even an unjust law until it can be changed by democratic processes. The Spaniard, even according to Madariaga, discussing basic democracy, bows to the authority of the King; but it is a hated authority imposed from above and so to be evaded as a naughty child, or an undeveloped adult, evades the authority of parents or police. In the individual we have learned to recognize such attitudes as proof of the adolescent revolt against too domineering parents. It seems possible to explain much in Cuba on the assumption that countries, like children, may suffer similar ills from too long a period of tutelage. There is no understanding Cuba without remembering that this island was Spain's oldest colony, *"La Isla Siempre Fiel"* (the Ever-Faithful Isle), which remained dependent some eighty years longer than most of Spain's American empire. It is true that islanders were restless under cover and that a complete picture of Cuba requires an understanding of her strong and noble revolutionary tradition, but much in the modern Cuban's manner of thinking can be explained on the ground that today's republic is suffering from a colonial complex.

Too often the popular reaction to affairs is that of the colonial who had no responsibility for his government. The *criollo* found it amusing as well as profitable to outwit the king and the peninsulars sent to rule the island. Smuggling was a great game as well as a profitable one. Conspiring was the recognized indoor and underground sport. This state of mind, oddly as it sits upon a people who wish to be recognized as responsible citizens of a modern republic, does persist. Of course it persists everywhere; our own country is not exempt from this any more than from any of the other ills Cuba knows, but in Cuba disregard of the law is very widely looked upon with light-hearted amusement.

The week I arrived in Havana the newspapers were filled with stories of a duel. Duelling is against the law. One of the contestants was Eduardo Chibás, a national senator and an intimate and honored advisor of President Grau San Martín. The other was a distinguished newspaperman whom Senator Chibás thought had insulted him. Their first meeting, ostensibly secret, but blazoned in all the papers and over the radio, and the theme of all conversation, was thought not to satisfy honor, so a second appointment was made with more publicity as to place, time, seconds, medical men, and terms. Cubans were enchanted with the affair. Cartoons, vaudeville skits, jokes running through the streets and cafés — all had to do with Senator Eddie and his honor. I heard nobody deplore the fact that the law of the land was being flouted by a legislator sworn to uphold it. On the contrary, a distinguished Cuban said: "It's as good as a bullfight, and we Cubans are too civilized to permit bullfights. In fact, it's better because in a bullfight somebody is apt to get hurt and in one of our duels the only danger is to the onlookers."

This sort of sly dig is typical of Cuba's humor. Jorge Ma-

ñach, one of Cuba's most brilliant prose writers, has made a penetrating study of his country's humor in a book called *Indagación
del Choteo*. This might be freely translated *Inquiry into Kidding*,
for the word *choteo*, a derivative of *chotar* (to suck) is so close to
our *kidding* as to suggest a similar hidden attitude toward life.
The Cuban, in his joking, is for pricking pretentiousness, pulling
down pomposity, showing scorn for superiors whom he cannot
destroy. Perhaps in this scorn for pretentiousness the *choteo* is
easiest for us to understand; it resembles the frontier humor that
runs through our literature from Lowell, via Mark Twain, Mr.
Dooley, and Will Rogers, to Bill Mauldin. Always it is taking
the starch out of the stuffed shirt, showing up the city slicker,
puncturing the pose of the politician, bringing the brass hat down
to earth. The Cuban's kidding is often more sharply barbed than
ours, less friendly, suggestive of the sword under the cape, ready
to kill as well as to kid. The *choteo* is wicked in the sense of being
both sexual and dirty; it spreads scorn of everything serious and
sacred. Nothing, in fact, is sacred. Jokes that run through Havana, and are originated or repeated in El Teatro Martí, leave
nothing inviolate: church, home, love, death, the most intimate
details of the lives of important men. Much of the meaning is
lost on the outsider unless a well-posted Cuban will explain the
background and interpret the slang. Jokes are light, allusive, gay
and completely irresponsible. They bring quick laughter and
often witty repartee or amplification; the gift for word-play is
almost universal. Mañach says that Cuba's *choteo* is not humorous because Cuba, a small country "that is not respected because
of its weakness causes all within it to respect each other less, de-
stroying the contrasts that invite humor."

One must bow to Mañach, but the casual visitor finds no lack
of contrast in Cuban life or in the *choteo*. In kidding themselves,
Cubans have created two stock characters as typical of conflicting traits in the national character: the *gallego* and the Negro.
The Galician is the Spaniard, who, coming from cool northern

Spain, is energetic, hard-working, and dependable. As a comedy figure, he is sturdy but stodgy. The Negro, likable but also exaggerated, appears in the guise of our cartoon darky. "No, sir, I don' wanna earn a quarter. I'se got a quarter."

In a daily radio skit, which no Cuban misses if he can possibly hear it, the plodding, stupid *gallego* is repeatedly out-witted by the Cuban Negro. Lazy, happy-go-lucky, full of wiles, the engaging Negro lacks all the *gallego's* sturdy virtues, but he wins every time.

Perhaps it is not too fanciful to see in these popular characters a reflection of the ages-old hatred of Spain that finally made Cuba independent. The *gallego,* coming at the end of the colonial regime, inherited the stored-up resentment against peninsular officials, for he came too to make money, to dominate through his very virtues, and at bottom to scorn the Creole, who had never learned those middle-class ways. To this day, the Spanish immigrant stands apart. He owns much of the retail business, a great deal of city property, and apparently all the hotels.

In the hotels the tourist notes how the Spaniard differs from the Cuban. Ask information from a hotel manager or clerk who lisps his Castilian syllables, and ten to one he will reply coldly, "No, I don't know. . . . He is out of town. . . . No, there is no way to get there." Then watch how a bystanding Cuban, whose speech is in the soft accent of Andalusia with the added gentleness of Cuba's elisions, will step up to offer aid. "Yes, indeed. . . . Certainly." (All his immediate reactions are assenting.) "He lives so and so; I shall be glad to show you the way." Often the Cuban is wrong, often he offers to do more than anybody could do. But he is kind, helpful, full of grace and charm. It is said that the Spaniard loses all his stiff-necked Spanish ways in one generation. I do not know, for then he is a Cuban, and as charming as all the others.

A related hatred of Spain appears in the anomalous attitude of many Cubans toward the Catholic Church. The Church, in all

Spanish America, came along with Spain. Every conqueror was flanked by both priest and notary; the cross was raised with the flag; Christianizing was as important as gold-seeking or empire-building. In many cases Catholicism was declared the state religion when the colony freed itself from Spain. Most of the populations are Catholic to this day. This is true in Cuba, but with important reservations. As everywhere, many educated and influential men are free-thinking agnostics or Masons, though they prefer convent education and church adherence for wives and daughters as a sort of moral and social insurance. Protestant missionaries continue to gain converts and establish schools, but, as in other Latin American countries, the dominant group is Catholic or nothing. Cubans are different from their neighbors in their insistence that the Church must keep out of politics. This may be due to American influence or to their own history. The Church in Cuba lost its greatest power and influence during the long struggle for independence because the clergy generally sided with the crown. In many American countries, certain clerics — especially among the lower orders — stood out boldly for independence, even led the forces of revolt, as Father Hidalgo did in Mexico. In Cuba the contrary was true. Most of the priests were Spaniards and active against revolutionists, and the Church lost confidence and loyalty which it has never regained. Lately the Church has been trying to restore its influence, but again it has chosen to ally itself with Spain; and Franco's Spain is not proving the best argument for Spanish culture and Catholic faith in Cuba, with its strong tradition of independence.

Four hundred years of feudal Spain and medieval Church have naturally left deep marks on the Cuban's way of thinking. An irresponsible subject lacks the foresight of the independent citizen who is going to have to see the thing through and pay the piper finally. Too often United States citizens refer to Cubans as "these people" in a tone that makes the rest of the statement redundant. It's purport always is that "these people" are definitely inferior to our people. Such thoughts pervade the atmosphere like a smothering gas that makes it very difficult for tender plants like international understanding and Pan American good will to flourish. That they grow at all may prove that they are not so tender, after all.

Perhaps it is time to recognize that the major differences between the United States and most other American countries are due to geography and the chances of history. One who knew Cuba well suggested writing a book on what would have happened if the Pilgrims had landed in Cuba and the conquerors on Plymouth Rock. In the case of the Spaniards, the answer is easy. One look at that stern and rock-bound coast, lashed by the icy storms of November, and those excellent mariners would have set their prows for the south and a land more amenable to human habitation. Of the English in Cuba, we might also hazard a guess, for we have seen in Hawaii what that breed could do with a tropical isle. Open the proceedings with prayer, set up a council of all males, put everybody to work, convert the natives to Protestantism, and get them into trousers and Mother Hubbards before nature produced original sin. More than likely the English in Cuba would have imported African slaves just as the Spanish did; in Hawaii they imported Orientals whose fate differed little from that of chattel slaves. The great difference in Cuba would have come, probably, from the facts that Englishmen expected to work and were determined to govern themselves. They came from a land where both traditions prevailed, and they came a century later than the Spaniards did. When Spain conquered and settled the New World, Europe was still Catholic, and unthinking obedience to King and Church was instilled into all. When the English came, Europe had been swept by protest; protesting was natural to people whose very coming was itself a protest. Moreover they represented many sects; Christianity had been split by disagreements that let in questioning and made scientific advance possible. Spanish America, held firmly by

Church and State, was, in a sense, the last stronghold of medieval Europe.

In civil life the Englishman in Cuba would probably have done as his stock did in the northern colonies: started with a small farm, worked by the farmer and his sons and a few slaves, but gradually, in a century and a half, built up great estates owned by wealthy owners and worked by tenant farmers. Few of us realize how strong this tendency is in the United States now. It is reported that in Iowa in 1945 there were more tenant than independent farmers. New and expensive farm machinery tends to force more little men onto the big men's payroll. Curious that our country today should be approaching the situation that prevails in Cuba as a result of her colonial pattern. The United States and Latin America seem to start at opposite ends of certain arcs; if we were more apt at learning from each other's experience we might attain a true Pan American civilization sooner.

The second incalculable advantage the United States had over America is geography, both physical and human. In the first place, the continent lay open to quick exploration and colonization. Even the Rockies offered no barrier comparable to that of the Andes, which men, with all their modern inventions, have even yet penetrated at only two or three passes. And when our forebears got to the Rockies even that comparatively easy crossing was made easier by the discovery of gold in California. With one final rush they made it to the Pacific. So the continent was crossed. It is important that it was conquered, not by armies led by noblemen and blessed by the Church, but by individual frontiersmen, often rough and unlettered, but always intrepid and willing to work. Without work they did not get there. So the United States was made by men who were used to work, not ashamed to work, and capable of dignifying work.

This is part of the human geography, of course. The rest is that the Indians were so greatly outnumbered that they scarcely stemmed the onrush of the white man or altered his cultural pattern. But the greatest boon, as though Providence had chosen this land for the definitive experiments in human development, was immigration. From the beginning of settlement on the Atlantic coast English colonials were mixed with other folk: Swedish, Dutch, German, French, Irish, Scotch, African, and even Spanish were fusing into that amalgam which will yet, we hope, make a true democracy. They all swooped across the Alleghanies, down the Mississippi, and over the Rockies; and all the way they lived, fought, bred, and died together, learning humanity's great lesson that folks are folks and it takes all kinds to make a world. The evil that went along was, of course, African slavery, which so blighted our whites that we still struggle under the hideous incubus of the fear of a colored skin. But the country was big enough to stand even that stress, to fight a civil war without wrecking the union, and in the twentieth century to begin to see better days.

All this time, what was happening to Cuba? Little or nothing. A few Spaniards came, but fewer cared to settle. Cuba is a fortunate isle where almost anything will grow, and full of potentialities. Sturdy hard-working folk could have made it prosperous from the start, but gentlemen and soldiers were not interested in potentialities; they wanted real wealth quickly acquired. Gold mines were discovered, but they were soon outshone by the vaster wealth of Mexico and Peru, and Spain reduced Cuba to a way station where ships could repair and revictual. An important business became the hunting of cattle that had been allowed to run wild; sugarcane culture soon followed, and every development demanded more labor than could be extracted from the Indians. Slaves from Africa seemed to be the only answer. Bartolomé de las Casas, ardent defender of the Indians, did not suggest the importation of Africans, but he did accede to it. Even this did not give Cuba parity with the other colonies, because Spain discriminated against the island by limiting the number of blacks, and the labor supply was always short. Smuggling naturally resulted; Yankees as well as Cubans and Europeans delivered many "sacks of coal" in quiet coves.

As Velázquez's original grants were ill-defined, the descendants of those grantors were forever in litigation, especially as Spain took more and more sugar and rum, and as land values increased. By the end of the eighteenth century, every *criollo* planter was a lawyer as well as a poet or philosopher and a widely traveled gentleman who believed in independence and owned slaves. The situation was like that in our southern states, except for several facts which have resulted in greater tolerance in Cuba.

In the first place, Spain, as always, got humane laws on the statute books. Slaves were to be given religious instruction; men and women were to be imported in pairs and married by the church; and punishment was to be administered only with official approval.

A thoughtful Cuban, comparing the modern attitude toward colored people in his country and in mine, said, "Both Spain and the Church deserve credit for our tolerance. According to Spanish law the Negro, like the Indian, was a human being and entitled to consideration as a man; according to the Church he had a soul to be saved. But it is more important that the Catholic Church teaches humility. No individual dares set himself up as the mouthpiece of God as Protestants do; one cannot imagine a Catholic priest invoking the 'curse of Canaan' as having forever damned any man to slavery. In the Spanish empire the slave, like the peon, suffered only from failure to obey or to enforce the law."

Early in the eighteenth century, slave trading was so widely approved that Philip II and Anne of England were royal beneficiaries of its enormous profits. It was good business because in Africa any cheap and unsalable trash could be exchanged for blacks, and blacks could be crowded into airless, stinking ships'

holds, packed too close for exercise, fed and watered like animals. When they died they were pitched overboard. Arrived in
Havana — where they usually landed — the slaves were lodged
in barracks where they were well-fed and allowed to bathe in the
sea and to exercise by playing their ancient games, dancing and
singing. Merchandise had to be put into good shape for marketing.

Once slaves were on the plantations, treatment varied according to the master or the overseer. Generally, of course, it was
bad. Despite the law, it became customary to import men alone
and to keep them in enforced celibacy, working under overseers
all day, locked into barracks at night. At one time there were said
to be five hundred men to one woman among the slaves. Illicit
unions between master and maid were probably as common as in
the United States; but in Cuba marriage between the races was
lawful; so Spain, in theory at least, encouraged legitimacy. Before his death in 1788 Charles III, mindful of the growing disapproval of slavery in all civilized countries, issued a royal cedula
designed to improve the slave's position. The slave could now
buy himself or his family at the original price paid for them, he
could petition to be taken from an unjust master and assigned to
another, he could appeal to the courts against ill treatment, and
he could hold property. Most of these provisions were not enforced: the Negro's position was so precarious that few dared to
take advantage of them. But they resulted in building up a considerable number of free Negroes.

The census of 1817, considered fairly accurate, lists 290,021
whites, 115,691 free colored, 225,259 slaves. Clearly the balance of power rested with the Negroes, and the whites lived in
that haunting terror of a Negro uprising which was intensified
by Toussaint L'Ouverture's success in Haiti and the arrival in
Cuba of colored men with revolutionary ideas. Such panic resulted in horrors comparable with our southern lynchings,
though Willis Fletcher Johnson, whose *History of Cuba* I have

followed in this discussion, compares it rather with the worst of the Spanish Inquisition.

The slave trade was abolished in 1820, but more and more Negroes were buying their freedom and becoming educated. Sporadic Negro uprisings all over the island kept planters in constant dread. Enough white women were violated, enough cane fields and plantation mansions were burned, to bring on hideous reprisals. Negroes, both slave and free, with and without proper trial, were beaten to death. It is said that Captain General O'Donnell in the 1840's was responsible for killing 1346 colored people. Negro women, especially, were without protection and there were orgies of violations ending in slaughter.

This was going too far. Many Cubans, striving constantly for their own independence, filled with the prevailing ideas of the rights and dignity of the individual, were revolted by O'Donnell's policy and came to the defense of the Negro. José Antonio Saco, author of a *History of Slavery*, was perhaps the most important and influential, but he was only one of many Cubans who openly advocated abolition. Frenchmen, even refugees from Haiti, brought to Cuba their civilized refusal to damn a whole race for the acts of some individuals. Frenchmen never drew the color line that Spaniards did. They appreciated the beauty and allure of mulatto women and often married them. French travelers are quoted as saying that the only women in Cuba capable of cultivated conversation were the *mulatas*.

Intermarriage was, and is, not unusual. Generally dark men selected dark women; the mixture is due to white men. Intermarriage naturally occurs most freely in the lower reaches of society, but Cuba's legal methods do not seem to be producing light colored people any faster than our extra-legal methods.

A Cuban, speaking of these matters, said, "Crossing the line is as common in your country as in ours, but here we are less hypocritical about it. In taking our census, we just ask a man what color he is; we figure he ought to know."

So Cuba, in the middle of the nineteenth century, was living in a plantation economy with highly cultivated rich men owning many slaves and living luxuriously on their half-cultivated fields. Here was no place for the poor white man. Cuba was receiving some peasant and artisan immigration, mostly from the Basque provinces, from Catalonia and Galicia, but all the arable land was in the great holdings. Cuba, the island, had no great hinterland into which the pioneer could push. The Spanish immigrant took to the city, to retail trade, and finally to acquiring city lots.

In one respect, fundamental for the future nation, the rich planter was as unfortunately placed as the poor white or the Negro. No Cuban was allowed to hold high office; the *criollo* was a second-class citizen compared with the peninsulars who came out to govern and to enrich themselves. The cruel Governor Tacón said in the 1830's, "I am here not to promote the interests of the people of Cuba but to serve my master, the King." Enriching himself may have been incidental but was certainly not disregarded. Spain's shortsighted policy was making resentful colonials, and conspiring against the government and the king became a recognized part of the Cuban's life.

Nor was Spain's policy developing spunky citizens for a future republic. In one town I was shown the city hall with chairs for the council. I asked how the government was conducted. "Oh," said my guide, "the mayor is always a member of the X family; the senator, too. They really rule us."

Even worse for the building of a modern state was that no different folk came bringing different ideas. Spain allowed immigration only of Spanish Catholics. So no tradition of self-government or of protest entered. There was only the sword under the cape; never the punch of the work-hardened fist. This kept on through the nineteenth century, when the United States was getting all the lucky breaks. For as our country opened up, the people who came were the best Europe had — not gentlefolk with silly notions, but peasants and artisans with all the skills to make land produce to capacity, to use and conserve, to earn and save, to build log by log a house, dollar by dollar a fortune, state by state a nation; always, because they were little people unaccustomed to much, to start simply and grow. This made the United States a land of the middle class. Cultivated folk of the other Americas often remind us that we lack the refinements, but no democracy has yet been made by a few exquisite gentlemen and an illiterate mass. The Spanish gentleman, filled with European culture, was inclined to start in the large and hope for the best. These two traits persist. Cubans still start with the biggest thing conceivable and gamble on a future to justify it.

The spirit that erected the Torre Iznaga in Trinidad, as tall as possible and for no use at all, persists. The national capitol cost some $18,000,000. Built of granite and marble, it glows with crystals, paintings, and gilding. Its culmination is the diamond set in the center of the rotunda's floor. From that diamond are measured the highways Machado built for his glorification rather than to open up Cuba for development. The same spirit is evident in institutions for the care of the old, the indigent, orphans. The Escuela Cívico-Militár, founded by Fulgencio Batista, is a vast plant, producing almost everything it needs, educating the orphaned children of soldiers in cleanliness, morals, primary subjects and certain manual skills. It is well run, but it reaches few children at best. Sociologists suggest that an equal sum of money spent in keeping children with their mothers and in improving general education would have much greater and more wholesome results. But the size of the Escuela Cívico-Militár is what appeals. One thinks of similar institutions in all parts of the republic.

Topping them all is Tope de Collantes, Batista's enormous tuberculosis sanitarium above Trinidad. A scornful English engineer commented on it: "They chose that site because Batista liked the view, and they did everything in the most expensive way. There was a fair road, but no, they blasted out a new one, making a twenty-mile haul from the railroad. They say it's the perfect altitude for the cure of t.b., but they seem to die or get well anywhere. Anyhow there are no sick up there, and probably never will be."

The property included seventy *caballerías* of land, on which it is planned to raise practically all the food required. A thousand orange trees have been set out toward the hundred thousand proposed. It is also proposed to grow apples and pears, besides cabbages, *yuca, malanga,* and corn. The building is to accommodate fourteen hundred patients at a time, whose care will require three hundred and fifty doctors, nurses, and other employees at an annual overall cost of $1,000,000 and, as the Cubans so grandly say, "a bit."

Money raised by the sale of t.b. seals and the lottery bought the land and erected eight floors of a stupendous building that stares blindly out of thousands of windows not yet glazed, provided with huge underground heating, washing, and cooking equipment not yet placed or connected. One is proudly conducted through miles of unfloored space, across great lounges and game rooms, operating theaters, and corridors of windows — the bedrooms form the spines of the corridors, away from light and air. I was assured that this is in accordance with the best Swiss theory. Nothing is finished, nor is any money in sight for completion now that President Batista has been succeeded by President Grau San Martín.

President Grau has been more interested in another project. During his first months in office he appropriated $750,000 for the erection of a "Labor Palace" in Havana. This seems especially shocking because one comes to trust labor in Cuba. Its young leaders speak so sensibly; they seem to see ahead, to demand what is just, to anticipate the democratic state that is building. But these very sensible labor leaders used their power with the new president not for improved housing for workers, not to eliminate the fearful slums in Havana and other cities, not for schools or technical training or roads or any of the hundred things that cry aloud to be done in Cuba, but for a "Labor Palace." And it would be a palace. The colonial complex operates among laborers as among the wealthy to build elegance rather than utility. Even the *guajiro* who belongs to no union and will never see the "Labor Palace" thrills to the grandiose.

A cartoon showed a poverty-stricken *guajiro* gazing at the pile of straw that was all the cyclone had left of his *bohío*. "Didn't the government promise you a new house?" asks a friend. "Oh, yes," answers the dispossessed, "it is building me a palace in Havana."

Building large, which is rooted in the splendor of Spain and the medieval Church, seems related to the gambling compulsion that is so much a part of Cubans that one is never, anywhere, out of sight of gambling. The national lottery is one of the government's principal sources of income; the Foreign Policy Association in its *Problems of the New Cuba*, states that before 1931 only the customs duties and sales and loan taxes yielded more than the lottery. The lottery is, besides, a fine instrument for administrative graft, and it presents a widespread social problem. The typical irresponsible Cuban does not save; he buys a lottery ticket, or a fraction thereof, and hopes.

Spain founded the Cuban lottery; the United States abolished it during the first intervention of 1898–1902; it was re-established in 1909. So much for the futility of trying to put one people's social *mores* over onto another! Ostensibly part of the Secretariat of Finance, the national lottery is actually a presidential prerogative with incalculable possibilities. The Foreign Policy Association compares it with our Post Office "in an earlier age." The evils of Cuba's lottery also belong to an earlier age; President Grau San Martín has demanded honesty of operation and thereby made himself a host of enemies. In the heyday of the lottery, the president assigned his chosen one a *colecturía* that was sold, at enormous advance, to jobbers who supplied the vendors.

How much the president and his cronies made and how they split the take never appeared in the public accounts. At its worst, under the Machado regime (1925–33), the administration depended so much on this source of income that when the public refused to buy lottery tickets it discovered that it held a potent weapon. In spite of reforms, the lottery is too dear to Cubans to be long dispensed with.

How could a Cuban be anything but a gambler? His climate, so idyllic when it is good, is the most untrustworthy on earth because the island lies in the track of the Caribbean hurricanes. Any October may produce storms that lay flat every tree except the durable ceiba, lift the roof off every house, destroy the crops. And any winter may produce a drought that destroys every crop except the dependable cane, and even cane comes through with less juice. In addition to these natural changes, the Cuban has always faced many manmade hazards. Nothing in Cuba's history has ever proceeded in orderly sequence from Cuban cause to Cuban effect. Long before the world began to think in global terms, little Cuba was the sport of cosmic forces, like a pretty glass ball tossed in a jet of water, rising from unplumbed depths. Life in Cuba was affected by European wars, Spanish politics, the character or caprice of a royal governor; all seeming as senseless as a cyclone. Fate. God. Ñañigo. Even the so-reasonable United States does little to give Cuba a sense of stability. During the last twenty years the price of sugar has fluctuated from 28 cents to 0.45 cent a pound. As such variations never depend upon the tried and true virtues, what can the Cuban do but gamble? He might sink into despair, but that is not in character. No, he jokes and plays.

The serious-minded comfort themselves with the knowledge that the lottery, however its receipts may be dissipated in transit, does support many worthy activities. In theory, seventy per cent is paid out in prizes, ten per cent goes to the vendors, ten per cent to administration costs, and ten per cent to the national treasury to be used for the public benefit. As many vendors have no other means of support, charity begins right there. The government receives only thirty-three and one third from the lottery and ninety per cent from other taxes, but the lottery is certainly the most painless impost. Far from evading it, the people would protest vigorously if they were deprived of it. To the Cuban, the lottery does not seem immoral (that's a Protestant idea): he finds it fun, rich in possibilities, and a suitable way to support institutions for orphans, the aged, indigents, and the insane. Corruption in administration of the lottery is accepted with that fateful irresponsibility of the Cuban; graft is taken for granted. People generally rejoiced when President Grau San Martín cleaned out some abuses. Only a few approved his suppression of the fly-by-night lotteries; most people, especially the poor, felt that he was depriving them of a low-cost chance at a good thing.

Penny gambling is a disease of poverty. Only the very poor risk their livelihood on the chance of a drawing. The rich gamble for fun, and Cuba offers them many elegant and exciting ways to hazard their surplus cash. *Jai-a-lai,* the fastest game in the world, which came from the Basque provinces of Spain, attracts nightly audiences in Havana and big stakes. The casino and the racetrack cater to the North American need to gamble. But the ordinary Cuban, who makes his country's character, takes less expensive chances. Cockfighting is his big game. Everywhere in the country one sees the basket-like palm-thatched rinks with horses hitched outside and a few jalopies, and men's bent backs eloquent of their absorption in the gallant and bleeding birds. The Cuban who lacks the price of a lottery ticket or one to the cockfight can always lay his penny on the chance that a fly will or will not light, or the shark show his head in the bay.

This Cuban who jokes and plays, irresponsible and complaining, is the descendant of the colonial who had no rights. He is also the heir of a society that placed no value on education. It was never safe to educate slaves. The white *guajiro* was so long denied education that he still has no particular use for it. Batista was much criticized for putting his sergeants in charge of rural schools. Those who approved his policy say that only military power could force the *guajiro* to send his children to school; that far from supplanting all teachers by sergeants, Batista often made sergeants of school teachers to give them the needed authority. But even with that impetus education has not gone far enough to remove the handicap of a twenty-one per cent illiteracy, according to the National Census of 1943. Nor has it produced a middle class to challenge the gentleman and his point of view.

The gentleman still thinks of himself as God's anointed, though he has relaxed a bit the hidalgo's scorn of business. That came with the good trade in sugar; many men of noblest heritage operated import-export houses both in Spain and in Cuba. Business is still not elegant enough for Cuba's best *señoritas;* the hidalgo tradition has moved over to the other sex. Cuban women, ambitious for a university education, have become *doctoras* of medicine, law, pharmacy, pedagogy, or the veterinary arts; scores of them write for newspapers or magazines, but few of them go into business.

These people, both men and women, are loyal Cubans and as a rule active in charitable or civic affairs. It seems unfair to labor the other point. But there is no understanding Cuba and Cubans without recognizing the handicap under which they suffer because of Spain's overlong dominance. One meets it over and over in private conversation about any subject at all. Cubans generally look to the central government to do everything; they blame all failures on government. This state of mind is changing so fast that it requires special discussion as regards the future of Cuba. But up to now many Cubans have tended to shift responsibility onto a higher, remote power, as colonials shifted it to

Spain. It is Havana if you live in the provinces, the United States if you are discussing the economic situation, especially sugar. The Cuban does not trust his own voting system, his own government, or even, one suspects, himself. Perhaps psychologists might find a connection between self-distrust and the extraordinary number of associations in which Cubans have united. Standing alone is not a Cuban trait; lack of trust seems to be.

Cuba has always been a problem child. Cuba feels that the problems have been hers and that their existence is due entirely to her dominant parent — first Spain, and now the United States, which, while hardly a parent, might be described as the interfering or intervening uncle. In any case, Cuba has a list of fully justified grievances and the psychology of the put-upon. Many Cubans, especially the young ones, are outgrowing it. But that story belongs to the revolutionary tradition, or to the future of Cuba, and not to the colonial complex.

# IV

# THE REVOLUTIONARY
# TRADITION

WE, IN OUR SMUG WAY, ARE LIKELY TO THINK OF CUBA'S freedom as something we stepped in and got for them, handing them independence as a condescension and then standing by with rewards and punishments to see that they did not mishandle the gift. We are wrong on all counts.

Cuba's fight for independence was not limited to a few months in 1898; Cubans had been in the field off and on since 1868. Sometimes they fought as guerrilla bands; sometimes as well-equipped and expertly officered armies. But there were few intervals in those thirty years that some Cubans somewhere were not dedicating all they had to the effort to free themselves from Spain. What the United States government did for them was to stop interfering with their efforts to free themselves, and then, at the last moment, to send them a small army and a few battleships which did give the *coup de grâce*. Jorge Mañach, a very fair-minded Cuban, said to me: "I do not think we could have won our independence without the aid of the United States; but perhaps we paid rather a high price for it."

We seldom remember that the long struggle for independence

in Spain's America began with the enslaved peoples. Most of them failed, though Tupác-Amarú in Peru led a dramatic revolt that was not forgotten. The first to win was Toussaint L'Ouverture, a Negro slave on the isle of Hispaniola, which France had won from Spain. The republic he set up, Haiti, was the first independent state in Latin America. Then white men, men of the upper classes, began to revolt. Among the first was Francisco Miranda, the Venezuelan, whose effort in 1806 seemed to fail. When Father Hidalgo in Mexico tolled the bell of his parish church and cried out for freedom, that clamor ran the length and breadth of Spain's empire. In colony after colony a few men inspired many men. Aristocrats and bourgeois, slaves and peons, men of white, black, and brown skins armed with *machetes* marched against Spain's regulars armed with guns, fought like guerrillas in country they knew, and finally triumphed. By the end of the first quarter of the century America was rid of European rule. All America, that is, except the islands of the Caribbean.

Cuba was affected by the virus of freedom as early as any. In fact, Cuba had had a taste of freedom before any. When the British captured Havana in 1762 and held it for a year, Cubans saw what free trade could do for a people. For the first time ships of all nations anchored under El Morro, commerce was stimulated, and everybody prospered. England withdrew in 1763, but that occupation, short as it was, implanted two revolutionary ideas in Cuba: freedom and *cubanidad*. For when the English had attacked, Creoles had rallied round the royal governor and fought gamely for Cuba. In 1807, when the French Haitians tried an invasion, Cubans, fighting again as Cubans, repelled the intruder. Spain was far away, Americans were beginning to sense their destiny as unrelated to Europe, and even the "Ever-Faithful Isle" was becoming restive. Intelligent Cubans were reading the French thinkers, the revolutionary leaders of both North and South America, and the news of their successes.

Spain's censorship, even backed by the Church, could not keep the glad tidings from seeping through. Cubans thrilled to Bolívar's spectacular advance from Venezuela's *llanos* up over the Andes, and they sent emissaries to beg the Liberator of Greater Colombia to free Cuba too. But that island was too easy for Spain to defend; Bolívar had all he could do on the continent. Cuba had four score long years to wait before her independence was attained. But there was constant ferment throughout the island.

The Free Masons were active, others formed the *Soles de Bolívar* with headquarters at Matanzas. This was in 1810. By August 1823 they had an uprising well planned. But spies betrayed them to Captain General Francisco Vives, who arrested all the leaders he could catch. Among them was Cuba's great poet, José María de Heredia, who was exiled to Spain. There he joined the revolutionists fighting for their rights in Spain, and there he wrote some of his best poems of protest. Many conspirators got away to Venezuela or to Mexico, where they organized *El Águila Negra* (The Black Eagle), with branches in the United States as well as in Colombia and Mexico. They met official disapproval in the northern slave-owning republic, where Spanish control of Cuba seemed safer than the influence of Bolívar who had freed his own slaves and who believed in freedom all the way. Lack of success was general. Spies reported regularly to the Governor General. Conspirators who were caught were often tortured; many were executed. Such stern policy naturally produced bitter grief and resentment to feed the freedom movement. But the growth was slow, slow.

Cubans were not all united. Many were out-and-out Spanish royalists. Many wealthy slave-owners favored annexation to the United States, especially during the decades when Southern slave-owners dominated the northern republic. Some hoped for an autonomous colonial government. Spain, blindly following the pattern of the "haves," who eventually lose all because they will not sensibly yield a little, thwarted every effort of moderate

Cubans to gain some modicum of self-government without a complete break.

Spain was not at one with itself either. Many people in that country, which personified repression and injustice to Cuban Creoles, were fighting for self-government and civil rights against the monarchy. Many of them hoped to extend self-government to Cuba as they won it for themselves. But the march toward freedom followed a wavering line in the mother country as it did in the colony.

In 1812 Spain had a liberal *cortes* that adopted a constitution giving the people a bill of rights, including the suffrage. So enlightened were the leaders that representation in the *cortes* was extended to Cuba, and the colonials sent their most distinguished citizen to represent them. Francisco de Arango, lawyer, planter, economist, scholar, and astute diplomat, actually succeeded in getting Cuba's ports open to foreign trade. It was a brilliant triumph, but short-lived. When the worthless Ferdinand VII returned to the throne, his first act was to abrogate the constitution. He appointed a governor general for Cuba who revived all the worst repressions and injustices. W. F. Johnson, in his *History of Cuba*, considers this repudiation of the constitution as the beginning of Cuba's revolution. Its effect on a high-spirited people must have been depressing in the extreme. Spain readopted her constitution in 1820, but it was too late. Spain's periods of civil rights were brief even as regards Spaniards; in her colonies, especially in Cuba, the policy of *oprimir para exprimir*, oppress to extort, reigned with almost no let-up. Under the liberal Charles III in Spain and a few governors in Cuba there had been an intellectual flowering and some betterment. Roads, bridges, ports, and public buildings were built or put in repair; certain asylums and hospitals were endowed or improved. But generally Cuba was expected to produce revenue in spite of a system that granted her no chance nor incentive to develop her resources.

After the North won the Civil War in the United States, our

volatile country was on the side of abolition instead of slavery. That made its friends different. The Peninsulars, as Spain's party in Cuba was called, were wealthy Spanish officeholders, merchants for Spanish goods, and bankers and Cuban planters. They were all opposed to freedom from Spain, freedom for Negroes, and free trade. Organized in Havana as the *Casino Español*, they enlisted their young men as *voluntarios*. A semimilitary troop open to all white men, it was really a social affair as correct as the Richmond Blues or the New York Seventh Regiment. Their leaders were a council of colonels, and they did good service at overawing city inhabitants and spying on patriots. Joseph Hergesheimer has given a good account of them in his highly colored *Bright Shawl*.

Mr. Hergesheimer's hero was a young American who went to Cuba to share in her revolution. Although of a later period, he was typical of many who kept hot and active the sentiment for Cuban freedom in the northern republic. One of Cuba's first prophets of freedom was Father Felix Varela, who advocated abolition, addressed the Spanish *cortes* in favor of recognizing Greater Colombia, and was finally forced to flee to the United States in 1823. In Philadelphia he founded a magazine, *El Habanero*, to win friends for Cuba's independence. Many Cubans lived in the States, propagandizing for independence, for annexation, or for the status of an autonomous colony of Spain. They always found it possible to raise money among Americans, often to enlist sailors to man the ships or soldiers to fight in Cuba.

Narciso López was most successful at this game. A handsome and cultivated gentleman and an experienced officer, he dominated men by his strength and prowess. It was believed that his leg-muscles were so strong that he could choke the breath out of the horse he bestrode, and he was a legendary lady-killer. Such a man easily became the idol of veterans of the Mexican War, who wanted more fighting, of idealists who burned to free some country, and of Southerners who hoped to gain another slave state. López was not a Cuban by birth. He was a Venezuelan who fought gallantly to hold Valencia for Bolívar, but who later fought with Spain and became a colonel in the Spanish army. As such he was sent to Cuba where he refused to swear, as all officers were asked to do, to adjure liberalism. Married to a rich Creole, López lived for a time in Spain, where he affiliated himself with the Liberal Party during the Carlist wars. When he returned to Cuba he stayed aloof from the conspiracies out of deference to his friend, Don Jerónimo Valdés, the Governor General. But when Valdés was succeeded by George Leopold O'Donnell, one of the oppressors, López felt free to act.

López's first attempt was a complete fiasco. His plans were unwittingly betrayed by a boastful boy, José Sánchez Iznaga, and they both barely got away. Later they were sentenced to death *in absentia*, but by that time they were in the United States. There López proved himself eminently fitted to raise money and recruit filibustering expeditions, especially in the South. He did not believe in freedom for Negroes, and his Southern friends assumed that he was an annexationist. Herminio Portell-Vilá suggests, in his scholarly biography, that López, an ardent advocate of Cuban independence, was capable of keeping silent when silence would best serve his cause. Moreover, his method was to deal with people of the highest rank. He invited Jefferson Davis, Senator from Mississippi, and then Major Robert E. Lee of the United States Army and of Virginia, to head an army to free Cuba. Both gentlemen declined, as did Governor Quitman of Mississippi, but only after serious consideration. López settled for lesser men, but he raised some eight hundred volunteers and collected $70,000 from Americans, which Cubans in Cuba augmented with $30,000.

These activities took some time, and were not unknown to the Spaniards, whose spies were everywhere. Spain naturally was incensed that a friendly nation should tolerate such goings-on. It is amusing to consider what would be the attitude of our country toward similar endeavors on the part of Russia or Germany, say, in Mexico or Canada. Spain protested. The United States promised and officially tried to control her nationals. But as usual she could not do so. López's plans went merrily along. Volunteers were promised pay equal to that of a private in the United States Army, a bonus of $1,000, later raised to $4,000, and free land in Cuba after it was won. The scheme appealed most to the South and West, and recruits were shipped down the Ohio and Mississippi to New Orleans, where others had gathered. There General López unfurled the new flag of free Cuba on the ship *Creole* and set sail with his army of eight hundred Americans.

After some misadventures, these confident warriors landed on Cuba's northern shore. López, blinded by his own shining convictions, expected all Cuba to rise as one man. But no Cubans rose to join him: some were royalists, some were apathetic, some were timorously mindful of Spain's punishments for revolt. Nevertheless the mettlesome invaders, officered by veterans of the Mexican War, fought a brisk engagement or two, captured the railroad station in an effort to cut communications with Havana, and called upon the garrison to surrender. The Spaniards showed a white flag, but fired upon the Americans sent to parley, which made the Americans so furious that they took the town. But López had counted on Creole reinforcements; his small force could not hold out alone. He realistically reimbarked on the *Creole*, eluded a Spanish ship that tried to intercept them, and reached Key West. There the survivors were met by an ovation on the part of the populace and arrest on the part of a worried Uncle Sam. The leaders were tried, but no charges would stick, no witnesses would stand, nobody remembered anything. The trial fizzled out, and López went to New York to start again.

American citizens thrilled anew to warlike adventure, contributed cash, volunteered, recruited others. More than ever, Southern gentlemen of the finest families flocked to join General López. One of them, General and Senator John Henderson, who had stood trial after the first expedition, wrote in urging the second: "As a Southern question, I do not think, when properly viewed, its magnitude can be overestimated."

The *Cleopatra* was surreptitiously bought, manned, loaded with supplies for war, and readied to sail from Savannah. Federal officers, acting more promptly than before, boarded the *Cleopatra* and arrested her officers before she sailed. So Expedition II died aborning. Again the courts failed to convict anyone.

Spain, clearly worried, ordered all officers in Cuba to be on the alert against "incursions of pirates." López's American supporters suggested that Cubans might play a part in this war for their independence. Some Cubans pluckily agreed. Don Joaquín de Agüero tried at Puerto Principe to raise an army of four hundred. But Cubans, still apathetic or timorous, again failed to rise. Only fifteen men responded to Agüero's frantic call, and they were all captured in the plaza and shot. Agüero lived to fight a couple of engagements, but was finally taken and garrotted with his officers. This execution so aroused the United States that López's third try met with quick response.

This time he raised $50,000 and equipped the *Pampero*. Garibaldi, who happened to be in the United States, declined to sail as commander, but Colonel Crittenden, veteran of the Mexican War, and a large contingent of others got away and landed López and his army at Morillo. López made the same mistake he had made before, and divided his army. Both divisions were captured by the same means. A slave reported to a master, who invited the Americans in, dined and wined them well, put them to sleep, and sent for the Spaniards. There were indignities, even torture, and finally fifty-two men were shot. Of the list given by Johnson only two are Spanish names, though many Cubans may have taken English names as a protection. López was garrotted.

So López failed? Perhaps. Many students believe that it was López's plucky effort and the cruelty with which the Spaniards met him that rallied thousands of lukewarm or even royalist Cubans to the cause of their own freedom. It also stiffened the Cuban party in the States, especially in the deep South. In New Orleans they openly advocated taking Cuba from Spain. Nor could Europe longer disregard the "Ever-Faithful Isle." England and France, both with American colonies, offered to patrol the waters of the Caribbean for Spain, who declined their aid.

In Cuba, Spain's policy was slowly throttling the life out of the colony. Wealthy Cubans saw its resources drained away in graft and in export-import duties. Emeterio S. Santovenia estimates that at this period the fraudulent official "take" at the ports amounted to some forty per cent at Havana, sixty per cent at Santiago. The whole interior was overrun by civil servants, nearly all Spaniards, who were on low wages and had almost autocratic powers. The result was inevitably flagrant peculation and mean repressive measures against those who dared to protest. Such conditions aroused many people who had no desire to separate from Spain, but who were goaded into demanding reforms. They were called *los reformistas,* and their organ was *El Siglo,* a newspaper expressly not anti-Spanish, but altogether Cuban.

Some Spaniards, as usual, recognized the justice of the claims of the colonials, and one minister of overseas affairs called a *Junta de Información* in Madrid, a meeting for discussion, to which Cubans and Puerto Ricans were invited. In Cuba the election was so manipulated that Spaniards who dominated industry and commerce got a larger representation than Cubans who owned land. Still, delegates were chosen and journeyed to Spain full of hope. But their hopes were soon dashed. With a change of administration, reactionary ministers disregarded the recommendations of the *Junta de Información,* declared that body dissolved, and decreed the raising of port duties. They also returned to the policy of suppression by the appointment of a raging absolutist, Don Francisco Lersundi, as Governor of Cuba.

Indignation in Cuba rose to fury. "Responsible Cubans," Santovenia writes, "had tried to avoid violent measures . . . they had encouraged the idea of making changes by evolution. This illusion was killed and buried by the conduct of the government of Madrid. Now those most interested in Cuban economy — the rich — who anywhere else would have been horrified of war, understood that they would have to invoke the final argument of force in defense of their very existence."

So rich men, in calm realization of its horrors and their own certain losses, undertook a war against Spain. It was a gentlemen's revolution in its inception, but it soon took on a different character. For its leaders, following Carlos Manuel de Céspedes, freed their slaves. Various provinces declared for abolition, and guaranteed the Negroes freedom, equal rights, prerogatives, and treatment as whites. One wonders if the result of abolition in the States had given Cuban planters hope that freeing slaves would not necessarily end their political and economic domination. In any case, Cubans were for the first time united. Recruiting among freedmen went well, and *mambises* were of every color.

Negroes at once displayed such patriotic devotion and military skill that many of them rose to commanding positions. Most notable among them was Antonio Maceo, the Bronze Titan, whose level head, disinterested persistence, and brilliance as a field commander won him a place among Cuba's most exalted heroes of independence.

A detailed account of the Ten Years' War that began in 1868 and apparently failed is of less moment now, outside of Cuba, than a consideration of the men who fought it and of how they made modern Cuba.

### *MAMBÍ*

CUBA's revolution, like every effort to make life better for men, had strong, true and noble leaders. Some of them, like Céspedes

and, especially, Martí, hoped for liberty that would really make
men free; for a country made strong by the strength of ordinary
Cubans, white, black, or brown. But the event betrayed that hope,
as events have so often betrayed the aspirations of simple people.

Many of those leaders are worth writing about — military
leaders because they were brave, adroit, persistent. I choose
Maceo rather than one of the white generals because he was a
brown man who stands high in Cuban annals and in those of all
people who strive for true democracy. Martí, more than any,
typifies Cuba's mystical fervor, fed from his own deep springs of
faith in humanity. But the man who fought the wars, stood the
gaff, literally lost his shirt, and lost all in the end was the un-
named, unknown guerrilla fighter whom Cubans call the *mambí*.
The real story of the Cuban revolution is in what the *mambí* did.

One sees him nowadays in every town where he has the Asocia-
ción Nacional de Veteranos, with headquarters often in the same
building as the city hall. It is a pleasure to call there, and visitors
are very welcome. Life must be fairly monotonous for old fighting men who sit rocking in their bentwood chairs, reading newspapers or talking interminably. There may be a billiard table,
writing desks, and racks of periodicals. Always there are pictures of the white Martí and the colored Maceo, Cuba's flag, and
frequently stained and tattered battle standards. Nowadays
most of the veterans remember service in Cuba's final war beginning in 1895; but among them are a few whose memories go back
to the Ten Years' War which ended in 1878. Like their battle
flags, they are past their pristine freshness, but they too still flash
muted colors; and like their heroes in the portraits they are white
men and black and men of every shade between. There is no color
line among men who have fought for freedom. Among Cuba's
veterans one always meets Englishmen, Frenchmen, or Americans who enlisted as youths to help Cuba Libre and who stayed
and founded families and are Cuban now in all but that long-gone
youth. Some of them have sent sons and grandsons in these last

years to fight for England, France, and the United States. As these old men rock and talk, they compare their wars with this, they speculate as to what this will produce for human freedom.

In one town, I spent several hours with the veterans. At first they were all quiet, crowding close around the table, listening eagerly, but deferring to their President, who answered questions carefully. But queries about how they went to war, how they lived and fought, aroused so many recollections that soon the whole concourse was at it, and Cuban Spanish, unleashed, ran away into conflicting and overlapping tales until it seemed impossible ever to sort it out into a coherent story. One remembered how he and his buddies had ragged the pro-Spanish Catholic brothers at school into a frenzy of rage and then had eluded them and run away to war at the age of fourteen; another told how his mother had fled from a burning home with four children and two slaves to hide in the jungle. One had assisted at a childbirth when he, at fifteen, was the only person old enough to help. Most of them remembered with pleasure how they slipped into Spanish strongholds at night and made off with pigs or chickens that might squeal or squawk, or food or clothes that were less exciting as loot. Some were quick to laughter, some to bitterness; all liked to tell the visitor about countrymen of hers who had fought well, been good friends, and stayed on in Cuba.

One summed it up: "We fought as all men must fight for independence and human dignity. But something went wrong somewhere. We did not fight for this." His gesture, I thought, was too wide to take in only Cuba.

These men are Cuba's long revolution, as little men are the heroes of every war to better man's condition. Their war was inaugurated and led by cultivated gentlemen and noble leaders, but to get the picture true one must know the *mambí*. That proud appelation of Cuba's revolutionary fighter was first applied to him as an epithet of scorn. Dr. Fernando Ortiz says it is a word of Bantu origin that the Spaniards applied to rebels in Santo

*If he can, he gets to a cockfight. Camagüey*

*Laughing Negro child*

*Children of all colors, Baracoa*

*At every halt, venders. Bayamo*

*We passed bohíos. Matanzas*

Domingo in the middle of the last century and brought from
there to Cuba. It meant rebel, bandit, freebooter, general bad
man, but the Cuban soon gave it honor. The *mambí* was the
freedom-loving Cuban who left his home for the wilderness,
there to live like primitive man and to put up a fight that stopped
the best Spain could send. It was not a proper war because the
Cuban had not the wherewithal for that. He could only harry
the Spaniards he was not strong enough to fight openly, and in the
end he lost, as his predecessors had lost the earlier efforts to make
Cuba free. But the Ten Years' War made a nation of Cuba, a
nation bound in time to be free.

The Ten Years' War began on October 10, 1868, a date celebrated annually as Cuba's Independence Day. At Yara Plantation in Oriente, a group of men, assembled around a heavy hand-
carved mahogany table, declared Cuba independent of Spain.
Nobody stood on a balcony and cried aloud as Latin American
liberators had typically done, but the tradition of taking off with
a shout was so strong that this quiet meeting of gentlemen in a big
country house was to be forever known as the *grito de Yara*. Being lawyers as well as planters, and well versed in history, those
revolutionists wrote a declaration of independence, made plans
for a constitutional convention and the election of officers. In due
time they called for the recognition of other nations. It was a
dignified proceeding, and among the actors were men whose
names stand high in Cuban annals and in those of fighters for
freedom everywhere.

Carlos Manuel de Céspedes, elected first provisional and then
"president" of Cuba, was acknowledged leader. Around him
were Salvador Cisneros, Francisco Auguilera, Tomás Estrada
Palma, and the experienced revolutionists from Santo Domingo,
Máximo Gómez and Modesto Díaz. Having performed all the
correct acts, those duly elected civil servants and duly appointed
military officers recognized perforce the hard facts that they had
no country they could call their own, no capital or seaport, no

army or navy, no arms or ammunition. The force that began a war that would last ten years was said to consist of 147 officers and men with less than a gun apiece, though most of them had the trusty *machete*. So they took to the *manigua*, Cuba's subtropical jungle, less dense than the tropical jungle, but thick enough to make good cover and productive of food for those who know it. The rebels also found refuge in the *monte*, the more open hardwood forests that then clothed the mountains. Their terrain was the mountainous end of the island that became known as Cuba Libre or *la tierra del mambí*.

Before those gentlemen turned guerrilla fighters they took a step more important for Cuba's future than the legal papers they signed. They freed their slaves. Led by Carlos Manuel de Céspedes, they not only abandoned their homes, endangered their families, and sacrificed their wealth; they proved themselves consistent in their demand for individual freedom. This was the act that made Cuba one in spirit. No longer a white-black Cuba, it was a unity. Cubans of color were now recognized as men, and naturally they came out to fight like men. As news of abolition ran along the underground, men of color and men of principle crossed the line from Spain's Cuba to Cuba Libre, and that handful of 147 men at Yara in October had grown, by the end of the year, to 26,000 men under arms. That is, there were 26,000 men; the arms were still illusory.

Spain naturally maintained that this was no war at all; merely armed bands disturbing the peace, slave insurrections, and, when help came from without, piratical incursions. Spaniards in Cuba tried to oppose the drift to the *mambí* by the formation of the *voluntarios*, with its appeal to race prejudice; it was limited to white men. These new regiments were generally assigned to guard duty in the cities or to other services in which they would free the regulars for fighting. This put them in close contact with the civilian population and made them a powerful spy organization, one that demanded even sterner measures against Cubans than peninsulars were ready for. More than one Spanish governor was returned to Spain at the behest of the *voluntarios,* who found his methods too mild. Consequently the *voluntarios* were more hated than the Spaniards; numberless incidents show how their acts kept the flame of insurrection aglow.

In 1869, the Spanish commander invited President Céspedes to a meeting to discuss terms. The President, expecting little, was willing to feel out his enemy and he sent Agustín Arango to Puerto Principe (now Camagüey) under a safe conduct issued by the Spanish government. Arango fell into the hands of a group of *voluntarios,* who, refusing to recognize the safe conduct, murdered the Cuban emissary. Cuban rage knew no bounds, and thousands of theretofore royalist or doubtful *criollos* joined the *mambí.*

Spain, then under a fairly liberal regime, tried again, asking the United States to get a statement from the revolutionists as to terms of peace. Uncle Sam declined the office. Spain sent Don Nicolas Azcárate to Washington with Spain's terms. They offered Cubans freedom of speech, assembly, and religion, emancipation of slaves, and even colonial autonomy and representation in the Spanish *cortes.* They also offered, in deepest secrecy, to disband the Volunteers. Uncle Sam still declined to take part. So Azcárate sent Juan Clemente Zenea to Cuba under a safe conduct from the Spanish minister in Washington and with orders to all Spanish authorities in Cuba to permit him to enter at any port and to travel freely. But the *voluntarios'* spy service was active in Washington as well as in Cuba. They captured Zenea in Havana, imprisoned him, and defied orders from Spain to liberate him. On August 15, 1870, they shot him.

Thousands more Cubans joined the army of Cuba Libre.

The Cuban leaders refused Spain's terms. Indeed why should they consider them? Certainly clever men would judge that a country whose own military officers would violate its safe conduct for a messenger of peace could hardly enforce terms of peace, however attractive they might look on paper. Cubans had less than no confidence in Spain. War continued.

In that very year, 1870, Queen Isabella was finally forced to sign an abdication and Amadeus, son of Victor Emmanuel II of Italy, was declared King of Spain. The royalist *voluntarios* were delighted, and got completely out of hand; they even refused permission to land to the Bishop of Havana returning to his see from Rome.

Organized in every town and many hamlets throughout Cuba, this white man's terror league claimed eighty thousand members. In Havana they published *La Voz de Cuba,* dedicated to diatribes against the patriots; it even descended to scurrilous attacks on Cuban women. One outraged Cuban challenged the editor, Gonzalo Castañón, to a duel and killed him. Later a group of students, mere boys, were seen near Castañón's tomb in the Espada Cemetery. A Spanish soldier, standing near, reported that the lads had made derogatory remarks about the deceased editor. As the story was repeated those remarks grew into defilement of the tomb, and by the time the case got to court it was fairly strong. Forty-three youths were tried, but were so ably defended by Señor Capdevilla that they were acquitted. The *voluntarios,* always bloodthirsty, were not content. They forced a second court martial and got convictions for all. Eight young men were shot, the rest imprisoned at hard labor. It is their names that figure on the tablet where Havana's Malecón crosses the Prado. It reads: "On the 27th of November, 1871, there were sacrificed in front of this place, by the Spanish Volunteers of Havana, the eight young Cuban students of the First Year of Medicine." All were young men of good family and fine promise. One can imagine how many young Cubans left Havana after that for *la tierra del mambí.*

Soon the war which had begun in Oriente's mountains involved all Cuba except Pinar del Río Province, and threatened Havana itself.

Although the United States was taking no official notice of all this, there was unabated interest among private individuals, especially in the South and border states, and ships loaded with men and supplies were constantly reaching the *mambí*. But no news came back, or very little. James Gordon Bennett, whose *New York Herald* was so successful at getting the news from everywhere, realized that Cuba Libre was a mysterious land of darkest horrors and known only through Spanish reports. These described a series of terroristic attacks on women and children and destruction of peaceful homes and crops, often belonging to Americans. Always the insurgents were pictured as lawless mobs of armed Negroes and a threat to white supremacy. Mr. Bennett decided to get the other side of the story, and he found his man in one of his own reporters, James J. O'Kelly.

O'Kelly was a fighting Irishman. Beginning as a Fenian in his native land, he later fought in Mexico with Maximilian, in France and Africa with the French; wherever there was a war Mr. O'Kelly went to it. Winding up in the United States, he got a job on the *Herald*. Sending O'Kelly to Cuba showed good judgment. He could be trusted to make friends with the Spaniards and then elude them. He could take care of himself in wild country, take long chances, talk himself out of fixes in several languages, and probably live to bring his story back.

In 1872, O'Kelly went to Havana and presented himself to the Captain General, Francisco Ceballos, asking safe conduct through the Spanish lines so that he could go on to those of the insurgents. Mr. O'Kelly, one can guess how smoothly even from a portrait taken in his bearded age, explained that he wanted only the truth, that the free press of the United States would print the truth, that he had such confidence in the Spaniards' gentlemanly conduct of the war he was sure His Excellency would facilitate his journey. His Excellency agreed with all Mr. O'Kelly said, but regretted that he could not give him a safe conduct; it would not, in fact, be necessary. Every Spanish official, both civil and military, would be entirely at Mr. O'Kelly's service. Perhaps the Captain General was too taken with Mr. O'Kelly's mild and humorous blue eye to notice the rocklike jaw. But there was nothing for James to do but to go on.

In Havana, which he described as a sink hole of filth, our reporter found two classes of people: Spaniards or peninsulars and Cubans. The Cubans were white Creoles, Negroes, both free and slave, Chinese, and all the intermixtures. He guessed at 700,000 whites, of whom not more than 180,000 were peninsulars; and 600,000 colored people, including Chinese, half of whom were still in slavery.

O'Kelly, dealing with Spaniards and even making friends with young officials, was well on the alert. "Between the peninsulars and criollos," he wrote, "there exists an intense hatred; if it is hidden and does not appear on the surface it is because the latter have been terrified by the bloody punishments carried out early in the insurrection. . . . Today acts of violence are rare because the necessity has passed; but the terror and hatred they caused remain. Nothing could exceed the abhorrence of the criollos toward the Spanish; and though the Cubans of the great cities do not dare to try any hostile act against the Spanish government for fear of losing their lives, they plot in secret to aid the rebels."

Even a few days in Havana filled the freedom-loving Irishman with fury at the treatment Spaniards accorded Cubans: irksome lack of consideration, petty annoyances of all sorts, and official injustice and dishonesty. He was struck by how superior the Spanish were to the *criollos* in physique and physical energy. They were, he said, vigorous, brave, bold, unscrupulous, and eager to get rich. Cubans he found weakened by the system of slavery, opposed to manual work, with no sports, and consequently with no physical stamina. They were, he said, more likely to be found gambling than indulging in manly pastimes. He was to change his mind about Cubans. Those he saw in Ha-

vana were the ones who had stayed under the Spanish power
and not taken to the jungle.

O'Kelly's prime objective was to find President Céspedes and
interview him. In New York, Señora de Céspedes had told him
that her husband's highly mobile capital was probably somewhere between Santiago and Cabo Cruz on Manzanillo Bay.
Where or how a reporter could cross the frontier between Spain's
Cuba and *la tierra del mambí* there was no way of knowing;
that frontier, real enough, was an unseen vacillating line. He
could, at least, go to Santiago. It is surprising to discover how
far he could go by train so long ago as 1872. The journey, as one
would surmise, was slow, dirty, and full of delays, but full also
in interest and worthwhile impressions.

During one delay, O'Kelly was entertained at a sugar plantation where he saw slavery in full flower. From dawn, when they
were let out of locked barracks, black men and women worked
under overseers armed with whips and guns until dark when they
were locked in again. He saw them herded in for a noon meal of
inadequate and badly cooked food. The slaves looked, he
thought, as low as human beings could, sullen, stupid, bestial.
Among the Africans were Chinese, and the inquiring reporter
learned how they came to be there.

White agents in China had signed up these ignorant laborers,
promising them freedom after eight years of work. Then the
agents shipped them to Cuba in vessels as bad as those that brought
Africans. O'Kelly saw a shipload of 900. As one man was worth
$500, and as the importer had paid out some $50,000 for the lot
in China, it was good business. On the plantations the Chinese,
like the Negroes, worked fourteen hours a day, including Sun-
days and holidays. Some seventy per cent of the Chinese generally died before their term was up. But they contributed to the
Cuban culture an ingredient that modern sociologists value as
Chinese heritage is valued everywhere.

By the time Mr. O'Kelly got to Santiago, he had a fairly com-

plete picture of the "Ever-Faithful Isle." There the commanding officer, Brigadier Morales de los Ríos, received him with all
Spanish courtesy, introduced him to his staff, young men most
solicitous and polite, and soon let him join a troop of soldiers
just leaving on a ten-day expedition.

They set out by train. Mr. O'Kelly was an honored guest; the
officers seemed worried lest he fail to understand how popular
they really were in Cuba; the *crème de la crème* of society, they
told him, was pro-Spanish. "My own observations, nevertheless,
contradict this, in that almost all young men of intelligence whom
I met hate the Spaniards with inconceivable bitterness."

All along the railroad he saw little wooden towers from which
watchmen popped up like jacks-in-the-box. Every sugar mill had
been turned into a fortress, well garrisoned, well armed. Mr.
O'Kelly did not see how the Cubans could ever win their war
against Spain's trained army. Like an experienced soldier he
judged Spain's chances by the privates. He found them well-
armed, not too badly fed, and with a doctor aboard who seemed
efficient and solicitous. But as he knew them better he realized
that it was a spiritless army. Of a hundred thousand men sent
to Cuba since the beginning of the war, only twenty or thirty
thousand were left. Disease had taken them, as well as the hazards of war. But these professional soldiers were suffering quite
as much from extreme frustration because their enemy would
not come out and fight. They seemed to be opposing phantasms,
unseen forces, black as the night they chose for their operations,
sneaking out of the dark to shoot or set fire, stealing, and disappearing again before a soldier could act.

"Strange comment on human intelligence that . . . a people
will make such sacrifices to the end that a few hundred men can
continue to enjoy their ill-gotten riches; because it is an incontrovertible fact that these thousands of Spanish lives and millions of pesos extracted from a people forced into poverty and
misery have been misspent in defense of a few hundred slave

owners. The Spanish nation gets no advantage from its connection with Cuba; a few government employees enrich themselves stealing as they pretend to serve, and that is all."

O'Kelly liked the Spanish uniforms, blue jackets, white trousers, often wide straw hats with red or blue bands. When the troop left the train to march through the greenwood, Mr. O'Kelly delighted in the beautiful color scheme they made. The Spaniards were presumably looking for Cuban rebels, but they did not find any. In fact, Mr. O'Kelly remarked that though every private could tell him where the *mambises* were, they never seemed to run them down. This, he thought, was because many of the volunteers were fighting for twenty centavos a day and food. As there was food of a sort, and native brandy was ten cents a gallon, it was too good to spoil by ending the war. Many, moreover, were not convinced royalists. The human frontier between Spanish Cuba and Cuba Libre was forever shifting. During O'Kelly's stay in Cuba he figured out that between three hundred and four hundred Cubans "with their families" had joined the insurgents. He wrote: "If this movement continues the Cuban chiefs will soon find themselves at the front of a numerous and well-armed host which will enable them to prolong the war, even against Spain's superior forces, during twenty more years if necessary."

O'Kelly's march with the Spanish army came to an end sooner than he wished. The expedition was ordered to return to Santiago. The young guest suspected that his presence was the cause of the sudden change, but he was playing a clever game and politely made no comment. Perhaps he was a bit too clever for his purpose. He had seen the Spanish army, but how was he to get to the *mambí* country, to interview President Céspedes? Brigadier Morales offered no encouragement; in fact when pressed he admitted that if Mr. O'Kelly were seen crossing the line either way, he would surely be shot. Politeness was giving way to sternness. Above all, O'Kelly seemed to have no friends among the patriots;

perhaps he had been too apt at making character among the Spanish; he could not be sure who were the Cuban sympathizers among the people he knew in Santiago.

Then entering his room one day he found an unsigned note directing him to go to a certain ceiba tree at dusk, bringing his hammock and blanket. Excited and torn between hope that a way was opening to *la tierra del mambí* and fear of a trap, O'Kelly set out as usual on his daily ride. He had ridden regularly hoping for a chance to cross the line. At dusk he neared the appointed ceiba. Darkness came quickly. Nothing stirred, but he felt someone near. Then a voice spoke the countersign he had been told to expect. He replied. A man approached, a man so black that he was all but indistinguishable from the night. He said little, but O'Kelly, hoping all was well, followed him.

Noiselessly as he could O'Kelly let his horse follow the silent guide, who slipped like a dark shadow through the darkness. Then he stopped and whistled. A birdcall replied, and other men materialized from the night. There were four, two of them white. The Spaniards were wrong then; the *mambises* were not all Negroes. O'Kelly was greeted courteously in a cultivated voice, and they went on. It was a grueling walk of many hours, but when they reached the Cuban camp it was not very far from Santiago. Many of the Cuban centers were within sight of the cities held by Spain, but well hidden, protected by Cuban sympathizers.

With *bohíos* in tidy rows, this one was clean, but unsanitary, as waste of all sort was just pushed over the edge of the *barranca*. The government was orderly too, and the people struck O'Kelly as very different from similar folk he had seen as slaves. Here were responsibility and a feeling of citizenship and their attendant dignity. *Mambí* men were generally out hunting groups of Spaniards small enough to attack, or rustling food. Women worked the small fields, kept house, patched up their wounded as they came in. There were physicians too, and O'Kelly thought that Cuban care of the sick and wounded had much to do with the rapid growth of the forces. No wounded *mambí* was abandoned to the enemy. Even children, down to mere tots, worked. O'Kelly saw them coming in at dusk, each with his burden, like long files of busy ants.

Here was a typical *mambí* camp, here were the method and the folk who were eventually to defeat the trained might of Spain. I thought of the old men I had talked with, veterans of these years, and of how discouraged they seem with the Cuba of today. Among them O'Kelly saw what could make a truly great nation of Cuba if her people had only a fair chance.

This was the second period of the Ten Years' War, after a series of defeats had convinced the leaders that they could not meet Spain in frontal attack and win. The leaders had made two important decisions. They must live on the enemy; Spain would have to supply their arms and ammunition. And they must levy tribute on the Spanish-owned towns and plantations. This had to be done without losing too many men; they had to steal what they could carry, burn what they could not, evade the Spaniards everywhere, and hope finally to weary them of the whole adventure.

Mr. O'Kelly, who had fought in many armies, found the Cuban system of supply original. The Cuban soldier got no rations, in fact he got no pay. There was no grousing about the commissary because each man was his own. There was fine respect for ownership and no communistic sharing except when an animal was slaughtered and the meat divided. Each officer had certain soldiers from among the *convoyeros* (bearers). These were too stupid or otherwise unfit for combat duty. They seemed devoted to their officers, and tireless. After an all-day march clearing a way through jungle with *machetes*, they made nothing of a night's foraging followed by another exhausting day. Mr. O'Kelly was hard put to it to maintain the prestige of an old soldier who expected to take it. He kept up, but he confesses that sometimes he thought he should drop. He wrote that a day's march in Cuba's spiny jungle made him look as though he had been worsted in a catfight.

What the foragers could find with luck sounds like a good diet; one must remember that there were many luckless days when only a tighter belt, if one had a belt, could serve. The wilderness provided cocoanuts, bananas, and palm for its many uses. Men who know how can almost live by the palm alone. Women manufactured rudimentary clothing from palm fibre, and sacks and hammocks and horse gear; part of the palm is edible; and of course it made the house. Any plantation or garden might yield *yuca* or *malanga,* yams, oranges, squash or corn, sugar cane, coffee, or tobacco. Ground corn, Mr. O'Kelly found, was nourishing, but "not very susceptible to mastication." The favorite drink, if coffee was lacking, was sugar-water spiced up with ginger. If there was any doubt of the ground water, one could cut a certain vine, thick as a man's arm, and drink the crystal-clear water that ran out of it. Hanging fountains, O'Kelly called them. Big days were marked by the capture of meat: a cow or pig from a plantation or the *hutía,* a native Cuban rodent that cooks up into a very delectable meal. Mr. O'Kelly concluded that Cubans could never be defeated because of their excellent commissary arrangements and the persistence of yams, which grew so generally and so fast. The fertility of Cuba's soil fought for her freedom.

Uniforms were even more sketchy than supply. He described one "fat dark brown man who moved me profoundly like the personification of heroic patriotism. His clothing consisted of the brim of a straw hat, through which his wooly head protruded. A rifle and a cartridge belt completed the equipment of this patriot." But they were not all garbed like Adam; officers he found well-dressed and "scrupulously clean, with a few dubious exceptions among colored officers." He found perfect equality between white and colored people, with colored officers taking precedence according to rank. Cuban fighters he found equal to the best. "These men bear the toil and fatigues of an unequal fight with a patience and valor which has seldom been equaled and rarely exceeded. If we wish to respect the Cuban character, we should observe it in the camps." This reminded him of the weakling Cubans he had known in the cities. " Between the men in camp and the effeminate folk of the cities there is a difference too great . . . it is hard to believe they are of the same blood."

President Céspedes was moving so fast that our reporter made many observations and several visits before he caught up with him. On the way he visited the camp of Major General Calixto García Iñíguez (he of the famous message). He found the general "tall, of delicate complexion; of thirty three years . . . of affable manner, he lacks no grace or air of distinction. Rapid and imperative in speech, and of nervous character, energetic and astute, he undoubtedly possesses the intellectual faculties needed by a leader in the sort of war made by the Cubans. Like most Cuban officers he has not had the advantage of officer's training, knows little of the science of war, except what they have learned during six years of fighting for liberty. Cuban officers know very well the fundamental principles of guerrilla warfare, thanks to the lessons which the Dominicans have given them: Generals Máximo Gómez and Modesto Díaz.

"General Gómez who now commands in the central province, is a brave veteran, energetic and of iron character. He lacks the high polish of an officer and seems to have less general education than his disciple, Calixto García. He has, nevertheless, the advantage of great experience in war and practical knowledge of irregular warfare. In great part the fortunate resistance of the Cubans during the first year of the war was due to the steady and unbreakable resolution of Díaz and Gómez; and whatever the outcome of the struggle, these men ought to occupy an honored place in Cuban history."

O'Kelly was seeing Cubans, not Spanish nor colonials; and he was good at picking up distinctive traits, many of which mark

Cubans today. "The cold dignity of the Spaniard," he noted, "has melted in this ardent climate and the grandiloquent forms of its language have felt the fertility of exuberance of the tropics . . . perhaps one of the most curious phases of [the Cuban's] character is his repugnance to admitting that he has been defeated. To believe him he personally has always come out victor. . . . The Cuban army may be scattered; but the soldier in his own eyes is never routed, and this way of thinking is to me one of the great reasons of the indomitable resolution of the men of the manigua."

Our reporter discovered also the Cuban ability to have fun in any situation. "The dance," he wrote, "seems to be the Cuban's absorbing passion. In that he forgets everything: suffering, weariness, and danger. There awake then the sleeping energies of the criollo and it seems that both sexes are absorbed in a passionate joy while they move to the melancholy and sensual measures of the native dance." There was dancing every night that the exigencies of war permitted. Once camp was established, the commanding officer would let the word go forth, and people would gather from miles around, slipping in through the forest in family groups. All night they would sing and clap the rhythm of ancient tribal measures, pounding the hard earth with bare feet, dancing with abandon until the bugle sounded *silencio*, when all sound would stop as if by magic and the company would fade out again into the *manigua*. Sometimes there were instruments: in General García's camp, they had captured the instruments for a whole band.

Mr. O'Kelly, white man from the north, was struck by the wildness of one dancing group. "Watching them it was necessary to make great effort to convince oneself that the place was America and not Africa . . . some dancers who moved with strange and singular movements, to the monotonous song of the musicians who seconded their vocal efforts with hand claps. The more rapidly the dancers leapt, the more did the enthusiasm of the spectators seem to grow until they gave vent to their emotions with hand claps and cries of 'ya, ya' and exclamations of joy. . . . This dance was known as the voudou, a sort of religious ceremony retained by the African Negroes but whose significance nobody was able to explain to me."

Arriving finally at the camp of President Céspedes, the northern reporter was received by young officers, among them the President's son, and passed quickly along to the chief magistrate's quarters. He occupied a *bohío* "larger than common, but which would not excite the envy of the most envious." It was furnished with a rude table, a hammock, several trunks and necessary books and papers. O'Kelly found the President a man of fine appearance. "Although a man of short stature, he has a constitution of iron. Nervous by temperament, he stands always erect. The features are small but regular. High and well-formed forehead, the eyes between gray and black, brilliant and full of penetration, reflect in his oval face the traces left by time and cares. His mouth and lower face are hidden in a gray beard and moustache, with a few black hairs still intermixed and on smiling he shows extremely white and well-preserved teeth."

Luncheon was served at a table "so rough the plates could not sit at ease. Most of them were tin, but highly polished and scrupulously clean; lunch consisted of a bit of roast meat, sweet potatoes, corn meal, casaba, and a sort of corn meal pie. . . . It was served with a formality suitable to the White House. . . . The affair had a character of moral grandeur which, in my eyes, compensated by much the absence of worldly pomp."

Among the men at table was a young officer, Tomás Estrada Palma, who was to become the first president of Cuba after she was free of Spain. A member of Cuba's congress and owner of large plantations, he had been educated in France, and he impressed O'Kelly as "of tranquil aspect and good character, and of practical intelligence." At the moment he possessed exclusively the clothes he stood in. Señor Estrada had as good cause as any for bitter hatred of Spain. His mother, a tenderly nurtured woman, had been captured by the Spaniards and had died of exposure.

From President Céspedes and his officers O'Kelly concluded that Cuba would win her war, however long it took. Cubans had no confidence whatever in Spain, least of all when Spain was temporarily a republic. They were agreed that their only chance of decent government was to win complete independence of Spain. The only point at issue was whether they should try to establish an independent republic or seek annexation to the United States. On this rock they split. Patriots equally ardent and devoted showed the basic distrust that was Spain's ugliest heritage; they fell apart; they even impeached President Céspedes. Cubans still argue about the rights and wrong of the case. The sad fact is that Cubans could not remain together to profit by the victory they might have won. The war ended with the Pact of Zanjón, signed on February 10, 1878. It ended ten years' exhausting and destructive fighting. And it promised only the sort of reform that Spain had promised before: a general amnesty, a mild form of autonomy, and emancipation of the slaves who had served in the war.

Several important leaders stood out against such a peace, notably Antonio Maceo, Cuba's military genius, and José Martí, whose greatest work was done in New York and who remains Cuba's idol. These two men knew that the Pact of Zanjón was only a truce. Martí in New York and Maceo in Costa Rica set themselves to prepare for the ultimate effort, which they considered inevitable.

Mr. O'Kelly? He wound up his Cuban adventure in the best Irish tradition of complete but gallant unreasonableness. President Céspedes offered to send him safely to Jamaica, whence he could easily have shipped for New York. But James the soldier of fortune declined such a tepid ending. Disguised as a *guajiro*, he made his way afoot through the Spanish lines and into Manzanillo, where he was imprisoned with rats and other discomforts. At last he was sent to Spain, and he finally made his way back to New York.

## *ANTONIO MACEO*

ON Havana's Malecón, mounted on a marble pedestal so lofty one can hardly see the massive bronze figure on top, is an equestrian statue of José Antonio Maceo. Chapman says he was the greatest military leader in Cuban history. Cuban historians praise him with characteristic lack of stint. His contemporaries valued him as a leader, often followed him in preference to other men, put themselves on record as his affectionate friends. This seems odd to us, for Antonio Maceo was a mulatto. They called him *el titán de bronce*, for he was a large man physically as well as a great military leader and a commanding personality. Possibly Maceo would have been Cuba's Bolívar or San Martín if he had been white. Cuban writers suggest the idea. The Marqués de Santa Lucía, who gave up his ancient Spanish title and became president of Cuba as Salvador Cisneros de Betancourt, said in 1895: "What a shame is Antonio Maceo's condition, because he is and will be a good leader; if he is not now he will be superior to Gómez; but the prejudices of the vulgar are the devil." Who could better sum it up than that? Jorge Mañach, in his biography of Martí, wrote: "Martí counted on the mulatto's courage as on his intelligence. For obvious political reasons Maceo's flag could not be the first."

The Maceo family came to Cuba from Venezuela, where two of the sons had served as Spanish soldiers against Bolívar. They were prosperous enough to make the move in comfort, and in Santiago one of the sons, Marcos, became a merchant and did well. In 1843, he married Mariana Grajales Coella, a *mulata* of a Santo Domingan family. When she married Marcos Maceo,

Mariana was a widow of thirty-five with four children. She bore Marcos seven sons and two daughters, all of whom were trained in love of Cuba and of independence. Marcos was soon marked as a rebel, and his good business suffered. Once, when a fifteen-year-old son was arrested as a conspirator, Marcos gave himself up to serve the term. Then he went to the *manigua*, and his sons, as they matured, did likewise. Two became generals — José and Antonio, who was the most notable. The others all served creditably as officers. Mariana followed her family to *la tierra del mambí*, where she lived the toilsome life of a peasant woman, nursing wounded men, inspiring those who weakened. Once when her own young son was wounded, she patched him up and sent him promptly back. "Now your wound is cured. Back to your duty." A Mother of the Gracchi was Mariana Grajales de Maceo.

In such an atmosphere, Antonio grew to magnificent stature. At the age of nineteen he married María Cabrales. It was a happy marriage, but Maceo's biographers tolerantly concede that such a man, much away from home, should not have been expected to remain true to even the most satisfactory spouse. Maceo had his affairs; doubtless María was always his true love. They understood each other perfectly; María gladly accepted the fact that *la patria* came first with her husband. When he was wounded, she went to him on the battlefield; after his death she spent her life collecting mementoes of his deeds and every published comment on them. At the time of his marriage Antonio Maceo was a fine-looking man, with a big head covered with tightly curled hair, broad shoulders, and military carriage. Later he wore a close-cropped beard and moustache around full red lips. In 1861, at twenty-one, Antonio Maceo joined the patriot army and was appointed Captain.

About the same time, Máximo Gómez, who had fought in the Spanish army in Santo Domingo, moved to Cuba. There he threw in his lot with the *mambí*, and President Céspedes soon appointed him commander of a large territory in Oriente. This made him Maceo's commanding officer, and was the beginning of a lasting friendship. It was a queer association, for the men were very different. Leonardo Griñan Peralta, whose *Análisis Caractero-lógico* of Maceo is very helpful, describes Gómez as of medium height, lean, with gray goatee and moustache, a gloomy old man, dry, imperious, of rapid speech and brusque and nervous manner. He was careless of dress and made an unmilitary appearance on a horse often too small for his height. Because of some fancied resemblance he was called *el chino viejo* (the Old Chinaman) or just *el viejo*. Untrained in military science, General Gómez brought Cuba years of experience in guerrilla warfare and a genius for strategy, to say nothing of a personal intrepidity that never faltered.

Maceo was a fighter too with "a crazy and intrepid courage," and he was often chidden by Gómez for taking unnecessary risks. But his manner was that of a finished diplomat in contrast with the Old Man's nervous irascibility.

Griñan Peralta relates an incident told by one Dr. Souza, whose father called on General Gómez, then encamped near the Souza plantation. Seeing smoke rising from his cane fields, the *hacendado* impulsively asked the General to countermand the order to fire that cane. The Old Chinaman, springing up in his stirrups, his voice rough with disdain, scolded: "What do you mean, coming to me about your miserable sugarcane when so much blood is flowing? When a people is trying to free itself, one does not think of canefields! In my house, there is no bread, but there is honor." And setting spurs to his horse, the indignant Gómez, with no word to anyone, sped off like an arrow, endangering all those who stood near.

Maceo gathered up the reins of his horse, Libertador, and before following his chief, addressed the offended Dr. Souza in a tone of the deepest and most urbane courtesy. "Excuse the General's impatience. He has a heart of gold. His responsibility is very great; that explains his language. If you meet him again you will see that he is a very fine man."

Dr. Souza, on this occasion, found Maceo "a magnificent man, carefully shaved, irreproachably dressed in rough drill, his expressive head covered by the finest Panama. Mounted on a superb sorrel horse tall enough to bear him, he was smiling, ceremonious, polite, of slow speech and gesture so quiet as to be almost caressing."

Maceo advanced rapidly in rank to lieutenant colonel, colonel, brigadier general. Spain recognized his importance by condemning him and his family to death and confiscating all their property. The history of the Ten Years' War is almost completely told in the advance of Antonio Maceo, both territorially and in rank. For he first swept eastward toward Guantánamo and then westward into the regions of Las Villas, Holguín, Manzanillo, and Camagüey. Everywhere Maceo showed himself a daring officer, with the sort of personal bravery that took no note whatever of danger and inspired men by leading them. He saw his brothers fall gravely wounded or dead; he himself was wounded repeatedly; his doctor said that he had the gift of convalescing while fighting. He expected to die in action. "We Maceos," he once wrote, "have to die for our country." Maceo had the guerrilla fighter's consummate gift of being always where he was least expected, of dashing in to do as much damage as possible, and of getting out again before he could be caught. He showed this brilliantly in 1874 when General Calixto García sent him into the Spanish-held city of Manzanillo. His friends expected Maceo to find there "a glorious tomb." But the Bronze Titan galloped into the very plaza and out again under a storm of lead.

In 1877 Maceo performed a feat that Cubans compare with San Martín's crossing of the Andes between Argentina and Chile. Learning that Brigadier Francisco de Borbón, a cousin of Alfonso XII, was at Baracoa, Maceo decided to attack. Ten days of slashing with *machetes* through spiny jungles impenetrable to daylight, with little food and little more water, the *mambí* reached Baracoa, raided the storehouses, burned what they could not take. I was reminded of the story of the old unreconstructed royalist I had met in Baracoa. Maceo left the Spaniards gasping, though not defeated. They were almost never defeated, but they certainly never won.

Through numberless such exploits Maceo grew constantly in the regard of his countrymen. The details of the war, so important to Cubans, seem of less moment now than the achievements of this colored man who won the complete confidence of both civil and military superiors and made for himself a place in his country's history second, perhaps, only to that of the sainted Martí.

It has been said that Martí was the brains, Maceo the brawn of the revolution. Maceo certainly contributed strength, but not only physical strength. He was invincible because of his conviction that Cubans could win without arms or supplies. "I bring no army, but I have faith in the grandeur of our cause; resolution will supply all lacks." "I never turn back." He had his convictions, one of which was unalterable: he wanted no aid from the United States. "We don't need intervention to triumph sooner or later. And if we wish to reduce that time to a few days, bring me twenty-five or thirty thousand rifles and a million cartridges. . . . If you succeed in getting that government [the United States] to protect the shipment, nothing will be needed except a person in Havana to let me know when they arrive. With this, you will see that the Americans will not be openly compromised and the Cubans will need no more help."

Maceo's personality and military achievements were such that few white men objected to serving under him. When one did, he lost. On social occasions, Maceo's urbanity was exceptional. A Cuban, whose father knew him well, says that Maceo occasionally appeared at smart restaurants where men gathered, and that his demeanor was perfect. As he never drank, his order was for milk; he let men come to him; he seldom joined a group. Once, as a guest at a *baile* arranged by Gómez's staff officers, General Maceo was urged to dance. So he bowed ceremoniously before a young lady, inviting her. She replied rudely that she danced only with her equals, an affront more distressing to his hosts than to Maceo, who passed it off with dignified disregard. On a similar occasion an officer, described by Griñan Peralta as "black as coal, brave as a lion, of little learning or intelligence, and always ingenuous," protested like treatment in a manner so noisy as to start a ruction. Maceo, strolling up, said quietly: "Nothing has happened here. No lady is obliged to dance with any gentleman she does not like. Tell the musicians to play; let the dance go on." In another like situation, Maceo is quoted as rebuking one of his own staff: "Your duties do not bring you here. Please return to your quarters."

These were social events, conducted by men of both races with the grace of Latins who manage such things well in a society still too undeveloped to judge men without reference to external markings. Cuba is remarkably free of racial prejudice, but to say that there is no color line there is to turn away from one of those hidden sores which we must finally face. It will profit us more to try to understand how Cubans have advanced so far along the hard road toward tolerance, which we only begin to see dimly ahead. Cubans, like us, had to overcome the silly sense of superiority that white men needed in order to bear holding colored men in slavery. But when those Cuban planters freed their slaves and declared for Cuba Libre, the leaders at least had the consistency to give colored men the right to win individual position and distinction. They descended to no such governmental double dealing as some of our states did. Caste was practically unknown, though class distinctions were as hard as always in Spain's colonies and most Negroes were inevitably in the lowest classes. It is still true in Cuba that dark-skinned people have political rights, though social *mores* run against them. Unhappily the bad example of the United States seems to be gaining influence just when we should be profiting by Cuba's good example; one meets too many Cubans who hasten to boast that they are just as prejudiced as anybody from Georgia.

Maceo met this social prejudice with equanimity as long as it was social discrimination, conceding, as Cubans still do, the individual's right to choose his associates. But when racial discrimination affected a man's rights as a citizen, especially when it threatened the unity needed for liberating Cuba, Maceo was quick to resent and to act. At such times his temper, usually so controlled, erupted into vigorous and effective rage.

In 1876, President Estrada Palma had been petitioned not to permit white officers to serve under colored ones. One wonders what the petitioners thought their callow lily-whiteness could offer better than the tried and proved military genius of Antonio Maceo. Maceo at once wrote the president a strong letter stating that if those who expressed such calumnies were not declared enemies of the Republic he would ask for his passport and leave for other lands, there to protest to the entire civilized world. Maceo made two points, still pertinent: that such a ruling would sow the seeds of division and discontent among the revolutionary forces, thus endangering the war; and that it would establish a dangerous precedent. Maceo, in 1876, recognized our problem of today, and he vigorously opposed the first step toward a race war. Who the petitioners were is unknown, though Maceo's prompt action is held to indicate that some of them were men "not far from the government," and of considerable power.

Fortunately the President was a man of intelligence and energy, and he scotched the petition before it had done serious harm. Maceo, thus, according to Griñan Peralta, "faced the problem that even today in Cuba confronts every colored man who becomes notable and who must win esteem by dignity and decorousness. Nobody like Maceo has succeeded in being the symbol of that sublime fusion which Martí so often invoked in his patriotic speeches."

In 1882, Martí wrote Maceo: "The solution of the Cuban problem is not political, but social, and it will be reached only through that mutual love and pardon of one race by the other and that prudence always worthy and always generous by which I know your noble and lofty heart is moved. For me he is a criminal who promotes hatreds in Cuba and profits by those which exist."

In 1878 the immediate problem was that of divisiveness and interprovincial jealousies, which were making it impossible to carry on the war. On the tenth of February the *asamblea de Camagüey* signed the Pact of Zanjón, and most revolutionary bands surrendered within a few weeks. But Antonio Maceo declined to have anything to do with such an agreement, and he proved his gift for leadership by heading a group of nonconformists and demanding an interview with General Martínez Campos. This was partly to gain time for organizing a new army and partly to learn which Cubans had held out against the signing. In his letter to the Spanish general, Maceo stated that all his associates "desire absolute independence" because he believed the Cubans, "favored by physical and moral conditions," were capable of prolonging the struggle indefinitely.

Martínez Campos, feeling his whiteness, wrote a friend suggesting that Maceo wished to surrender individually. "As a mulatto, he is extremely vain." But the Spaniard was eager to get the capitulation of every leader, so he accepted Maceo's invitation to a conference at Baraguá. Arrived there with his staff, he found the Cubans ready to receive him with utmost courtesy. Martínez Campos asked for Maceo, and the General came forward with extended hand, offered the Spaniard his hammock under a spreading mango tree, and waited for the other to speak. Martínez Campos, whose suavity and alluring promises had succeeded with other Cubans, found "this mule-driver turned general," as he called Maceo, impossible to convince. The interview got nowhere. Martínez Campos was forced to leave with the knowledge that "this Maceo is the key to real peace," as he wrote. So the Pact of Zanjón led to a truce, not to peace.

Maceo and his friends escaped from Cuba one by one to set up little centers of Cuban propaganda and recruiting all around the Caribbean. The Spanish authorities paid Maceo the compliment of heading their list of wanted rebels with his name. Efforts were made to assassinate him, but Maceo's time was not yet; his war went on through seventeen years of ostensible peace.

The Pact of Zanjón, despite its promises, changed little for Cubans. Gerardo Castellanos, in *Resplandores Épicos*, sums it up tersely: "Cuba kept on being the same oppressed colony as before Zanjón. Identical proconsuls with the same attributes as Vives, Tacón, O'Donnell. As many or more taxes than before. A daily stream of gold flowing toward the peninsula as a tribute of conquest. The volunteers of the island as aggressive as in the insane days of the murder of the eight students."

Maceo had to earn his living, but his constant preoccupation was renewal of the war in Cuba. He was in Jamaica, Haiti, and Honduras, always received as a distinguished officer. He served as an officer in the Honduran Army. In Costa Rica he was granted permission to establish a colony for Cuban refugees on that little country's eastern shore. Spain, convinced that Maceo's presence anywhere on the Caribbean would menace Spanish control of Cuba, brought pressure to bear, and the Costa Rican president revoked his permission and accepted a Spanish decoration. In Panama, Maceo established a successful business as a builder of frame houses, also for Cuban patriots.

Polavieja, Governor of Cuba, described Maceo for Madrid as "the ringleader who achieved greatest prestige in the first separatist war because of his audacities, his cruelty . . . and who because of this and because he belongs to the colored race . . . this so-called General Maceo must be recognized as the bloodiest enemy of Spain." The Spanish were right; as long as Antonio Maceo lived, there would be war or war in the making.

In 1884 Maceo was in New York, where he met José Martí for the first time. This was the occasion of a quarrel between Máximo Gómez, man of war, and José Martí, man of words. Martí was raising money and inspiring men to a new revolt in Cuba. Gómez wished to send Martí and Maceo to Mexico to stir up Cubans there and perhaps win approval and aid from the Mexicans. One can easily imagine the scene in the New York home of a Cuban. The crusty old general, carelessly dressed, inept at expression, but confident in his experience and leadership, and the enthusiastic young man — Martí was only thirty-one — brilliantly expressive, able to foresee and outline a whole propaganda campaign. He talked and talked. Finally the old man, outdone and jealous for his lieutenant Maceo, burst out: "Look here, Martí; you stick to instructions. General Maceo will do whatever has to be done." And off he went, towel over his shoulder, to the bath his servant had just announced.

Martí was equally furious. He had spent years of effort to enlist financial and other support for Cuba; it was intolerable that *el viejito* should assume that Cuba's war was his private affair. It was Maceo who tried to soothe them both, for Maceo was a friend of both. But Martí refused to take part in the Little War, an abortive attempt to land troops in Cuba in 1885.

The war of 1895 was held to begin with the landing of Maceo. His old and admiring enemy, Martínez Campos, said: "I admit the importance of the landing of Antonio Maceo because I recognize the prestige he enjoys and his prowess in the earlier campaigns."

The Ten Years' War, fought in the jungles and mountains of Oriente, had not reached the center of production. Too many Cubans, apathetic and untouched, were content to live secure under Spain or to assist without really endangering their comfortable livings. Gómez, with the invasion of 1895, planned to carry the war the length of the island, to show every Cuban the smoke by day and flame by night of burning villages and mills, and to force them into the fight. He would also show Spain and the world that this was an all-Cuban war and not a series of sporadic uprisings. Gómez and Maceo were just the pair to put it over: the *chino viejo*, relentless and ruthless, the Bronze Titan, reckless and dashing.

The two men were not entirely agreed on method. Gómez favored a scorched-earth policy, the destruction of the plantations and mills that were supplying Spain; Maceo advocated demanding money under threat of destruction. Some students hint that Maceo had wanted supreme command and was disgruntled; others that he was not altogether scrupulous in money matters. It is related that José Martí's diary records Maceo's arrival at a conference with the observation: "He has already got silver trappings for his horse," and that the next day's entry, which should have revealed what went on at the meeting, was found cut out after Martí's death. Somebody, perhaps even Gómez, may have destroyed an entry not flattering to Maceo. In any case, Maceo showed himself again a first-rate military leader and a brilliant strategist, especially in dashing cavalry attacks.

Between April, when Maceo, Gómez, and Martí landed in eastern Cuba, and December, when Maceo was killed in the West, Gómez and Maceo had, by a series of daring raids, invaded every province, outgeneraled every Spaniard. Their method was enough to drive any academic soldier frantic. They would dash into a village, capture it, infuse the inhabitants with enthusiasm and mark them as anti-Spanish and consequently subject to Spanish reprisal. They would then let the Spaniards recapture the town and appear at another far away. The *machete* attack came into its own. A *mambí* on foot armed only with a *machete* could decapitate a mounted Spaniard, slice off his sword-arm, or disembowel a horse.

As recruiting, these measures proved highly successful, Gerardo Castellanos, who estimates that during the Ten Years' War ninety-five per cent of Cubans were apathetic if not opposed to the *mambí*, states that these methods brought the Cuban forces within measurable equality with the Spaniards. Spain had shipped to Cuba some three hundred thousand soldiers under their best officers, but diseases and climate thinned their ranks continually. Gómez planned to subject the untried Spaniards to the worst possible swamps and torrential storms, and he counted cynically on his best allies, yellow fever and malaria, to which Cubans were considered immune. It was such recruiting and devastation that the Spanish General Weyler tried to combat by establishing his infamous concentration camps, which aroused warlike horror in the United States. If the *mambí* demanded that Cubans leave their villages and fight, Weyler ordered that they stay in their villages or suffer horrible consequences.

By such methods Gómez and Maceo threatened every town, including Havana, and broke through the *trocha,* which Spain had counted on to confine the fighting east of Las Villas. But that series of blockhouses, barbed-wire entanglements, and ditches proved no more effective than the later Maginot and Siegfried lines. Maceo broke through and set about devastating Pinar del Río Province, whose tobacco *vegas* had heretofore been unburned. The Spaniards then hoped to bottle up the Cubans in Pinar del Río, but they broke the lines again and again.

Maceo, who seldom boasted, was betrayed into one gloat when he wrote: "The invasion . . . has been realized with little difficulty and few losses in spite of fighting a sharp combat every three days. . . . The report I enclose will show how we have managed to reach the extreme end of the island, from triumph to triumph, returning to this province through the traps the enemy set to catch me, sure I'd never get through."

Historians, especially Cubans, are fairly well agreed that the Cubans had the Spaniards outmaneuvered and outfought, that they could have won their independence without intervention from the United States if that country had granted them recognition and permitted the shipment of arms and medicines. The Department of State was consistently gentle with Spain and uninterested in the plight of revolutionists, a situation very reminiscent of another revolution against the forces of conservative and Catholic reaction in Spain.

José Antonio Maceo was killed in one of those heedless rushes of his. Leaving most of his troops in Pinar del Río Province, he set out with a small escort to meet Gómez for a conference. In San Pedro, a spot important only for what happened there, he and his handful of men ran into a Spanish patrol. They fought, of course, with their usual courage and dash. But the heart was taken out of them all when they saw their General fall, not to rise this time and convalesce fighting. Maceo died, saying: "It goes well."

When he died, Antonio Maceo was fifty-one years old. He had been working and fighting for Cuban independence for thirty years. He had campaigned the length of the island, he had figured in one hundred and seventeen battles and an uncounted number of lesser engagements.

In the first letter Martí wrote him, he said: "I do not know, General Maceo, a braver soldier or a more tenacious Cuban than you."

Griñan Peralta writes: "Antonio Maceo was far from being that confused mixture of valor and vanity which is generally the Indo-American *caudillo*. One would need a new word to describe the personality of this gentlemanly spirit, of this magnanimous man who united in himself, along with the *caudillo*'s best qualities, the endowments of a man who could control his emotions and who, along with the small virtues of little souls, had the great virtues of great souls."

Máximo Gómez, in an order of the day, wrote: "Our country weeps for the loss of one of her forceful defenders; Cuba the most glorious of her sons; the Army the first of its generals."

## *JOSÉ MARTÍ*

THE VISITOR to Cuba is soon made aware of the widespread devotion to the national hero, José Martí. His name is invoked on every occasion, literary as well as patriotic; his words are quoted like Biblical sayings; scholars devote symposia to considering Martí in every guise: as liberator, religionist, philosopher, educator, writer in prose and poetry. Comment is always laudatory, even adulatory. Cubans call their hero *el apóstol*, venerate him as a saint. A typical example of the style is an editorial by Eduardo Abril Amores in *El Diario de Cuba* of May 19, 1942:

"Martí is the liberator of always and forever; the warrior of every epoch and the eternal thought of Cuba. Nobody has said, since Martí's death, anything that he had not said. He was the pinnacle of Cuban liberty, of the Cuban ideal, and of Cuba's political genius. Martí was Cuba's Infinite. Martí reached a point beyond which there is nothing."

This way of thinking illustrates one of the fascinating conflicts between the Nordic and the Latin mental habit. The Latin requires a faultless ideal to adore; he resents the sort of probing that seeks to know the man as he was, to show any shortcomings or failures as well as his nobility and achievements. The Nordic, as least since the passing of the Parson Weems school, tends to investigate a great man's whole nature, seeking to establish why he triumphed in spite of frailties or handicaps. Martí, approached in this spirit, arouses several baffling questions.

Why do we know so little of him? José Martí lived more of his adult life in New York than he did in Cuba. He wrote penetrating criticisms of our life and literature, discussing such different men as Emerson, Grant, and Walt Whitman. Yet few of our writers give Martí more consideration than to refer to him as one of the Latin American liberators or one of its poets. There is no collection of his writings in English. It is our loss that we do not

know Martí. Much that he wrote of the democratic ideal, of tolerance, and of personal relations in a political world is freshly
applicable to today's problems.

Martí's eminence in Cuba raises questions too. National heroes
are generally military men or those whose accomplishment was
concrete. José Martí was not a general of genius like Washington, San Martín, or Bolívar, a law-giver like Jefferson, or an
emancipator like Lincoln. Like them he led and inspired his
people though he may not have been — as his most ardent disciples maintain — a greater man than all of them combined.
Martí's preeminence consists in his personality: he was a great
and pure spirit, and he had an extraordinary gift of expression
both as orator and writer. Perhaps his growing fame is a tribute
to his countrymen's maturity of judgment. For his legend appears
to be in the making just now. And one gets the impression that
Martí is still more in the minds of intellectuals than in the hearts
of the people.

José Julián Martí y Pérez was born in Havana on January 28,
1853. His father, Mariano Martí, was from Valencia, and his
mother, Leonor Pérez, from the Canary Islands. Their house,
which is preserved as a shrine, has three rooms downstairs, a
patio with open kitchen at the rear, and three rooms above. Don
Mariano, a Spanish civil servant, must have lived in comfort with
a servant, perhaps a slave or two. In the front room upstairs, now
furnished with furniture of the period, Doña Leonor "gave
light," as the Spanish has it, to her only son; three daughters
completed the family.

Little Pepe was sent first to an infant's school, which stayed in
his memory because the teachers there pulled his ears out of shape.
Don Mariano saw no point in his son's going farther, but was
persuaded to enter him in a new school for boys, whose director,
Rafael de María Mendive, was to be one of the greatest influences
on the boy's life and the man's thought. For in that teacher Martí
first met the revolutionary ideas for which he was to live and die.

M. Ysidro Méndez, whose biography of Martí is by many considered the best, gives a revealing picture of this home and childhood. He explains that the parents, being Spanish and reconciled to belonging to a lowly class with no chance to rise, were quite out of sympathy with a child who was as sure to rise as tomorrow's sun. Always the father, who was often out of a job, thought Pepe had better leave school and go to work. Doña Leonor, described by Méndez as professing "customary Catholicism," opined that "a man should ask God for work suited to his class"; she thought that the best rewards came in another life anyhow.

Mendive saw possibilities in the boy and made an intimate of him. In his teacher's home the lad heard talk of freedom. Once when Mendive was arrested for conspiracy, Pepe visited him in jail. He read his mentor's poems and contributions to the underground magazines. When Don Mariano removed his son from school and apprenticed him to a shopkeeper, Dr. Mendive gave him a scholarship that enabled him to continue into secondary school. It also prepared him for the life of a revolutionist.

Once, when a group of women appeared in a theater draped in the colors of Free Cuba, Mendive's pupils cheered them with boyish abandon. The authorities decided this school had lasted too long; it was closed, and Mendive was sent into exile, where he continued his propaganda, mostly from New York. Martí had already published his first poem, *Abdala*, an allegory on Spain's treatment of Cuba, and when he and his friend, Fermín Valdés Domínguez, were caught exchanging incendiary letters, both were arrested with a large group of students.

Young Pepe, among others, was sentenced to six years at hard labor. The one room remaining of the prison where he was held stands in the little park where the Prado comes into the Malecón. Today Martí's cell seems quite a pleasant place with its iron bars open to the morning sun instead of onto the foul hallway that must have been there. Each morning the prisoners were marched out for a long walk to the stone quarry where, as the boy swung

*180*

*Variety of terrain. Habanilla Falls, Cienfuegos*

*Los Mogotes de Viñales, Pinar del Río*

a heavy mallet all day, the gyves cut deeper and more festeringly
into his flesh until they made sores from which he never recovered. The scars on his spirit were quite as enduring but more
creative. Blind Spain was tempering another tool for her humili-
ation.

Mariano Martí was an officer in the Spanish police, and he had
friends. One of them was Don José María de Sarda, who operated a line of small vessels from the port of Boniato, near Havana, to the Isle of Pines. In the fall of 1870, young Pepe's sen-
tence was commuted to exile and he was paroled to Don José
María, who took the maimed and disillusioned youth home to
his wife.

I was privileged to see that home with Judge Waldo Medina,
who has made it his service to preserve this refuge and all that is
known about the young hero's stay there. The Sarda family
still lives on the place and farms it. The present owner was a
baby when Martí was there; he remembers only what he has
heard. But one can see much and sense the rest in Dr. Medina's
account; he has worked out almost to a day the two months of that
exile.

The two houses, the one occupied by the family now and the
one in which Martí slept and worked, stand on a gentle hill. The
view is across rolling fields, which rise to the hills described in
*Treasure Island.* Cuba's tall palms lift their crests to the high
breeze, and there is a quietude of sun and shadow that must have
been very healing to the lacerated spirit of the young idealist.
His sores were bathed and his body nourished by the mother of
the family. They say she bothered little about her own husky
sons while she mothered the visitor, whom she may well have
turned from corroding bitterness to the certainty that human nature was worth struggling for. All psychoneurotics are not the
products of an age that has invented the term, and all the ways
of saving them did not wait for us either. Señora de Sarda gave
the young man care and quiet and left him much alone. For

hours every day he paced up and down the flagstones in front of his door or circled the sundial that still marks the hours in London and Madrid as well as on the Isle of Pines. He was only seventeen. But he knew that he had work to do against all injustice and in favor of human dignity. He wrote little about this period.

Then blind Spain contributed again to the preparation of her rebel leader. It was decreed that José Martí must leave Cuba, but that he might live in Spain. That was just what he needed. It gave him an opportunity to study at the University of Madrid and later that of Saragossa. He took degrees in civil and church law, in philosophy and letters; he perfected his always beautiful and facile literary style while he supported himself as a journalist; and he exposed himself to all the revolutionary currents that were sweeping Europe. With his friend Valdés Domínguez he was in Spain from 1871 to 1873. During that time also he learned to the point of mastery both French and English. The flaming youth with the festering sores on his ankles and a Cuban secondary education had, by the grace of Spain's stupidity, been turned into a man of the world, a finished scholar, a practiced writer, a polished poet, and an eloquent speaker.

In 1875, José Martí returned to America, knowing that what he meant to make his life work — Cuban independence — could best be done there. During the next twenty years Martí roamed widely, first in Mexico and Guatemala, where he acquired fame as writer and orator, and where several love affairs inspired some of his most charming poetry; in Venezuela, where he thought he might settle; in Costa Rica and Santo Domingo to confer with Cuban revolutionists, and in the United States where he was to live most of his adult life.

He first went to Mexico, which was full of Cuban refugees, in 1875. There his cultivated tastes, literary gifts, and revolutionary fervor opened all doors to him. Not tall and very thin, Martí was a romantic figure whose slight limp recalled his prison experience and whose charm was felt by men and women alike. He was described at this period as "fragile, nervous, loquacious." His head was large, and as his hair retreated his lofty brow became the dominating feature that sculptors make much of. But in life his eyes were most remarked. Dark and deep, they could brood with sadness, twinkle with laughter, flash with rage, see right through falsity. His voice was vibrant, and when Martí spoke everybody else was silent.

Such a man in such an era was marked for romance, and Martí had plenty. His lovelife was of the very stuff of poetry; secret, sad, or unsatisfactory. Being a poet he told all. In his *Versos Sencillos* one can trace his development from a boy's first love, through an idyllic tragedy, to a man's disillusionment and the reward of mature understanding.

The first love was *"la blonda y distinguida señorita"* whom he knew in Saragossa, that Moslem-Spanish city with gardens overlooking the Ebro. Ysidro Méndez called it "a local love, which never rooted itself deeply enough to rise above time and distance." But it produced a lyrical poem or two.

In Mexico, Martí was soon well known as writer on European affairs, poet, and orator, and a member of the most esteemed intellectual circle in the capital, that which surrounded Rosario Peña, a beauty most famous because Manuel Acuña had committed suicide for love of her. Older than Pepe Martí, she favored him as "the golden-tongued Cuban . . . whose eyes held captive all the sun of his native isle." It must have been pretty heady for a youth. Martí was a homesick exile, absorbed in his dream and his work for Free Cuba, but he was only twenty-two, and, as always, needing tenderness. But Martí, destined to be always beloved of women, was a man whose loves, however numerous, must be pure. He soon, as Méndez puts it, retired honorably from the tourney with Rosario Peña.

Perhaps it was natural that in his retreat from Rosario's overheated salons the young idealist should be attracted by a well-bred and simple girl, the type of wife rather than mistress. Carmen Zayas Bazán y Hidalgo was the daughter of a Cuban aristocrat who had no sympathy with the revolution he had fled from. He received Martí for his skill at chess, but violently opposed the young plebeian's suit for his daughter. Martí became persistent. It seemed an eminently suitable alliance between a poor and not too healthy intellectual and a young lady with an assured income. Surely he did not think of it so. He must have been, however briefly, in love; too enamored to realize that Carmen's innate conservatism would make her forever unsympathetic with his mission. Few young men in love see in the pretty girl promising serenity the future wife demanding a stable home, a settled income, and conformity. But Martí was soon writing verses that indicate some premonitions.

> *Mas si tu quieres que esté bien afana*
> *Mi pobre corazón en ti sonría.*
> *Mírame hoy, desdéñame mañana,*
> *Pero, por Dios, desdéñame algun día.*

> Wouldst make me over-anxious, yearn,
> My poor heart turn its smile on thee?
> Gaze then on me today, then turn
> Away, by Heav'n, away from me.

He also wrote: "She who is to become my wife has already begun to suffer." They became engaged, nevertheless, and Martí went to Guatemala to teach in a school conducted by Cubans. There he taught French literature, English, Italian, German, and the history of philosophy, but he was best remembered for his liberal ideas. Most of the pupils were under twelve, but for special courses in art, music, and in literature older students were admitted. Among them were Señorita María García Granados, and Máximo Soto Hall, who has written his recollections of the inspired young teacher. He describes Martí's first public appearance in Guatemala.

A new liberal society, called El Porvenir, The Future, was presenting the opera *Robert le diable*. Everybody was there. The streets were jammed with carriages bearing ladies in their most elaborate Paris gowns, sparkling jewels, waving fans, spreading scent; and gentlemen whose white linen shone against formal black while gleaming tiles rose above sweeping capes. The theater, which had known Adelina Patti, Julián Gayarré, and Rafael Calvo, had never seen a more brilliant concourse. Nor had a Guatemalan audience ever been stirred to such enthusiasm as that aroused by an unknown speaker. Presented by the introductory orator, José Martí came forward, bowing, and spoke on his dearest theme, a future world dedicated to freedom and justice. Máximo Soto Hall wrote that from Martí he learned how one could give "color and flavor to words." The Mexican poet, Luis G. Urbina, described the Martí of that period as "pale and nervous, with dark wavy hair, a thick moustache under a Greek nose, a broad brow, small deep-set eyes shining with starry brilliance. When he smiled, what a childish and luminous smile! It seemed that an electric halo surrounded him."

In Guatemala, as in Mexico, Martí soon became a vital part of the city's intellectual life, especially among Cuban exiles. Thus he knew his pupil, María García Granados, whose portraits show a delicate narrow face with large eyes, sensitive mouth, and framed by long ringlets. Unlike Carmen waiting in Mexico, María was a revolutionist. Her father was a Cuban patriot who had left his country only when illness made it imperative: he was dying of tuberculosis and able to be out of bed only a few hours a day. During those hours he received liberals from everywhere and challenged to chess all those worthy of his skill. Among these was Martí, who engaged the father at chess while he fascinated the daughter in the fragrant flowery patio.

This was an idyll — a tragic idyll, Soto Hall called it. For

Martí was engaged to Carmen Zayas back in Mexico, and his honor would not let him fail her. Returning to marry Carmen he doubtless told María how it was. After he left, María grew more and more languid; as delicate, Soto Hall said, as a butterfly's wing. Then they heard at school that she was gravely ill, and finally that she had died. Martí wrote *La Niña de Guatemala,* which is known to every school child in Cuba:

> He returned with his wife;
> She died of love.

> She went into the river in the evening,
> The doctor drew her out dead;
> They say she died of the cold,
> I know that she died of love.

Well, it was a romantic age; who so crude as to remember that María like her father had tuberculosis? María died, and Cuba lingers still over the romance of that pure and sacrificial love. There is even a national scholarship that brings a maid of Guatemala to Cuba every year. So ended the love that, if not the deepest of Martí's life, was perhaps the sweetest and the saddest.

After the treaty of Zanjón, Martí returned to Cuba, but his stay was brief. As soon as it became apparent that Spain was not going to abide by the terms of the treaty, Martí was again deported. Carmen was growing weary of her role as the wife of a revolutionary. She wished only that he would use his talents to make a living and a dignified position. Her father stood ready to help. Even José's devoted mother thought that her son might well think less of others in order to give more time to his own family. But the patriot was on his way again.

Martí went to Venezuela, and Carmen refused to accompany him. One is helplessly impressed with how sensible Carmen was. Imagine taking a two-year-old child on a sailing ship to such a country as Venezuela then was, with all the tropical diseases and no sanitation! Carmen returned to her father's home in Camagüey, and the event justified her judgment, for Martí soon got himself deported from Venezuela as a dangerous alien. Most Cuban writers are gentle with Carmen; she simply was not of the sturdy stuff required in the wife of a martyr to patriotism. Martí thus described his ideal of the martyr's wife:

> *Amor? Eso es un voto! Es un espíritu que a otro se libra,*
> *Como una monja que en las aras jura bodas divinas,*
> *Como Jesús, la generosa novia serena, a la cruz mira,*
> *Y al novio ofrece, si en la cruz lo clavan las fieras de la vida,*
> *Colgarse a él, y calentar su cuerpo y si en la cruz expira,*
> *Morir con él, los nobles labios puestos sobre su frente fría.*

> Love? A vow. A spirit's self it gives to hold
> Like the divine troth pledged by a nun with prayer.
> Like Christ, the serene sister does the cross behold
> And if the fiends of earth must crucify Him there,
> She clings to warm him and, if death breathes ever cold,
> She gladly dies, her lips pressed on His brow so fair.

That, definitely, was not Carmen.

Carmen's sister wrote to Martí: "Carmita did not abandon the home of a poor husband; with the prudence of a woman of judgment she left her husband the liberty necessary in poverty, imposing upon herself the pain of a separation she thought would be compensated when you summon her to a stable home."

Thus freed of family cares, Martí returned sadly and alone to New York. His real task was working toward a free Cuba. To earn his living, he served as consul for Argentina, Uruguay, and Paraguay; he wrote for many magazines and newspapers, including *La Nación* of Buenos Aires. He was also a regular contributor to *The Hour* and the New York *Sun,* writing in succinct and expressive English. Charles Dana was his friend. Those articles show how keen a mind was judging the American scene, how appreciative a critic was reading Whitman and Emerson, how unprejudiced eyes and ears could recognize beauty in modern art and daring new music. In New York, José Martí reached the apogee of his powers both as a writer and as a person.

Critics, both Spanish-American and Spanish, laud Martí's writings, but never fail to emphasize the grandeur of his personality. Rubén Dário called him "a superman, great and virile . . . in communion with God and Nature." Miguel de Unamuno named him "the apostle of the eternal and universal quixotic *hispanidad*," Fernando de los Ríos "the most moving, profound, and pathetic personality that the Spanish soul has so far produced in America." Federico de Onís, in *La Antología de la Poesía Española y Hispano-Americana,* says that Martí's life was "one of the most intense, pure, and noble that have been lived on earth." Of his work, Dr. Onís writes: "Martí is one of the most profoundly original writers that America has produced so far," and adds that Martí had one of the most individual styles in all Castilian literature. This is especially surprising because all Martí's prose was journalism; but according to Pedro Enríquez-Ureña, it was "journalism raised to an artistic level that has never been equaled in Spanish or probably in any other language. . . . The style he achieved was entirely new to the language . . . he shuns pedantic words, his syntax is full of unexpected but racy constructions." Thus Enríquez-Ureña in *Literary Currents in Latin America.* One might ask how much Martí's Spanish style was affected by his experience in writing crisp New York journalese.

Martí won acclaim as an orator soon after his arrival in New York in 1880. He was one of several speakers at a Cuban mass meeting in Steck Hall. It was a snowy January night, but the place was crowded with Cubans of all classes, including many Negroes "at the back of the hall." Martí began to speak, as was his custom, quietly, in close-knit, precise phrases. But soon he passed, as Jorge Mañach described the episode, "from sententious argument to telling detail and lightning-like metaphor. That clear voice exploded in the air an electric effluvium that dazzled his listeners and took their breath. . . . In revolutionary meetings no language like this had ever been heard. Even," Mañach goes on, "the *hombre de machete* understood why 'first was the word.' "

From this time on, Martí was the recognized leader of Cuba's independence movement. His personality, his febrile zeal, and his unquestioned integrity and singlemindedness dominated even men older and more experienced than he was. He was strong and self-reliant; he often disagreed with his associates, but he was a skillful advocate and adept at reconciling conflicting points of view. In 1879 he had refused to join two of Cuba's most influential military men, Máximo Gómez and Antonio Maceo. Against his advice they started *la guerra chica,* the Little War, which ended in disaster. Martí was accused of backsliding and challenged his detractor to a duel, but the affair was settled without a fight.

Off and on during these years, Martí had a home of sorts in New York, where Carmen and his little son, also José Martí, joined him several times. But it was never satisfactory. Martí was more and more torn between his public vocation and his private devotion. Carmen was always unhappy in the northern city. Her husband was forever away from home, attending meetings, lecturing or conferring with other revolutionists. Several times he gave up lucrative employment for his work for Cuba. Carmen's protests, at first suppliant, grew more reproachful; finally she returned to her father's house in Camagüey, leaving Martí deeply humiliated. Their last effort to make a home was when Pepito was twelve years old. The boy had been educated by Jesuits and trained in the Spanish tradition by his royalist grandfather. A friend of Martí related that the boy showed his father a watch engraved with the Spanish crest; his grandfather had given it to him so that every time he looked at the hour he would be reminded that he was Spanish. What a thrust for the man whose life was dedicated to warring against a hated Spain! He wrote a poignant poem, *Ismaelillo*, addressed to that beloved son.

This poem is considered by many Cuban critics the first example of Spanish modernism, which is generally held to have begun in Spain. Enríquez-Ureña agrees with the Cubans. "In poetry he was an innovator as much as in prose. With him, verse definitely gave up the now stale ornaments of romanticism and became again a fresh and living thing." Dr. Onís concurs: "The simplicity and freedom to which his poetry attains consists in giving the purest and most elevated concepts with complete force and originality. . . . Martí's spirit is of no epoch or school; his temperament is romantic, full of faith in nineteenth-century human ideals without shadow of pessimism or decadence, but his art is rooted, in a manner entirely his own, in the best of the Spanish spirit, both classical and popular and in his wide modern culture into which enters much that is English and American."

Added evidence of Martí's modernism, and perhaps of the American influence, is found in his freethinking and anti-clericalism. Dr. Emilio Roig de Leuchsenring, in a scholarly study that I follow, quotes Martí as writing "religions are all equal . . . outside of historical and purely human dogmas, man will seek the harmony of the religious spirit with free judgment, which is the religious form of the modern world."

Martí was a Mason, and as such excommunicated by the Church, a fact that poses a problem for devout Cuban Catholics. He spoke out freely against clericalism and even against the Catholic Church. "Christianity has died at the hands of Catholicism." "The only religion worthy of man is that which does not exclude any man from its breast." "The tyrant is the Catholic who holds himself above a Hindu, and the Methodist who hisses at the Catholic."

Martí's vigorous anti-clericalism was most frankly expressed in an unpublished book, *Hombre de Campo, Country Man,* in which he wrote:

"Don't show this book to your village priest, because he wants to keep you in the dark so you will have to ask him about everything.

"And as he charges you to put water on your child's head, to say that you are your wife's husband, which you already know because you love her and she loves you; as he charges you to be born, to give you unction, to marry, to pray for your soul, to die; as he even denies you the right of burial if you don't give him money, he never wants you to know that all you have done is unnecessary because on that day he will have to stop charging money for all that.

"I don't ask you to believe what I believe. Read what I say, and believe it if it seems right to you. The first duty of man is to think for himself. Therefore I don't want you to believe your priest; because he won't let you think."

Martí was, nonetheless, a truly religious man and a student of religions. From his studies of Jesus he extracted a social doctrine which infuses all he wrote.

He believed in the dignity and equality of man, and made practical suggestions for the development of the individual. "There is no better religious rite than the free use of human reason." "To believe in the unknown does not better the world, but to work for it does." Naturally he advocated universal and "elementarily scientific" education. "Schools of trades and crafts will help to solve the human problem now that we see falling those ancient trees — monarchy and the church — under whose branches so many men have lived comfortable lives. Now neither courtiers nor friars! A trade or a craft . . . is the firmest foundation of personal independence and of public dignity. The general happiness of a people rests on individual independence." Martí seems to have been that rare combination, a political mystic offering such practical ideals as Cuba, and all of us, most need.

Martí was never truly settled in New York; to him it was a way station on the road to Cuba Libre. He had many friends, he shared in the intellectual and artistic life of the city, but he complained much of the cold. He missed Cuba's sunshine, but he suffered from more than physical cold. Martí needed warmth; only in love or in action did he find his proper temperature. Once he wrote: "God pity the heroic heart that does not find at home a welcome for his noblest purposes."

That he found such a welcome finally is an open secret which Martí's biographers touch lightly. I heard the story, most circumspectly told, from Señora Blanca Z. de Baralt, whose *El Martí Que Yo Conocí, The Martí I Knew,* was published in Havana in 1945. I have the book, and I have used it freely, but I like best to remember her as she read me certain chapters in her Havana home.

In 1884, she said, her music teacher asked her father's permission to present Blanche and her sister at a Cuban soirée. (Blanche had not then translated her name into the Spanish Blanca.) The host was Luis Baralt, Martí only one gentleman among the guests. The sisters, elegant in curls and bustles, rendered several selections, Blanche singing to her sister's violin obbligato, the professor accompanying on the piano. The young ladies were acclaimed as musicians, complimented as conversationalists, and adopted as Cubans. At least Blanche was, for her host of that evening became her husband as soon as he could manage it.

That first night, Blanche was deeply impressed by Martí. "Within a few moments, with a skill I have never seen equaled, he had ascertained, without questions, what were my tastes, my inclinations, my hopes. . . . He discussed with me pictures, music, and books . . . with absolute simplicity without letting me feel the difference between a girl and a scholar.

"At the same time he revealed himself to me. I could appreciate in an instant that he was a superior man of vast knowledge and a great soul."

Later young Blanche saw Martí often, for he was living in a boarding house conducted by Doña Carmen Miyares de Mantilla, a cousin of Luis Baralt, who found many excuses to take her there. This was a Carmen very different from the wife in Camagüey. Carmen Miyares, born of a Venezuelan family, had lived in Cuba until she was fifteen. She then married a Cuban, Manuel Mantilla, and went with him to New York, taking her four orphaned sisters and brothers. There she lost them all; four children died. But Carmen Miyares de Mantilla was greatly endowed with courage, strength, and unselfishness. Her husband had a small and not very profitable tobacco business, so Carmen took in boarders to supplement the family income. Among the boarders was Martí, who once wrote: "In the Mantilla home, Carmita always had a large fire in the fireplace. Fires of home." There young Blanche met all the leaders of Cuba's revolution until she had her own home and received them there.

Of the wife Carmen, Señora de Baralt speaks compassionately. "Between them there was that unbridgable gap, failure of comprehension. He had to go ahead; if his wife would not stay with him he still had to go ahead."

Of Carmen de Mantilla she wrote: "He found in her support, an advisor who offered him a friendship that never ended, and which was to Martí a great help and even a force in his life as liberator."

In private conversation, Señora de Baralt spoke more freely. "Carmen de Mantilla," she said, "was truly a great woman, strong, steady, capable of appreciating what Martí had to do. Ugly things have been said of her, but I never allow a slur in my presence. She was a great and good woman, and she gave Martí the tenderness and understanding that his wife could not give him. . . . Her fourth child was born while he was in her house. María. I think Martí never loved any being as he loved that child."

I asked more about María. "She grew up in her mother's house and married a Cuban named César Romero. . . . Yes, she is still living. A widow now, she lives in Hollywood with her son, also César Romero; you may know the name." She smiled as the name clicked into place. "He would like to play Martí; perhaps some day he will, but he does not look the part at all."

Martí, who had opposed the Little War, believed that war was the only solution of Cuba's problem; but he held out for a well-organized, adequately-financed effort, which the fiasco of 1879 was not. Moreover, he had two fears. First that a "generals' war" might result in "a rule of personal despotism that would be more shameful and lamentable than the political despotism then prevailing in Cuba." And he feared Yankee imperialism. United States haters in Cuba like to quote his saying: "I know the monster; I have lived in its entrails." He insisted that Cuba's revolution must be a people's war in which Cubans would triumph because they were animated by a true sense of destiny and ready for the establishment of a republic firmly grounded in the rights of men and true justice.

During the eighties and nineties Martí lived the exacting, exhausting life of organizer and money-raiser. As president of the Comité Revolucionario Cubano, he addressed Cuban rallies from New York to Key West and as far west as New Orleans. He organized illiterates into *ligas de instrucción*, night schools where he taught whatever was asked, never failing to sound the call for independence and for contributions. In New York he wrote, lectured, conferred with Cubans, and sent many of them off to rouse others all round the Caribbean. Money flowed in from everywhere. At last Cuba's "men of the *machete*" were willing to admit that the dreamer's worth was computable in what generals most need, cash. In Florida, Martí found a rich source of income. Wealthy Cuban tobacco men had set up factories and brought in expert cigarmakers to avoid the high tariff on *habaneros*. In the cigar lofts and clubs Martí enrolled thousands of Cubans, many of them Negroes, in the cause of Cuba Libre. Almost unanimously they tithed themselves; the first time, Cubans boast, that so many people have given so faithfully to an impersonal cause. So Martí made Cuba's war a people's war. Now the youngest tobacco worker was a patriot whose nickels and dimes would roll up into a golden flood to float ships and liberate Cuba.

In 1891 Martí founded El Partido Revolucionario Cubano, which included Cubans of every stripe and which, through Martí as its leader, dominated preparations for another effort to rid Cuba of Spain. By 1895, Martí was ready. Máximo Gómez, in Santo Domingo, accepted the post of commander-in-chief of the revolutionary army. Antonio Maceo and others were ready to come from Costa Rica. In Cuba, Juan Gualberto Gómez had had considerable success in arousing and enlisting the patriots. Still others were organized in Florida. Martí had succeeded in purchasing three yachts, which were loaded with arms and munitions in the port of Fernandina, Florida.

Then came the bitterest disappointment. Spain's spies reported to the United States authorities, who had no alternative as neutrals. The yachts were captured, the cargoes confiscated; even Martí was taken into custody for a short while. This disaster might have been irreparable. But Martí never shone more convincingly. As Cubans in every province were ready to rise, he decided to go ahead. The date of February 24, 1895, was set for the general uprising, and on that day another *grito* rang out, this time at Baire in the province of Camagüey.

Martí, in New York, insisted upon going to Cuba as a soldier. Characteristically he refused to ask other men to make sacrifices he was not ready to make. Señora de Baralt remembers that at the last supper where his intimates saw Martí there was a sense of foreboding. He sailed for Santo Domingo, where he conferred with Gómez and Maceo. Not a military man, Martí was recognized as supreme chief of the revolution, and helped plan the campaign. Maceo headed for Guantánamo, and Gómez and Martí landed at Las Playitas, also in Oriente, on April 11.

The advance moved slowly. On May 19, near the hamlet of Dos Ríos, a small band of Cubans was attacked by Spanish troops. Gómez, about to lead a counterattack, urged Martí to stay behind, but that patriot insisted upon exposing himself to fire. It was first reported to General Gómez that Martí had been wounded, but he had been killed by his first bullet.

So Martí was killed at the age of forty-two that he might live forever as the symbol of Cuba's aspiration. That apparently needless sacrifice placed him beyond the hazards of living too long. He could now be Cuba's ideal and stainless hero, apostle of her future greatness.

Unhappily the world knows Martí only fragmentarily. Writers in Spanish mention him as a writer oftener than as a liberator. Nobody has yet studied his influence on those elements in the United States which were sympathetic with Cuba's war for independence. Even Cubans venerate rather than evaluate Martí, and a study of Martiana suggests that Martí has dawned rather slowly upon his own people as the national hero, that his apotheosis has been recent. Señora de Baralt bears out this impression. "It is curious that during a quarter century the figure of Martí was little studied in Cuba. Everyone admired him as patriot, framer of independence, but in the popular mind the outline of his personality was not very clear."

Oddly enough the first biography of Cuba's national hero was written in English and published in Chicago in 1899: *Martí, A Story of the Cuban War,* by Anna Maria Barnes. The first biography by a Cuban did not appear until 1923, when Nestor Carbonell's *Martí, Su Vida, Su Obra, Martí, His Life, His Work,* appeared. Meanwhile there had been only collections of his writings. Martí's close friend, Gonzalo Quesada y Aróstegui, began a collection in 1900, but he finished fifteen volumes only in 1919. Others have been made since; the *Obras Completas* is not yet complete at fifty volumes. Articles and pamphlets began to appear in the 1920's, almost thirty years after Martí's death, but not in numbers until the 1930's. The titles are suggestive. Following Carbonell's emotionless *Life and Works* came studies of Martí as journalist and of his pedagogical, social, and economic ideas. In 1933, emotionalism crept in when Jorge Mañach named his book, *Martí, el Apóstol;* Felix Lizaso followed in 1940 with *Martí, el Místico del Deber, Martí, The Mystic of Duty;* in 1941 Mauricio Magdalena published *Fulgor de Martí, Refulgence of Martí.* Carlos Márquez Sterling, in 1942, enlarged on Mañach's idea, calling his book, *Martí, Maestro y Apóstol, Martí, Master and Apostle.* The beatification had already been completed by Luis Rodríguez-Embil's *José Martí, El Santo de America,* published in 1941. Perhaps the end is not yet.

# V

# INTERVENING UNCLE

*THE WAR*

CUBAN HISTORIANS HAVE TWO BITTER COMPLAINTS against the United States: that the United States does not intervene in Cuban affairs and that it does. Equally bitter is the complaint that intervention, when it does occur, is at the wrong time, badly managed, and leads to no good end. Happily these harsh criticisms are not all buried in Spanish, which too many Americans do not read, but are quite as sternly voiced by our own writers. Indeed Cubans are often gentler than North Americans for they nearly always draw a distinction between our government, which consistently refused to recognize Cubans as belligerents, and our people, who were sympathetic enough with Cuba's long travail to send men and munitions and the ships to carry them. Such popular brotherliness was too scattered to move the government until jingoes in Congress and a sensational press gave it a spearhead and a voice. Meanwhile at least two incidents offered better reason for war with Spain than the explosion of the *Maine* in 1898. These were the episode of the *Black Warrior* in 1854 and the *Virginius* affair in 1873.

The *Black Warrior*, plying between Mobile and New York, called at Havana where her master failed to submit a manifest declaring his cargo; a formality required by law but generally dispensed with. This time Spanish officers demanded the manifest and threatened to confiscate the ship and her cargo. A first-rate cause for war, and our minister to Spain, Pierre Soulé, a Louisianian of French extraction, who hated Spain and had supported López, made the most of it. Spain, faced with war, made a financial settlement with the owners of the *Black Warrior*. Soulé with his colleagues, our ambassadors to England and France, then proposed to offer Spain $120,000,000 for Cuba and if she refused, "to wrest the island from Spain." This, through a letter to Secretary of State William L. Marcy, was allowed to leak out as the Ostend Manifesto. Marcy repudiated the suggestion: "The robber doctrine I abhor."

Marcy's lofty dictum had little effect in the back country where Americans kept right on sending what aid and comfort they could. In 1869, Spain, harassed beyond endurance by this continuing aid, authorized her officers to capture any vessel of whatever nation that was carrying supplies to the rebels, and to execute as pirates all persons aboard. Strong words. We had once fought a war for such utterances. The United States threatened recognition of the Cubans as belligerents. Spain retreated, of course. But it took a long time to cross and recross the Atlantic, and meanwhile the *Virginius* had been captured. She was flying the United States flag and she was taken either on the high seas or in British waters off Jamaica.

Taken to Santiago, the captain and fifty-one others were shot after a trial so quick that the American consul could not be notified. Ninety-three others were in line for execution when a British man-of-war under Captain Sir Lambton Lorraine sailed into Santiago Bay. An advocate of direct action, Sir Lambton sent word to the Spanish commander that if one more English or American was shot he would shell the city. That stopped the shootings. But the American position was not so clear. Spain, always able to reform in a crisis, had just become a republic again, and the United States had recognized her. Besides, it appeared that the *Virginius* had no right to fly the American flag. Spain finally paid $80,000 to the families of the executed men. But she promoted General Burriel, the officer responsible.

Many other American families had tragic reason to protest Spain's high-handed methods, and with less result. Spain complained that many Americans fighting in Cuba were very recent citizens. Portell-Vilá estimates that 30,000 Cuban families moved to the United States during the Ten Years' War. Thousands of their men returned as naturalized Americans to fight for Cuba while demanding United States protection.

Cuban historians, indignant over United States failure to intervene on these occasions, do not fail to note that popular sympathy with Cuba's cause increased as commerce grew, and North American shippers began to complain of high import duties. It was actually cheaper to ship flour from the Mississippi valley to Spain and thence to Cuba than to ship it directly. Another force more potent than sympathy for a people fighting for freedom was that of American property owners in Cuba. Constant sufferers from the *mambí*, who took what they needed and burned the rest, they naturally inclined toward Spain and they never ceased demanding that Washington give them peace.

Thus there was no lack of causes for war. And there were men in power who wanted war to further the expansion that they called the "manifest destiny" of the United States. There was constant tugging between citizens who thought one continent was enough and those who wished to dominate all the Caribbean islands, build a big navy, play a world role equal to that of England, Germany, or France. These imperialists criticized Cleveland, whose policy was consistently pacific toward Spain, as pusillanimous, and hoped that McKinley would take a stronger stand against Spain. But he, gentle soul, proved almost as hard to force into war as his predecessor. In fact, his Assistant Secretary of the Navy, Theodore Roosevelt, described his chief as having no more backbone than a chocolate eclair. Roosevelt, perhaps to compensate for a weak youth, brandished war words like weapons, demanding a fight to stiffen the national spine. He had the astute guidance of Senator Henry Cabot Lodge. Such men provided an ideology, but they could not prevail until the vast inert mass of public opinion had been heated to the point of explosion. This was done by two young men from the West who developed a new school of journalism in the process. When the *Maine* blew up in 1898, the thing was already done. People who had reacted not at all to Spain's actual execution of American citizens, were thrown into a frenzy of belligerency by the sinking of the *Maine*, which may have been entirely accidental. But by that time public opinion was the game of two jingo newspapers, dominated by bitter rivals and clever men.

Joseph Pulitzer, a German immigrant who had worked with Carl Schurz and who then owned the St. Louis *Post Dispatch*, bought the New York *World* in 1883. He proposed (according to Joseph E. Wisan's study of the press of the period) "a journal that is not only cheap but bright, not only bright but large, not only large but truly democratic — dedicated to the people rather than to purse-proud potentates." That involved entertaining the people, and Mr. Pulitzer invented many a trick to that end: enormous headlines, lurid style, and illustrations drawn from hearsay. This method developed some remarkable illustrators, and had the advantage of permitting a free play of the imagination. Mr. Pulitzer sponsored causes, interviewed notables, magnified crime and scandal, and increased the *World*'s circulation from 15,000 in 1883 to 5,000,000 per week in 1895.

It was too good a thing not to breed imitators. William Randolph Hearst also came out of the West with millions in money and a yen to serve the people. Mr. Hearst, then only thirty, had already made a success of the San Francisco *Examiner*. His own paper, the New York *Journal*, sold for a penny, ran colored supplements, and introduced cartoon serials. The combination of color and the "Kid of Hogan's Alley" gave a name to the new journalism: the yellow press was born. Mr. Hearst beat Mr. Pulitzer's circulation with over a million a day.

Both *Journal* and *World* began pumping up feeling against Spain in the early nineties; and when Weyler, "the butcher," arrived in Cuba to end the revolt, both papers ran horrifying illustrated accounts of Spanish barbarities. Walter Millis, whose *The Military Spirit* is frankly sarcastic, presents the case for Spain and Weyler. That general, he avers, was really a kind man, intent only on stopping the fighting. Even the concentration camps, of foul renown, were one of General Weyler's efforts to save Cubans from the scorched-earth policy inaugurated by General Máximo Gómez. Mr. Millis seems a bit inclined toward the superior Nordic tone. Similar treatment could with reason be given the leaders of our Revolution. Washington was also a "rebel chieftain": his armies deserted, he ordered many an act not approvable by the Geneva Convention; if he had not won, history might estimate him very differently. But Cuban patriots, like Washington, won their war; they deserve equally dignified treatment.

Looking back as coolly as one may after half a century it seems clear that the United States could have avoided war with Spain by merely allowing Cuba to free herself. President Salvador Cisneros de Betancourt declared that the island was "peaceful, law-abiding, and well-governed, except where the Spanish invaders were making trouble." Cuban historians agree that if the United States had permitted them to ship in arms, ammunition, and medicines they could have run those invaders out. Enrique Gay Calbó, acrimonious critic of the United States, writes: "The northern statesmen . . . were only awaiting the right moment to obtain without much sacrifice of men the most rapid and splendid triumph of their fleets and armies." But it was not quite so clearcut. Imperialists who were ready to fight Spain on any pretext were restrained by the peace-at-any-price thinkers, who continued to deal with Spain and to refuse to recognize Cuba. President Cleveland offered a solution that would permit Spain to retain her sovereignty while granting autonomy to Cuba. Spain refused as the Cubans would probably have refused. Spain's pride would not relinquish the last vestige of her American empire; Cuba would settle for nothing less than independence. It was a stalemate until the pacifists were swept aside by the rising tide of popular opinion roused by lurid tales in the papers.

David Graham Phillips wrote a series for the *World* on Spanish cruelties, showing starving women and potbellied children dying slowly in the filthy concentration camps. Richard Harding Davis, Hearst's man in Havana, cabled a story of indignities suffered by American women when ships were searched by Spanish officers. Frederick Remington illustrated it with a drawing of a lissome nude surrounded by Spaniards.

Finally the *Journal* discovered the perfect cause, the romantic tale of Evangelina Cisneros. This aristocratic girl held with her father and sister in a penal colony on the Isle of Pines had, according to the *Journal,* been brutally assaulted by the Spanish commander, Colonel Berriz. Set upon and beaten by outraged Cubans, Berriz retaliated by charging Señorita Cisneros with rebellion and removing her to the Recojidas, the women's prison in Havana. The *Journal* featured her wrongs both journalistically and editorially. "This tenderly nurtured girl was imprisoned at eighteen among the most depraved Negresses of Havana, and now she is to be sent in mockery to spend twenty years in a servitude that will kill her in a year. . . . Miss Cisneros is, according to all who have seen her, the most beautiful girl in Cuba . . . almost a child in years, she is as ignorant of the world as a cloistered nun. . . . Berriz is a lecherous and foiled scoundrel."

The *Journal* telegraphed Weyler, asking mercy for the girl. Better still, it appealed to American women to come to the aid of violated innocence, and they responded nobly. Julia Ward

Howe, Mrs. Mark Hanna, Mrs. Jefferson Davis, Clara Barton, the President's mother, General Grant's widow were quoted by the *Journal*. Mrs. Ormiston Chant, an English temperance leader, took up the cause in England. The *World*, having a spell of rectitude, denied everything, got a retraction from Weyler, and suggested that Señorita Cisneros had led an innocent Berriz on. The Queen Mother in Spain asked General Weyler to remove the girl to a convent pending her trial, and the General refused.

Then, when there seemed little more to be said, suddenly, in late August, Hearst went into action. A *Journal* reporter went to Havana, scaled a roof adjourning the prison, lifted the maiden out and smuggled her aboard ship dressed as a boy. The *Journal* had scooped the world, and especially the *World*. The lovely Evangelina received an ovation in New York, all the notables who had signed petitions now wrote congratulations, and Mrs. John A. Logan, widow of the Civil War general, presented the maiden to the President.

McKinley, who took office in March, 1897, was a pacific man who hoped to avoid war, but who was constantly beleaguered by the imperialist faction in his own party. Americans in Cuba were making ever stronger appeals for protection, especially Mr. Edwin Atkins, whose book, *My Sixty Years in Cuba*, presents an appalling picture of savage Cubans. Finally, largely at Mr. Atkins's behest and at the request of the consul general in Havana, the *Maine* was sent down to Havana for the protection of Americans. There she blew up. It happened the evening of February 15, 1898, just as her Captain Sigsbee was finishing a letter to his wife. The explosion was forward, the whole ship rocked with it, and in a moment men were screaming in agony and leaping into the sea. As soon as possible, Spanish craft of every category were speeding to the scene. Spanish officials ordered all civil and military services into rescue work, and the Governor and his staff called upon Captain Sigsbee to offer aid and condolences. That night 286 officers and men were lost.

Captain Sigsbee accepted all Spain's good offices and wired Washington: "Public opinion should be suspended until further report." But who could suspend Pulitzer or Hearst? Headlines, stories, and drawings of unspeakable horror crescendoed to a hysterical demand for immediate retribution against those guilty of planting "that secret infernal machine." Or who could stop Roosevelt and Lodge, who at last saw a way to force the vacillating McKinley into war?

A court of inquiry found that the vessel had been "destroyed by the explosion of a submarine mine," but admitted that it had been "unable to obtain evidence fixing the responsibility upon any person or persons." This report was drowned out by the jingo chorus. After a second inquiry, in 1911, the wreck of the ship was towed out to sea and sunk too many fathoms deep for further investigation. How the *Maine* was destroyed remains one of the great mysteries, with a strong probability that she blew up by an internal explosion.

Spain, fully informed of opinion in the United States, agreed in 1898 to suspend hostilities pending an armistice to be directed by Washington, to grant Cuba autonomy, and to submit the *Maine* matter to arbitration. It was McKinley's chance to make a strong bid for peace. But his message to Congress was ready; he added only a weak final paragraph telling of Spain's acceptance of every demand; the general tone of the message was warlike. Congress, through a joint resolution of the two houses, declared war on Spain on April 21, 1898. The people, egged on by the yellow press and speaking through their duly elected representatives, had demanded and secured war.

The joint resolution, which studiously omitted any recognition of the Cuban government, did carry an amendment which for honorable disinterestedness was new in history. On motion of Senator Teller of Colorado it was stated "that the United States hereby disclaims any disposition or intention to exercise sovereignty, jurisdiction, or control over said island, except for the pacification thereof, and asserts its determination . . . to leave the government and control of the island to its people." The United States, that hydra-headed monster, had spoken sense and honor through one mouth. It would be a question whether the "great Christian nation" would keep its word. European nations did not think it would. Cuban patriots hoped it would, but doubted. Cuban and United States annexationists hoped it would not.

The United States was enthralled at the prospect of a real war. North and South forgot their differences, citizens of Spanish heritage burned to fight against Spain as their cousins had throughout the hemisphere. Newspapers prophesied the landing of 50,000 men in Cuba, though the entire standing army consisted of 28,183 officers and men. Roosevelt anticipated "a splendid little war" with glory enough for all. Imperialists at last saw us emulate England by shouldering the "white man's burden" and bringing enlightenment to our little brown brothers in an ever wider world. Religious leaders thrilled to the prospect of advancing Protestantism; the national missionary zeal awoke. The echoes also awoke as the whole country sang "There'll Be A Hot Time in The Old Town Tonight," marched shouting "Remember the *Maine*, to hell with Spain," and promised to lick a degenerate Spain without half trying.

Only a few worried and unheard men knew how woefully unprepared for war we were. Thanks to the Indian wars our Army officers were West Pointers who knew their business, though because of the style of Indian fighting few of them were experienced in handling large bodies of men. The country relied on volunteers, and governors demanded the right to recruit both officers and men in their own states. The basis of this army was the National Guard, 100,000 strong, but far from being a professional army. In fact, they scorned professional officers and refused to serve under those spit-and-polish snobs from West Point. As many officers of the guard enjoyed the highest social prestige and as all the National Guard had votes, overriding the states to build a national army was impractical.

General Nelson A. Miles, who knew that soldiers needed food, arms, ammunition, care of health, and sanitation, urged a national mobilization and advised waiting to invade until Cuba's dry season began in September. He also knew that Spain had 80,000 professional troops in Cuba under experienced officers, and he urged a few months of training. But politics was more potent than military science, and the state regiments were on their way. There was no overall policy, no plan of mobilization, no provision for assembling, transporting, or supplying an army. The Quartermaster's Office in Washington complained that they had had everything in excellent order and now came this war and upset all their arrangements. Their arrangements were far from up-to-date. Guns were lacking; many southern regiments appeared with old Civil War muskets; all carried old style rifles, which belched black smoke. The uniform was still of heavy blue wool with overcoat and a blanket roll. But there was not enough of anything, and volunteers appeared in all sorts of garb; one Missouri company showed up with some barefooted recruits.

Conditions that affected the enlisted men were shameful. Everybody old enough remembers the scandal of the "embalmed beef," the preventable deaths in vilely unsanitary camps in Georgia and Florida, which produced typhoid, malaria, dysentery. Yellow fever took its toll long before the troops embarked for Cuba, though that dread disease was usually diagnosed as malaria. No plans had been made for sanitation, potable water, adequate medical inspection, or hospitalization.

These scandals came out little by little in the press as the war went on. Meanwhile recruiting proceeded and the handling of troops became more and more of a personal affair. Perhaps not typical, but certainly revealing is the case of the Rough Riders. As soon as war was declared, Theodore Roosevelt resigned as

Assistant Secretary of the Navy and set about getting an appointment that would give him real action in Cuba. He had no luck in New York, and another aspirant to active duty was having even less. Leonard Wood, a captain in the medical corps who had won distinction in the West, found that his own state of Massachusetts had nothing to offer him. Nor had New York. But Arizona had. Bucky O'Neill was recruiting a troop in Prescott; and Senator Warren of Wyoming, chairman of the Senate Committee on Military Affairs, got the Army Bill to include three regiments "to be composed exclusively of frontiersmen possessing special qualifications as horsemen and marksmen." Secretary of War Alger offered one of these regiments to Roosevelt, who did not consider himself capable, but strongly recommended Leonard Wood.

The Quartermaster's Office being as it was, and Wood knowing what he had learned along the Mexican border, he set out to recruit, equip, and train his own regiment in his own way. He first spent some time in the War Department's musty purlieus, presenting his requests in such detailed, intelligible, and ready-to-sign lists that he got practically all he asked. Some of his requests were curious. Instead of heavy woolen uniforms and tight hot caps, he settled for "stable uniforms." Of cotton and dun-colored, they were not effective on parade, but comfortable in a hot country; and a western hat was to prove as all-round useful in Cuba as in Arizona. In fact, the Cuban army still wears it.

Colonel Wood then went west to check up on the recruiting, leaving Roosevelt in Washington. In record time Wood's regiment was on a drill ground in San Antonio, Texas, and learning to take orders. He had told his medical men to reject any man "whose stomach is bigger than his chest." Otherwise requirements were not rigid. The regiment included cowboys, bartenders, miners, tramps, scions of old Spanish families and sons of newer pioneers, migrant Yanks and Rebs, Negroes, Indians, and a sprinkling of youths from the Fifth Avenue clubs and the most aristocratic universities. This added the lustre of names, and most of the young aristocrats shed their stiff collars, patent-leather shoes, and derbies, and soon overcame the natural suspicion of the Westerners. Colonel Wood, who was equally facile with a Harvard accent and frontier profanity, sweated long hours working his 1,200 individuals into a regiment. Then he wrote his wife: "These are the best men I have ever seen together and will make the finest kind of soldiers." The men were spoiling to get to Cuba: "Rough, tough, we're the stuff. We wanna fight and we can't get enough."

Roosevelt in Washington had become a national figure. Because he was always spectacular, not averse to publicity, and with a good cartoon grin, his name was inevitably attached to the tough western regiment. Teddy's Terrors progressed through Rocky Mountain Rustlers to Roosevelt's Rough Riders. They were known by their Colonel's name only once, on a sad day in Cuba, when they dubbed themselves Wood's Weary Walkers. Alliterative to the last.

Roosevelt joined the regiment in Tampa, where Wood had managed to arrive by sheer force of personality and savvy. From the Spanish *saber*, to know how, this old southwestern word still seems more cogent than the newer know-how. Because of the general snarl and lack of direction, every officer had to do the best he could for his troops. Wood, thanks to his western experience, was one of the best. A German official observer reported that the Rough Riders were the smoothest and most orderly regiment he saw. What else he reported to the Kaiser about American skill at making war would make interesting reading.

Lieutenant Colonel Teddy found everything to his taste: "Bully." His special enthusiasm was for his own kind, those nobly-born youths who had left New York's countinghouses and clubs to lead the country bumpkin into battle. Imagine an officer of 1945 writing seriously that these lower class fellows from the West and South comported themselves quite as well as Roosevelt's friends of the best families!

In Tampa, officers and correspondents made themselves very comfortable in the best hotel, where many of their ladies joined them for dinners and dances under the tropic moon or long lazy days rocking on piazzas, flirting under the palms. Richard Harding Davis, reporting for Hearst, was in his element. Affecting white duck trousers stuck into cavalryman's boots and a campaign hat, strung all over with binoculars and cameras, he consorted only with officers, wrote stories that made or broke reputations, and established the war correspondent as a featured star of the war.

While the Army was waiting to get to Cuba, the country up north was more worried about the Navy. Our observers had seen the Spanish fleet under Admiral Cervera get away from Spain and beyond the Cape Verde Islands. Then it disappeared. The press threw the seaboard into a dither, lest Atlantic City or Newport should be shelled from the sea. Roosevelt complained that the very congressmen who had voted against all naval appropriations now demanded a battleship apiece to guard their particular beach, resort hotel, or private home. Commodore Winfield Scott Schley was stationed at Hampton Roads with a "flying squadron" ready to dash at a moment's notice. The *Oregon* left Seattle on her historic run around Cape Horn, hoping to reach the Caribbean in time. Admiral William T. Sampson with the heaviest squadron waited at Key West ready to engage the Spaniard whenever and wherever that wily enemy should be sighted.

As Admiral Cervera did not emerge from the mists of the Atlantic, Sampson finally got off to Puerto Rico, where he shelled San Juan, hoping for such a triumph as Dewey had recently achieved at Manila. But the annoying Spaniard was not there. Then he was sighted, and Sampson sailed west in case Cervera should make for Havana. Schley meanwhile had cruised the tropic seas, up and down, invested a couple of harbors, run out of coal, run afoul of Washington by disregarding orders, and had finally brought up outside Santiago Harbor on May 26. There Admiral Cervera's fleet was in plain and taunting sight, with his flagship, the *Cristóbal Colón*, blocking the bay's narrow entrance under El Morro.

Admiral Sampson, who had arrived by that time, conceived the maneuver of sinking the old collier *Merrimac* in the mouth of the harbor, and so bottling up Cervera for certain. At dawn of June 3, Richmond Pearson Hobson, a naval constructor, sailed gallantly into the harbor's jaws with seven men. Shooting was heard, and later observers saw the *Merrimac* under water, but she had drifted too far to block the passage. Nothing was heard of Hobson until Admiral Cervera, with true Spanish courtesy, sent an officer to inform Admiral Sampson that all eight men had been picked up unhurt, and were prisoners of war in El Morro. Harbor-blocking was a failure, but the press had a glamour boy in Captain Hobson.

Orders then went to General William R. Shafter in Florida to make for Santiago and attack the bottled-up Spanish fleet by land. Richard Harding Davis wrote glowingly of the stupendous feat of getting 12,000 men shipped off for the wars. Later writers give less admiring accounts. General Shafter was a Regular Army officer with experience in Indian wars, but he was getting old, he weighed some three hundred pounds, and he suffered cruelly from the heat. He was hampered at every turn by lack of a plan and of adequate preparation. Again everything depended upon the regimental officers. Roosevelt recounts how he outran and outsmarted other officers to get the Rough Riders into a train; how Colonel Wood boarded the *Yucatan* and held her until the regiment arrived on the double. Fortunately, Wood had hit on a ship that actually reached Cuba. Many civilian ships' captains, wearying of war, had turned and sailed for their home ports again.

The Army was bound for Santiago with the actual landing-point still undetermined. General Shafter, who was not inured to reporters, antagonized Richard Harding Davis by refusing him a front seat in the landing boats. Davis, indignant at being classed as a civilian instead of a "writing observer," missed no chance thereafter to discredit the General. Shafter's apologists, notably Stewart Edward White, gave him full credit for the Cuban campaign and described him as a "soldier's soldier." Recriminations between Army and Navy officers and between the two services filled the papers and split opinion at least four ways. Scanning these accounts, one is embarrassed at how little was written about the Cubans who had been outwitting and outfighting Spain's best for thirty years or so. It is salutary to read what Cubans have written about this invasion. Again I quote Gay Calbó:

"At this time the Revolution was triumphing alone, with its own resources, which were very scarce, as most of the arms and equipment had to be taken from the enemy in daily combat. Many towns in Oriente were in Cuban hands before a single United States soldier disembarked.

"The North Americans lacked military organization, and counted only on their immense resources. The Spaniards had in Cuba nearly 300,000 men of the regular army and some 200,-000 volunteers, all veterans. . . . To conquer this enormous force required a tactic possible only with Cuban cooperation. Without this, the invasion of Shafter's green troops would have failed whenever the fleet withdrew its protection."

Of General Shafter, he wrote: "The North American commanding general was a man absurdly fat and terribly incapable of that sort of warfare, as was recognized by his subordinates, many able and competent men."

Our Army and Navy disagreed as to where the landing should be made. Admiral Sampson wanted the Army to land under El Morro's guns and take the city by assault. General Shafter re-

*Cane-cutters work three months a year*

*The* bruja *casts the shells to reveal my fate*

alized that in that case all the losses would be his and all the glory the Admiral's when the Navy should sail in and clinch the victory. He thought a better landing could be made at Daiquirí or Siboney. General Calixto García, consulted on this point, advised Daiquirí. He agreed also that Santiago should be captured with all speed; the yellow fever season had begun; the Americans, unlike the *mambises*, had no immunity.

Gay Calbó puts it more strongly: "The site chosen for the landing, the plan of combat and methods of preventing the other Spanish armies from rushing to the defense of the besieged city were all conceived by Cubans, under Calixto García as chief, and executed with the constant support of the [Cuban] army of liberation."

The landing was unopposed, and once ashore the Rough Riders found themselves in camps just like home with horses staked out, canvas shelters, and cook fires. The cocoanut grove was beautiful, but how they hated the land crabs and mosquitoes! One, when he learned that mosquitoes were mosquitoes in Spanish too, opined that he supposed the Spiks couldn't find a meaner word.

General Shafter ordered Colonel Lawton to take the beach of Siboney and hold it until all troops were landed there and at the more sheltered Daiquirí. Curiously, the Spaniards did not take advantage of their good position to oppose the landing. Colonel Lawton, a Regular Army man, held as ordered, but General Shafter's plan was upset by individual initiative. Major General Joseph Wheeler, whose command included the Rough Riders, had held the same rank in the Confederate Army. He longed to beat that Yankee Lawton into action. So, by forced march, he brought his troops up ahead, and by dawn they were facing unexpected fire from well-entrenched Spaniards who had smokeless powder, Mauser bullets, and military acumen.

General Wheeler was finally persuaded to ask Colonel Lawton for support, but fortunately for the honor of the Confederacy, the Spaniards broke before reinforcements arrived. General Wheeler, pardonably confused in the heat of battle, was seen to wave his saber as he charged, yelling: "Come on, boys, we've got the damned Yankees on the run!"

This was the battle of Las Guasimas which put Roosevelt and the Rough Riders in the headlines back home and incidentally showed the *mambí* how useful his allies could be to him. Old Cuban officers like to tell how the Yanks advanced through Cuba's steaming heat shedding their dark blue woolens as the snake his skin. Especially they sloughed their greatcoats. Followed the *mambises*, whose clothing was of the sketchiest. How they pounced upon all those sturdy garments! In jig-time the Yankees were stripped to what the climate demanded, and the *mambises* marching proudly, were for the first time completely clad, often in dark blue greatcoats that trailed on the ground.

To reach Santiago there was only one more height to cross. San Juan Hill. General Shafter sent Colonel Lawton with one division to take El Caney and thus protect the flank of the two other divisions, which were to storm the hill. It was tough going through the jungle, where slimy mud alternated with trails running like creeks, and where one company commander could not keep in touch with another. Supply had failed completely. Officers with savvy were requisitioning wagonloads of food from teamsters who often did not know where they were bound anyhow. There was only one narrow road, and there the troops destined for San Juan Hill were almost completely bogged down. And the Spaniards, who were expected to quit when they saw the Americans, were holding Lawton at El Caney. This was the situation when the advance on San Juan Hill was ordered at nine o'clock on Friday, July 1.

A confused army in a dense and steaming jungle was facing a wide dusty plain that would have to be crossed with no cover. The Spaniards were firing accurately and well. They had two excellent targets: the black smoke rising from the Americans'

antiquated guns and Uncle Sam's first air force. The Signal
Corps had tethered a balloon above the jungle, and from it the
observer called now and then; once he even indicated a trail.
Happily a Spanish ball punctured the balloon, and that menace
was mercifully removed.

By mid-afternoon the situation looked bad, as casualties
among the Americans had been heavy, the advanced troops had
run into barbed wire strung from tree to tree, untrained volunteers were confused, no orders came from Shafter. Then somebody called for the advance, and the famous charge up San Juan
Hill was on. Colored troops from the Ninth and Tenth Cavalry,
and the Rough Riders led by Lieutenant Colonel Roosevelt,
charged from Kettle Hill through a watery depression and up to
the ridge. *Mambises* provided strong support. At about the same
time, Colonel Lawton had entered El Caney. The road to Santiago was open. But the Americans had suffered 1,475 casualties,
many because of inadequate medical personnel, and Santiago
was still to be taken.

Clara Barton was in Cuba. For the first time the Red Cross was
officially with a United States Army in the field. She, with a few
doctors and nurses and some hospital supplies and food, had
landed through the surf on "dilapidated flat boat scows that had
been . . . cast away by the Engineer Corps . . . mended by
the Cubans." They had requisitioned and loaded two six-mule
wagons and so reached the front after "two fearful nights had
passed." "The sight that greeted us . . . was indescribable
. . . a few little dog tents . . . and under these lay huddled
together the men fresh from the field or from the operating tables,
with no covering. . . . Those who had come from the tables
were entirely nude. . . . As we passed, we drew our hats over
our eyes, turning our heads away . . . for the delicacy of the
poor fellows who lay there with no shelter either from the elements or the eyes of the passers-by."

This comes from Clara Barton's book, *The Red Cross,* which

reveals a remarkably intrepid woman, tactful with doubting officers, deferential and reasonable, but firm in getting her job done.

There still remained the question of whether the Army or the Navy should bear the brunt of a head-on attack on Santiago. General Shafter and Admiral Sampson agreed to meet at Siboney.

This left Commodore Schley in command of the battleships guarding the entrance to Santiago Bay. It was a calm Sunday morning, July 3, when suddenly the entire Spanish fleet came grandly filing out through the bay's narrow mouth. Under orders from Madrid, Admiral Cervera refused to surrender without a fight. He considered the attempt suicidal, but he executed it so well that his whole fleet was out and away with the surprised Americans in pursuit. Soon his wooden decks were all ablaze; ship after ship turned into a tower of smoke and flame. Their crews fought valiantly, serving hot guns on burning decks, but even Spain's pride could not survive. As the *Vizcaya* went down, Captain Phillips of the *Texas* uttered his unforgettable: "Don't cheer, boys, the poor devils are dying!" Thus the Spanish fleet went down to defeat in a burst of magnificent defiance. The battle was won. And Admiral Sampson and Commodore Schley were in position for the ensuing battle over who won the great victory of Santiago.

The city did not capitulate for a couple of weeks. An illuminating account of the situation and one unknown in our text books is that of the Cuban Gay Calbó: "Twenty-six days, from June 20 . . . until July 16, when Santiago was surrendered, proved completely Shafter's lack of the gift for command and Calixto García's skill. The Spanish . . . forces were moving there from Holguín, Guantánamo, and Manzanillo. Only those from the last arrived because Shafter ordered that they be allowed to advance. They were 5,000 men when they left Manzanillo. . . . During that really frightful advance, there was not a single day in which the Spaniards did not have to face Cuban attacks. Only 4,000 troops entered Santiago . . . where they served only to increase the suffering and want of the city. . . . The other Spanish reinforcements could only hold on . . . where they were . . . which made possible *the capture of El Caney and of San Juan Hill by Calixto García's troops and the North Americans in co-operation.*" [Italics mine.]

If it is true that General Shafter was an inept military leader, he must have been a good poker player. For he demanded and received the surrender of Santiago, quite unaware of how desperate was the city's situation. Thus the war ended, and the American Army prepared for its victorious entrance without inviting the equally victorious Cubans to participate in the ceremonies. I quote another Cuban, Alberto Arredondo: ". . . and when the Cubans, drunk with patriotic emotion, powerful allies in the Yankee triumph, started to raise their flag — that glorious banner of Narciso López, Agramonte, Maceo, Martí, and Máximo Gómez — a terse order from the Yankees prevented their unfurling the Cuban standard to the air." As though the French at Yorktown had accepted the surrender of Cornwallis without the presence of George Washington, the United States Army marched alone into Santiago. This clumsy discourtesy has left deep wounds. School children know of it. Men who honor the memory of Máximo Gómez and Calixto García, who were insulted that day, do not forget.

Clara Barton found plenty to do. Santiago had been cleared of civilians, who were massed in hideous conditions at El Caney. There she and her long-skirted nurses set up soup kitchens and fed 10,000 in one day. Miss Barton also offered nurses to a United States hospital, but the commanding officer declined; he thought he and his assistants could do all that was necessary. Fifty or sixty wounded or sick men lay on the floor with no bedding, and one orderly sat on the porch smoking. It was more, he stated, than one man could cope with. The Red Cross nurses then sought out General García who accepted their aid with courteous appreciation. "With pails, scrubbing brushes, soap, whitewash and disinfectants," they transformed an old Spanish hospital into such a place of "peace, cleanliness, and comfort" that the United States soldiers raised a "kick" that overrode their officer and put the Red Cross at the service of our own wounded. Later the Red Cross served the starving and infested Cuban populations until it returned to the United States in September.

Nothing in our conduct of that war was so unbecoming as our ending it. The slight of Santiago was topped by calling the war Spanish-American, not conceding Cuba even a syllable in its naming. The official end came with the Treaty of Paris, whose terms, according to Alberto Arredondo, were "to fix what Spain had lost and the United States had gained. . . . By this treaty Spain and the United States achieved the slavery of Cuba . . . none of the articles mentions the independence of our country, none fixes the time during which North American troops should remain in Cuba, none mentions the Joint Resolution."

Arredondo represents the irreconcilables, going so far as to lament that the two leaders who might have stood out against Yankee domination had died: "Maceo, the heroic mulatto . . . to launch against those Cubans who were prostrating themselves at General Wood's feet, his curt maxim: 'Liberty is not begged, but won at the edge of the machete,' " and Martí, "leader of thought, builder of stamina, dynamic revolutionary, to co-ordinate the forces, take advantage of every opportunity, and give the final blow — political or economic — to that perverse . . . monster in whose entrails he had lived." Other Cubans are not so stern in their judgments. But one lays down the books on this war wishing that our country could do fine and helpful things without arousing so much resentful hatred in the doing.

## THE OCCUPATIONS

So the United States set up a military government to occupy Cuba until "the people should be able to govern themselves." Naturally such an announcement aroused deep resentment. Many Cuban historians are still concerned to prove that all their country's ills are caused by Uncle Sam. Nor need one turn to the Cubans. Our own writers, like L. H. Jenks in *Our Cuban Colony* and Carleton Beals in his angry *The Crime of Cuba,* make out a good case against the United States, both government and corporations.

The occupation began with the appointment in July 1898 of Brigadier General Leonard Wood as military governor of Santiago. This act, like the Treaty of Paris, completely ignored the Cuban government, which faced the usual difficulty of bad feeling between the soldiers, from General Máximo Gómez to the least *mambí,* and the civil authorities. According to Portell-Vilá, the United States was quick to take advantage of this, playing off one group against the other. But General Wood's primary concern was not with politics. He faced a job that the Cuban government was quite unable to cope with. Santiago must be cleaned up and made safe to live in, and that needed both autocratic power and ready cash. Four problems were immediate: to feed the starving, care for the sick, bury the dead, and clean up the city.

As a physician, General Wood recognized sanitary conditions throughout the island as one valid reason for the occupation. Even Havana was a source of infection that might menace our southern ports. Santiago was worse, one of the most pestilential spots in the world. Ships' captains used to say that they could smell the city's stench ten miles out at sea. After months of siege, years of war, centuries of maladministration, conditions were noisome beyond description. The water system the Spaniards had made centuries before was out of repair. There was no sewage-disposal system. Even the rich, living in beautiful, prettily tinted houses, drank water from wells near the cesspools in their patios, dumped their garbage into the street, pouring dirty water after it, and picked their way through the streets among piles of refuse, dead animals, and (after the siege) even dead people. Rains had, every summer, washed those streets more or less clean by carrying the refuse down into the bay, where it rose and fell with the tide. The lower reaches of the city were never clean. Disease was spreading; an epidemic was highly probable. As a doctor, General Wood understood the dangers. As an officer, an autocrat, he tolerated no nonsense. There was little time for mannerliness, but the General usually kept his voice down and saw all comers, annoying the important by making them wait their turn.

For the clean-up job, he nominated Major George M. Barbour, a major by courtesy, a westerner, and one who never dallied. Given authority to recruit whom he needed, Major Barbour soon had several thousand Cubans digging out filth and proving themselves less lazy than had been anticipated when they were given food. They wielded picks and shovels, pushed or drove carts, burned refuse, and cremated bodies. Major Barbour took stern measures with many a householder whose Spanish pride revolted at a rule invasion of his flowery patio for cleaning out of the cesspool and elimination of the accustomed smells. Some bewailed the lack of culture of these North Americans, whose minds, blind to the beauties of the spirit, centered on sewage. But in time garbage cans were introduced, used, even appreciated.

In September, General Wood wrote his wife, as quoted by his biographer, Hermann Hagedorn: "The old town is at last clean, and we are down, so to speak, to modern dirt which, while not attractive, is of a less offensive character than that of 1520."

It had been a costly experience for the North Americans. The occupation had cost more deaths than the war; five deaths daily were reported from yellow fever alone; General Wood himself was often ill; he probably had yellow fever without so diagnosing it.

General Wood had more distant objectives, though perhaps he was touched with our national vice of assuming that our ways, being best for us, must be best for all. As a New Englander, he was always trying to awaken a sense of citizenship, a willingness to work for the whole, a realization that if any were in danger of an epidemic, all were. He abolished sinecures, cut down salaries, even that of the Archbishop, and ended profiteering, not neglecting American soldiers who were buying freely with Confederate bills. Perhaps eighty per cent of the people were illiterate; he managed to get four thousand children into school. Whatever he tried to do, the new governor was faced with what Spain had left. Indifference amounting to cruelty, cynicism, scorn of Yankee directness, and distrust not only of foreign rulers but of themselves. This seemed to him the most tragic handicap of Cubans. In a letter, General Wood described the men he dealt with: "These men are emotional and hysterical; collectively they are timid."

As an offset to that Anglo-Saxon opinion, I quote Portell-Vilá again. "Cubans, generous of heart, laborious, impulsive and brave without being vengeful, and respectful of law and order, did not try to commit outrages, to persecute their ancient and despised rulers in person or property, to claim indemnity for their own goods or lives lost or to provoke disturbances that would assure them a predominant position in the new society that was beginning to arise." Perhaps Portell-Vilá was thinking of certain high-minded and competent Cubans, not of the mass of the people, many of them recently out of slavery and with no experience in self-government.

Despite this sort of criticism, General Wood slowly won his way until many Cubans and Spaniards recognized that he was

really honest, that he kept his word, that neither he nor his subordinates were bribable.

In October, General Wood was raised to the post of governor
of the province of Oriente, which brought him added problems.
He was now in command of a huge mountainous and forested region where distances were great, roads non-existent, trails practically impassable, plantations reverting to jungle, and the
jungles and mountains filled with discharged soldiers living now
by *machete* and terror.

General Máximo Gómez asked $60,000,000 from the United
States to pay off the *mambises,* who were in a destitute condition.
The United States offered to appropriate $3,000,000 which had
been left over from the war. The Cuban army, supposed to consist of 30,000 men, swelled rapidly in the warmth of financial
expectations to 48,000. In due course that estimate was reduced
to just under 34,000, who were paid off as they turned in their
arms, at the rate of $75 apiece for privates, from $7,000 to $12,-
000 for each officer.

This did not quite settle the problem of the disbanded army.
General García registered indignation because the North Americans were not feeding his veterans, and even threatened war.
Then a wise Cuban, Colonel Francisco Valiente, proposed the
establishment of a group of rural police, like Porfirio Díaz's
*rurales* in Mexico. Wood was delighted to accede and Colonel
Valiente soon had corps of 2,000 mounted Cubans chasing pil-
fering Cubans. Someone put it rather crudely: "Let the Cubans
kill their own rats."

On January 1, 1899, Major General John R. Brooke had taken
office in Havana as Military Governor of the whole island. A Regular Army man, he had little use for Wood, who was by rights
only a medical captain; his promotion for meritorious service
was irrelevant to the West Pointer. The two men were constantly
at cross purposes. General Brooke, pursuing the policy of governing as little as possible, surrounded himself with Cubans

whom Wood characterized as unscrupulous. Brooke reestablished Spanish law, and Wood wrote Roosevelt: "Nothing more idiotic can be imagined than the attempt to establish a liberal government under Spanish laws." Brooke revived the Spanish custom of having all revenues sent to Havana to be disbursed from there. General Wood, who had been collecting taxes in Oriente and using them for Oriente's benefit, resented the new policy. In the end, Wood won; in December, 1899, General Brooke was relieved and General Wood was appointed military governor of Cuba.

As he left Santiago, General Wood was presented with a memorial that stated that "the greatest of your many successes is that you have won the confidence and esteem of a people in trouble." The new governor met a hearty welcome in Havana where he made a first gracious gesture by accepting the escort of *mambises* rather than that of American officers. He plunged at once into work; Wood, like Roosevelt, was of the strenuous school. He gave his subordinates authority, but he knew what was going on; he was indefatigable in visiting every place of which he had a bad or dubious report. No jail was too foul, no hospital or insane asylum too tragically neglected for the governor to visit in person. His recommendations were always sensible, marked by the doctor's attitude and for immediate execution. His staff was notable.

He began with Frank Steinhart, who had worked with General Brooke and who was to make a vast fortune and a deal of history in Cuba. His children still enjoy the fortune in the silent splendor of a stone-and-iron mansion on Havana's Prado, but it was their father who had all the fun. Hagedorn describes him as "a Bavarian, a portly person with a moustache that curled at the ends, an aggressive chest, and a simple-hearted warmth that gave no hint of the acute encyclopedic mind." He also says that Steinhart in his prime "looked as cherubic as an innkeeper and as astute as a Mandarin."

Steinhart was an immigrant who began as a newsboy, advanced to office boy at Wanamaker's, and then joined the army and went west, where he rose to sergeant. He was a superlative poker player, an avaricious reader, who studied law at odd times and even took a degree. But he stuck to the Army, either because he loved it or because he thought his commanding officer, whoever he might be, needed a keeper. By the time General Wood took over in Cuba, Frank Steinhart was completely at home, knew everything and everybody, spoke Spanish like a native, had a few enemies and a host of friends. He initiated Wood into the mysteries. And there were plenty.

President McKinley's instructions to Wood were to prepare Cuba as fast as possible to handle its own democratic government and with a good school system. It was a departure in administering a conquered state; all the world was watching what the idealistic United States would do when it had a chance to keep as rich a prize as Cuba.

*In government,* General Wood raised and spent $58,000,000 during his two-year tenure, and left more than half a million dollars in the treasury for the first nationally elected Cuban president to start with. His appointees were ninety-eight per cent Cubans, and they learned, as the *santiagueros* had, that government employment was no longer a Spanish sinecure. The inevitable *choteo* advised: "Don't stop for a drink, to spit or scratch or smoke, come early, work till dark . . . whoever seeks a government job is one who wishes to die."

Wood, with his Anglo conviction that the basis of self-government is in the smallest unit, ordered in 1901 that all municipalities should pay their own officers from their own taxes. It was the first break in the old Spanish system of complete control from Havana, and it persists today except for the schools, hospitals, and sanitation, which still depend upon the national government.

He was just as hard on Americans. A case that had noisy re-
percussions in the United States as well as in Cuba was that of
Estes G. Rathbone, "a Hanna man," who as director of the Cuban
postoffice was permitting large-scale graft. Wood, against advice
of politicians in Washington, proceeded vigorously against Mr.
Rathbone, who was removed along with many of his Cuban un-
derlings. Politicians in the States were amazed to discover that
open action against dishonesty could be good campaign material.
Cubans were divided between those who gained admiration for
Wood and confidence in his administration and those — mostly
those who had been hurt — who sniped at him thereafter.

*Education,* President McKinley's second desideratum, had
started with a rush under General Brooke, who had Alexis
Everett Frye draft a school law and establish schools. Mr. Frye
has been described as a pink-faced bubbling enthusiast who in
no time had 3,000 schools on the books and local politicians
happily appointing teachers. Wood accused Brooke of accepting
reports of progress for actual performance. Portell-Vilá, advocate of General Brooke and especially of Alexis Frye, claims
that Wood disapproved of Frye because of his sympathetic attitude toward Cubans. As governor, Wood put the educational
program in the hands of Lieutenant Matthew Hanna, who had
been a teacher in Ohio and who set up a system modeled on that
of his native state. He succeeded in getting some 4,000 schools
to function with 254,000 children between the ages of six and
fifteen. Before the occupation ended, Wood had spent some
$4,000,000 on education out of the revenue of $17,000,000.
Some of that money took 1,500 teachers, 900 of them women, to
Harvard for a summer course. Curious how many of the later
good neighbor policies were first tried by Wood in Cuba. In the
University, General Wood found some 400 students and almost
100 professors, mostly old men, who appeared only at their convenience; some even lived in Spain and hired substitutes. All this

was changed. Much of the success of the school program was due to the active and intelligent cooperation of Enrique José Varona, Secretary of Instruction.

*Public works,* under Governor Wood, went on apace. He followed up his road-building in Oriente with similar work throughout the country. He laid out the Prado and the Malecón in Havana. He cleaned up and bettered public institutions of all sorts. He pardoned many poor wretches who had for years been held in filthy jails without trial. Chief Justice White, a student of Spanish law, recommended quicker trials, *habeas corpus,* and abolition of the custom of holding prisoners incommunicado for causes unknown to them.

*The Catholic Church* naturally posed an important problem. Its power had been second only to that of the Spanish government, its influence in many respects greater. General Wood started well in Santiago by walking in a religious procession with the Bishop. He caused much criticism in Havana by allowing payment to the Church for church buildings that had been used for mundane purposes. This amounted to $21,000,000 from Cuba's slender revenues, an item that still rankles today.

*Health* was where Wood the doctor shone. Cuba, like all tropical countries then, was the victim of endemic malaria and of terrifying epidemics of yellow fever. Martínez Ortiz writes: ". . . yellow fever . . . was a constant threat to foreigners, and its annual victims were counted in many thousands. . . . In Havana itself . . . all the littoral of San Lázaro, where the picturesque walk and elegant buildings of the Avenida del Golfo beautify it, was converted into an immense dunghill, infected and bad-smelling." Even during the war years, Cubans had been studying yellow fever. As early as 1881, Dr. Carlos Finlay had published his revolutionary theory that yellow fever was transmitted by the mosquito and was not a filth disease. Wood the doctor was struck by this theory, especially as Havana suffered a serious epidemic of the disease in 1899, by which time it was perhaps cleaner than most cities in the United States. So he approved a grant of $10,000 for research on Dr. Finlay's theory. Walter Reed, James Carroll, and Jesse Lazear, all physicians experimenting first on themselves and then on volunteers both American and Cuban, proved beyond a doubt that mosquitoes were the carriers. Dr. Lazear died of the disease, and Dr. Carroll had it in virulent form, but Dr. Finlay was fully justified. War was then declared on mosquitoes, and Major William Crawford Gorgas, later famous in Panama, directed a sanitation program that succeeded in ridding Cuba entirely of yellow fever, and in greatly reducing malaria. Indeed, it transformed the island from one of the most dangerous into one of the safest spots on earth; the death rate in Havana was cut in half. This seems to stand up as one of the few Yankee achievements about which there could be no dispute.

Martínez Ortiz sums up Wood's record: "Neither favor nor gifts counted with him. No one dared propose any unclean business to him or ask him to take part in any matter of doubtful character." Adverse critics say that Wood sometimes carried matters with too high a hand; Cubans distrusted his motives. His most consistent detractor, Portell-Vilá, dubs him a "decided annexationist"; and Arredondo writes: "Always his words were stamped with the threat of intervention."

Portell-Vilá's *Historia de Cuba* should be required reading — at least in part — for all students of Latin America. It is a brief against the United States, generally well documented. The book's importance for us lies in its theme, which is carried by the sour note, "thus they were teaching us to govern ourselves," recurring so frequently that its insistence almost destroys its effectiveness.

General Wood, however annexationist inwardly, acted according to the Joint Resolution of 1898, and called for an election to choose members of a constitutional assembly. Thus the United States, in a world of imperialisms, honorably fulfilled its promise to withdraw from Cuba when the new Republic of Cuba should have been established. But there was a joker. The United States demanded that Cuba should include in its constitution the basis of its future relations with the United States. Many Cubans opposed such a measure as inappropriate in a constitution and as limiting Cuba's sovereignty. The United States, in the person of the Secretary of War, Elihu Root, feared European influence in a free but inexperienced Cuba, wished a more legalistic expression than the Monroe Doctrine. He certainly drafted if he did not write the Platt Amendment, which was introduced by Senator Orville Hitchcock Platt of Connecticut. This infamous document granted the United States the right to pass on any foreign loans Cuba might contract or any treaty with a foreign power. It granted the United States the right to intervene "for the preservation of Cuban independence, the maintenance of a government adequate for the protection of life, property, and individual liberty." All acts of the United States during the occupation were to be ratified by the Cuban government. The sanitation program was to continue. Naval bases were to be ceded to the United States. The Isle of Pines was specifically omitted. And the Government of Cuba was obligated to embody all this in a permanent treaty with the United States.

Statesmen in Washington saw the Platt Amendment as a reasonable measure. To Cubans it was an insulting denial of the self-government they had been fighting for. Root said that it gave the United States no powers the Monroe Doctrine did not imply. The Amendment, then was redundant, besides being the sort of Yankee overinsistence that is our most egregious error in dealing with sensitive people. Cubans naturally protested, but vainly. It is hard to see what the United States gained to offset the chronic running sore left in Cuban minds. "Down with the Platt Amendment" was always good for a campaign slogan; even after its abrogation, in 1933, its recollection still rankles as an unjust conqueror's demand.

Despite this disappointment, the Cuban Republic was declared a nation, and Cubans made ready to elect their first president. The favored candidate was Don Tomás Estrada Palma, who all critics agree was an honorable, unselfish, and pure patriot. His advocates admit that his own high integrity may have blinded him to much that less pure eyes might have seen. His enemies dubbed him "more Platt than Platt"; he had lived for twenty years in the United States, first as a teacher and later as representative of revolutionary Cuba in New York City.

The opposing candidate, Bartolomé Masó, campaigned on such charges and on many promises to disgruntled groups such as Spaniards, the old autonomists, and Negroes. Many Cuban liberals believed that Masó embodied the nationalistic and liberal viewpoint, but he certainly lacked that confidence in the ballot on which democratic government must be founded. When Estrada Palma's election seemed assured, Masó and his henchmen refused to go to the polls. Naturally Estrada Palma had a smashing majority, and his opponents began undercover talk of revolution. Such events mark all Spanish American history. Lack of experience with the ballot makes for lack of trust in it; people turn instead to that traditional Spanish weapon, the sword.

Despite this hidden opposition, President Estrada Palma made a triumphal progress from Bayamo to Havana, where he was received with wildest demonstrations of patriotic fervor. The Military Occupation was over. In an impressive ceremony on May 20, 1902, the stars and stripes fluttered down and Cuba's new flag broke out to the breeze. Old Glory had come down where it had once been raised. This was no retreat, but an honorable act, one unprecedented in history. General Wood sailed for New York saying that he left Cuba "a going concern." It remained only to see how well Cubans could maintain their independence and develop their democracy.

The results of the military occupation of Cuba have been variously assessed. Jenks says that it saved Cuba from starting her independent career with the colony's vast debt, which Spain wished to saddle upon her. Albert Robinson, one of the bitterest critics of General Wood, says: "Beyond question . . . the United States left in Cuba an immeasurably better and surer foundation . . . than any upon which the Cubans could have built had they succeeded, without American aid, in expelling the government of Spain." Certainly Cuba enjoyed peace and better health and sanitation than before or since, and there was money in the treasury. In the long run it may be that the corrosion of resentment and hatred left by the Yankees was worse for the country than poverty, yellow fever, and bandits. But the new president could begin his administration in a peaceful country with courts and schools in operation, with local governments functioning, and with cash in hand.

The first administration of Tomás Estrada Palma was highly creditable. Chapman calls him worthy to be Cuba's Washington, "or Cuba's Estrada Palma, which is quite enough." He carried on all the projects begun under General Wood, and so economically that he left the treasury with a balance of millions estimated at from ten to twenty-five. It was Cuba's great opportunity. Unhappily the President's political associates were not as scrupulous as he was, and they set out to win the election at any cost, and by any means. Their most intriguing figure — in every sense — was General Fernando Freyre de Andrade, Secretary of Government. Active, intelligent, and a political gamester, he showed himself master of the *choteo* when he gravely explained to William Howard Taft later that his party had entered some 150,000 extra voters on the rolls "in a spirit of mischief."

A strong opposition grew up: the Liberal Party. It had no very definite platform, though it appealed to the less privileged groups and was outspokenly anti-United States. Its leaders have been adjudged noble patriots, fighters for Cuba for the Cubans, and also dangerous incendiaries, risking the very life of their

country for personal advantage. They certainly threatened to
"take to the woods" in armed revolt and to cause if not to invoke
intervention. Perhaps one of the worst effects of the Platt Amendment was that it gave Cubans a stick to beat each other with,
threatening to call in Uncle Sam.

By election day, December 1, 1905, the President's Moderate
Party had been caught in such flagrant frauds that the Liberals
again refused to vote. This left the President's ticket with embar-
rassing majorities, in some places larger than the entire voting
population. The Congress declared the Moderates elected, and
Estrada Palma was inaugurated for a second term on May 20,
1906. Then the Liberals did take to the woods, and by the middle
of August armed revolt had broken out in every province except
Matanzas, which remained loyal to Estrada Palma. Russell Fitz-
gibbon, in his *Cuba and the United States,* estimates that between
15,000 and 20,000 rebels were in the field.

Cuban history reads like one of those novels whose tragedy
depends upon the shortsightedness or complete blindness of the
characters. Why, oh why, could they not have seen that they were
bringing on their own destruction? A people schooled in self-
government might have conducted fair elections, demanded
honesty in office, and so made the Platt Amendment a dead letter.
Perhaps it is fanciful to suggest that a few austerely economical
administrations could have managed their finances without falling into the clutches of Wall Street. After all, if you do not borrow from a banker he has no power over you. But Cubans were
neither austerely economical by nature nor politically experienced enough to see whither they were drifting. The outs drew
the sword. Civil war was an actuality.

This posed the Roosevelt administration a pretty problem of
the sort that was to bedevil every succeeding administration.
Shall the United States throw its influence behind the duly elected
government or shall it heed the protests of the revolutionists that
the election was fraudulent? Opinion on this question differs ac-

cording to which side the critic or the government favors at the moment. Roosevelt wanted no intervention: he was sufficiently under fire for his recent achievements in Panama. But pressure from Cuba was increasing as the foreign owners of some seventy-five to a hundred million dollars worth of sugar lands and *centrales* began to cry for protection. Leaders of the revolt had threatened to resort to that old *mambí* trick of the torch.

The American Minister, Edwin F. Morgan, was on vacation, and his assistant proved unequal to the occasion. So Frank Steinhart took over. By that time General Wood's old sergeant was wealthy and the most powerful American in Cuba. He was also consul general. Portell-Vilá charges that Steinhart was deliberately working for intervention as a first step toward annexation. He was certainly the constant advisor of President Estrada Palma, who also desired intervention as the only way to shore up his collapsing government. Portell-Vilá finds that events had changed "the old, kindly, simple, and frugal man into an ill-humored person annoyed with any opposition." The cabinet he describes as "hampered by that unhealthy anxiety which the Platt Amendment had left in the Cuban soul."

On September 8, Consul General Steinhart telegraphed Washington, as "absolutely confidential," that President Palma requested President Roosevelt to send two vessels, one to Havana, one to Cienfuegos. "Government forces are unable to quell rebellion. The government is unable to protect life and property. . . . Congress will ask for our forcible intervention." Washington hesitated, but Steinhart continued to insist and finally sent the decisive message: "President Palma, the Republic of Cuba, through me officially asks for American intervention because he cannot prevent rebels from entering cities and burning property."

Roosevelt, hoping to avoid actual intervention, sent Secretary of War William Howard Taft and Robert Bacon to try to restore peace to Cuba. These two gentlemen conferred with leaders of both factions and finally offered a compromise by which all officers chosen in the recent elections should resign except the President and Vice-President, the insurgents should disarm, and a new electoral code should be drawn up. The government refused to sign on the ground that to treat with the insurgents would violate the President's "personal decorum and the dignity of the government." The Liberals accepted the terms as a victory for their side. The whole affair put the so-correct United States in the position of conciliating rebels; but the judicious Mr. Taft could hardly uphold a government elected by such notorious fraud as Freyre de Andrade admitted. Quickly members of Congress resigned, the Cabinet resigned, and the President, after calling on the American commissioners to take over the treasury, also resigned. Cuba was left with no government, no agency capable of calling an election. On September 29, the United States took over, and Taft sailed for home, greatly relieved that those "dreadful twenty days" had ended. Roosevelt then appointed Charles E. Magoon, who had been governor of the Canal Zone, as provisional governor of Cuba.

Portell-Vilá, whose phrases are irresistible, describes the new governor as "an obese giant born in the solitudes of Minnesota, whose childhood was passed on a farm on the frontier of the Far West Indian plains of Nebraska" and at a time when "Cuba had known contact with European civilization for almost four hundred years." A popular *choteo* states that Cubans thought they knew all about dirty politics until Magoon came along to teach them new tricks.

Magoon's job, as he saw it, was to keep Cuba quiet until a new president was elected and he could go home. Keeping Cubans quiet seemed to mean giving them political jobs, pardons, and work on public projects. As the Liberals were the noisiest, they got most of the political jobs. As Magoon thought many prisoners had been unjustly jailed for political reasons, he issued many pardons. As actual want among the *guajiros* — this was the panic year of 1907 — made new revolts more than likely, he inaugurated a large program of public works. Magoon is credited with building more roads in two years than Spain had in four centuries. He propitiated labor by advocating wages in American currency, thus raising purchasing power about ten per cent. Most United States historians agree that Magoon was honest. Jenks says categorically: "No evidence has been adduced to convict . . . Magoon . . . of corruption in the exercise of his office." But all these public works brought to Cuba a rush of contractors looking for a new West where a bright man with few inhibitions could make a killing.

The United States had tried to prevent just such unrestrained exploitation. The Foraker Amendment to the Army Appropriations Act of 1899 had prohibited the granting of "property, franchises, or concessions of any kind whatever" during the United States occupation of Cuba. During Magoon's administration clever lawyers found loopholes, and both American and European capital flooded in to finance docks and dredgings, railroads, and street railways; North American contractors had their day. To sugar interests, which had been growing rapidly, the United States now added public service corporations whose power was leading to what Jenks describes as *Our Cuban Colony*, politically independent but financially bound. All this seemed naturally right and good to the North American. That was the way a new country was opened up.

Perhaps Magoon's most amazing achievement had to do with Cuba's legal code. As a lawyer he was appalled at the confusion of Spanish laws, Spanish and United States military orders, the Cuban constitution, and later statutes. He imported another lawyer, Colonel Enoch H. Crowder of the Judge Advocate's Office. Crowder, with a committee of Cubans and Americans contrived a legal code as incomprehensible, according to the *choteo*, as the Einstein theory; only four men could understand it. It provided for a civil service, for well-supervised elections, and for a census to establish the basis of voting.

Three parties entered candidates, and a vigorous campaign and a peaceful balloting showed an overwhelming majority for the Liberals, headed by the chief of the revolt of 1906, José Miguel Gómez. Cuba was again a "going concern," and Governor Magoon could at last go home.

Magoon's rule was the first under the new "preventive policy" in Caribbean affairs. Our Uncle Sam, more like a fussy old maid aunt than a benevolent uncle, now undertook to forestall trouble which might lead to intervention. Such a policy naturally led to more and bitterer Cuban animosity. Cuban historians almost unanimously blame Magoon for all succeeding evils, though Emilio Roig de Leuchsenring admits that "Cubans were to blame, the intransigeance of some, the thoughtlessness of others, the passion of all."

Portell-Vilá's diatribe against the United States is the most revealing of basic Cuban psychology. The public works program he dismisses as designed only to "satisfy the ambitions of politicians, contractors, and influential people"; and he complains that "there was not the least attention to . . . ending the domination of the sugar industry, of encouraging the cultivation of food plants and of primary materials . . . of creating other sources of wealth and of causing finally the rise of a Cuban middle class economically independent, intelligent and progressive, not subject to political fluctuations and with a supreme interest in keeping public peace, and a rule of right and duty under a decent and responsible government."

It is touching that a Cuban has such faith in the ability of the United States to make everything right for his country. It is laughable in view of the vociferous protest that is raised against any similar measures for the folks at home, even now, forty years later. To Cubans, Uncle Sam is all-powerful. He can; therefore he should.

For the United States government in Cuba our historians have made out a case that is not too bad. The Teller Amendment, to assure our leaving, and the Foraker Amendment, to hold down private exploitation, both showed the government willing and able to back its idealistic claims. For the first time in history a conqueror withdrew leaving its conquest in condition to continue as a self-governing unit. But even during the occupations, business was there with its different standards. It is commonplace that no man does well if his heart is not in it. If his business is in it, buyer or borrower must indeed beware. It was too easy to lend large sums of money to dictators in Cuba. Too many officers of our government were also officers of the banks that lent the money or of the great corporations that came soon to dominate Cuban business and Cuban life. It is not a pretty story from the point of view of the Cuban "little man." However sugar may fluctuate on the international market, the price the ordinary Cuban has had to pay has been consistently too high.

# VI

# THE PRICE OF SUGAR

A SUGAR PLANTATION IS A LOVELY SIGHT. THE CANE-
fields ripple like water over rolling hills and ruffle their tufts in
the breeze like ocean spray. One can almost feel the rocking of a
boat. And *ingenios*, sugar mills, rise like islands in the delicate
and moving green, flaunting banners of smoke and pulling unto
themselves lesser smoke banners from ships and trains. For each
sugar mill is a *central*: a center to which tenant-growers, *colonos*,
bring their sugar to be ground; and a link with the vast world of
sugar consumers.

The casual eye does not recreate the primeval forests of hard-
woods that covered most of those hills before United States and
Cuban business men, piped along to the tune of quick profits,
peeled them off regardlessly and turned Cuba into the world's
sugar bowl and a one-crop country. A sugar man boasted to me
that his company had planted cane only on virgin land, not dis-
possessing a single Cuban. He did not mention the hundreds of
thousands of acres of timber, much of it hardwood, that the sugar
companies burned off in Camagüey and Oriente to plant sugar.
Thus in the rush to make quick money, an irreplaceable resource

was destroyed. Only God can make a tree, but even He cannot restore a hardwood forest under a hundred years or so. This is part of the price, not always considered, that Cuba has paid for sugar.

Still, growing sugar is a pretty sight and a plantation's operation, like any successful operation, is thrilling and gratifying to see: people at work with beasts and machines in orderly and calculated processes to produce one of mankind's great needs. A plantation such as that of the United Fruit Company which I visited at Banes in northern Oriente arouses only admiration. Questions lurking underneath obtrude their ugly heads only on later consideration.

Banes and Preston are United Fruit's two great plantations, each with its own sugar mill, its own pouch bay with docks, and its own set-up for human living on a civilized scale. I reached Banes by train, and was taken at once to the Employees' Club. It is always fun to visit one of these transplanted patches of United States in a foreign land; they are so much alike, so altogether like home. Wide porches with screens, doors that really catch and shut tight, rows of high-backed rocking chairs; indoors all the home magazines, ping-pong tables, an out-of-tune piano, and a faint scent of antiseptic. The beds are good, the baths shiningly clean, and the presiding genius is nearly always a man of color. In Cuba he is Jamaican, speaking English with the British accent of the Caribbean. My companions at dinner were several young engineers and office workers, two Cubans among them, and the ubiquitous Scotsman without whom no engine is properly operated anywhere in the world. After dinner, the office workers, who were girls, disappeared with a couple of the engineers and another offered to show me the two towns. Company town and Cuban town.

Company town is like any garden village at home with flower and vegetable beds, a lawn, clotheslines, and a driveway. In Banes there is a palm in every lawn, hibiscus and butterfly bushes, and rampant bougainvillea, royal purple or candent red, hanging heavily on fences. Young people were coming home from tennis or swimming, older people from golf, pianos sounded from the houses and chatting from the screened porches. This is the way salaried folk live. Later I should see the workers' homes.

Cuban town is still pleasantly colonial except where company influence has led to a few separate houses with lawns. The company has invested $47,000 in a sewer, put up a slaughterhouse, provided a playground, and given material aid to the Friends School. But Cuban Banes is still Cuban. In the evening people were sitting in their long windows with iron grilles. Beyond were lighted rooms with tiled floors, tidies on pianos and tables, artificial flowers in tall vases, and painted or plaster saints on the walls. Heavy doors folded back in the cool evening revealed patios full of flowers. Children ran and shouted, girls giggled in groups, pairs strolled and spoke low.

In the morning the busy manager himself took me to see how sugar is produced. Mr. E. S. Walker is a company man, making sugar, but doing as much for the people concerned as is compatible with making sugar. We stopped at the company store, which has had an influence in all retail merchandising. Early in the century young William P. Field came here to manage the store. Methods, he found, included much squeeze. The landlady expected to pay less or get more for her money. Clerks sold things to themselves at less than the marked price. There was, in fact, no marked price. So Mr. Field inaugurated a new system. It meant a couple of strikes and one direct assault with guns. But he won, and the young men who worked with him under the new and honest system are now middle-aged admirers and still loyal employees of United Fruit. Mr. Field himself says: "The merchandise department is a model for all the world, not alone because of the assortment of merchandise, but because of the quality of the goods, full weight and reasonable prices, it being literally true that the department exists for the benefit of employees and not to exploit them as is still being done in many places and as always was done only yesterday."

The hospital also exists for the benefit of employees. There are fifty beds; about thirty were occupied by Cubans of all ages, from those just born to those about to die. Old folks with nowhere else to go are kept clean, fed, and comfortable for their last years. One woman, vacant-eyed, was grieving herself to death for a son who had been drafted in the United States. We were greeted by a jolly doctor who amuses himself studying ancient Indian medical practices, and shown about by a starched and businesslike nurse.

We visited the model dairy, whose normal production is a thousand liters daily, though drought had cut that down one fourth. Because of that drought I was milk-starved and begged a glass, which was cool and fresh and creamy. A thousand liters does not provide enough for all, but they make it go as far as it will, beginning at the top.

In the afternoon we drove out to see how the workers live, Mr. Walker honorably showing me the floorless, windowless *bohíos* that were the first the company provided. A few are still in use. There is a second type of frame cabin, better than the *bohío*, but not as good as the newest house, in which anybody could live with comfort and cleanliness. These cottages, with two bedrooms, living room and kitchen, have water piped in, a shower, and electric light. Everywhere there were small vegetable gardens, so many that I inquired.

"Yes, they've all got gardens now," replied Mr. Walker with a sigh that indicated bother rather than pride. "But you ask Brickley about that; he's the agricultural man. He's sweated enough over those gardens to have his name engraved on every carrot." Another sigh. "Cubans urge us to go into the vegetable market. They kick about Yankee developments, but complain because we don't go into more. They could produce enough on waste land in Cuba to feed the population well. But you won't see any Cuban capital going into that business! Well, we won't do it. We'll stick to sugar.

"Cuba is a natural sugar country, the best in the world. Cane here needs neither water nor artificial fertilizer, as in Hawaii, and there is no danger of frost, which is a constant hazard in Louisiana and Florida. But sugar here, as everywhere, requires what the United States can supply and Cuba cannot: great capital investment in vast plantations and expensive plants, to say nothing of engineering and managerial training. And yet they hamper us in every way; the new laws work against the foreign companies, not against the little fellows who are mostly Cubans. That makes it practically impossible now to employ more U. S. people. As money comes from the States, investors demand U. S. management. If that ever becomes impossible the money will be withdrawn. You'll see. And they'll see, and be mighty surprised!

"Another thing is this recent raise of thirty-two per cent in all salaries as well as wages. A rise in wages was all right; labor needed it. A man making $1.21 a day now gets $1.60 a day. The price of sugar had gone up. Fair enough! But salaries! A doctor, for instance, who was getting $500.00 a month now gets $660.00. Impossible! And everybody gets the raise, your lazy loafer as well as the fellow who's hitting the ball. Impossible now to weed out the deadwood. It shoots your morale all to pieces. It used to be a pleasure to watch a gang of men digging a ditch, for instance, and promote the one who was really throwing dirt. Now the loafer, who is often a labor organizer put there for the purpose, just spoons a few pebbles around, looks you in the eye and dares you to do anything about it. Brings down the morale of the whole lot. Naturally nobody is going to work harder and steadier when no rewards are possible. He'd be a fool to do it."

Mr. Walker cheered up in the mill. Here the mechanized process was in full swing. Machines set the pace for everything from the farthest reaches of the fields, where men swing *machetes* to cut cane which other men load on oxcarts that move in a steady procession to the rail line or directly to the mill. The mill is a big factory where one gazes into boiling vats, watches oily men with long-nosed oil cans tending the shining steel while engineers keep an eye on the temperature gauges. It all moves the sugar along from the cut cane through boiling juice to crystals, and finally into bags that huge cranes swing aloft and dump into ships waiting to steam off to Boston. Cuba still lives in the colonial economy of the producer of raw materials to be finished by the industrialized nation. This too may be added to the price of sugar.

In all this operation nothing is wasted. Yankee ingenuity has never ceased making new inventions, introducing new processes, until the very last bit of squeezed cane serves either as fuel, fodder, or fertilizer. It is good to know that the last waste generally considered in economic development — human waste — is of concern at Banes, where ten thousand people feed and serve the mill during the grinding season. As the grinding season is so short — only two or three months — the crying human problem is what is to happen to all those people during the dead season. Under slavery they were at least fed. At Banes a more modern method is being tried. The *guajiro* is learning to garden so he and his family can eat between *zafras*. About that I was to talk to Mr. Brickley.

Mr. Brickley was more than willing to talk. Men on the production end sigh less than managers; they deal with results rather than costs. Mr. Brickley showed me a couple of human results as we drove away from Banes. He introduced a tall smiling Cuban, and later told me that he was one of the highest-paid employees on the plantation, a Banes boy. We stopped at the store Mr. Field had put on such a sound basis where all the clerks and bookkeepers were Cubans. All Cubans on technical jobs get exactly the same pay Yanks get.

As he swung the wheel to skirt a water tower, suddenly Mr. Brickley braked and hailed a man in a truck. Also a Cuban, this was Señor Torres with excellent English and perfect aplomb, but clearly too busy for a long conversation.

"He's one of the district superintendents," said Mr. Brickley, as we drove on. "There are four. One American, one Englishman, one Jamaican, and this Cuban. And nobody does a better job than Torres. He's the son of illiterate *guajiros*. He started with us when he was fourteen years old, cleaning out the stables. He'd been to school until then; learned to read. He's picked up the rest as he went along. Soon he was straw boss over fourteen men. Then he was promoted to *mayoral*, overseer of forty to a hundred men. He proved that he could handle men, get out the work, handle money. So in a few years he was a farm overseer supervising 1,500 to 2,000 acres of cane and handling from 500 to 600 men. Now as district superintendent he's got 1,200 acres of cane and pasture land, and about 2,000 men under him. The farther that fellow goes the better he gets. He earns $4,000 a year now; it's really a $5,000 job. The company gives him a house with electricity, water; you'll see it. His wife runs a nice home; they have a cook."

Suddenly he stopped the car, hard. A slim tower of smoke, black and murky, rose in front of us. A few yards ahead was the railroad crossing with a man in a box. Yes, he said, it had been reported.

Mr. Brickley turned to his chauffeur in the back seat. "Sorry, José, that you'll miss the ride." He gave the man no instructions. José saluted me and disappeared down the road toward town. "I didn't expect to show you a cane fire, but since we've got one, you might as well see it."

One of the young men I had met before passed us in a car filled with men with *machetes*. Then a red truck, charging as to battle. We were constantly passing men on horseback, afoot, all with *machetes*, all waving happily as we sped by. The smoke cloud was still billowing up, black in the center, paling out toward the edges. It moved heavily before a slow breeze. We passed several houses where women stood watching. At every crossroad and trail more men came along armed with *machetes* or caneknives.

"The fire signal calls out everybody," Mr. Brickley explained. "They get paid the prevailing day's wage, whether they're on a regular job just now or not. Yes, they turn out well; everybody's got an interest in saving the cane."

Another truck dashed by us, coming in obliquely. "Torres!" said Mr. Brickley with satisfaction. "I knew he'd be on the job. He's been down along the stream bed to start a backfire. It'll soon be under control now. See! That cloud is getting lighter already. It's larger but it's losing intensity. That smell? That's the hot sap in the cane. It does smell like fudge boiling over." Mr. Brickley's eyes never rested. "No, that crackle's good. That's the backfire starting along the stream bed. It won't leap the stream now. It's under control. Good old Torres! I knew he'd get it."

We must have seen a hundred men running along the roads. Mr. Brickley estimated that the fire would have brought three hundred converging from all directions. Each one knew what to do. It had been done. The fire was out with a minimum of loss.

Then I relaxed and remembered the gardens. Mr. Brickley laughed. "Yes, they've all got gardens now. But we had a lot of work, I'll tell you, getting them to do it. During the depression we had to lay off so many that we knew the only way to save them from real starvation was to make them raise their own food. But would they? You should have seen the struggle we had. We gave them land, seed; they had time — nothing but time. We said: 'We can't sell our sugar; we're on a quota; we can't help you. If you're going to eat you'll have to produce food.' We gave them tools, we even ploughed the land. And they wouldn't produce! They're just beginning now, but it's a hard pull still; we have to keep a man on the job all the time to see that they work their gardens, bring in the stuff, eat it. You can't imagine such

*Wilfredo Lam. Background, his painting* The Jungle, *now in the collection of the Museum of Modern Art, New York*

Jesús y Luis, *by T. Ramos Blanco*

Rumba Rhythm, *by T. Ramos Blanco*

complete indifference to his own welfare as the typical *guajiro* shows. But they're doing better."

"How many gardens are there now?" I asked.

"Eleven hundred and thirty."

"And how many *guajiro* homes are there?"

Mr. Brickley's chuckle was a bit grim. "Eleven hundred and thirty."

I had seen one of the best sugar plantations in Cuba, though I am told that many United States operations are as well conducted and take as much care of their men. As about seventy-five per cent of Cuba's sugarlands are owned and operated by North Americans, this is heartening to know. Cuban plantations are less admirable, as any Cuban readily admits. Their plaint that only rich northerners can afford such luxuries comes just as easily from a Cuban sugar man who has just sold the last *zafra* for half a million dollars. Closer examination reveals that all these luxuries — hospitals, schools, decent housing, fair hours and working conditions — are required by Cuban laws. And laws are better enforced for foreigners than for homefolks.

What goes on on the plantations is not all there is to the price of sugar in Cuba; nor can the Cuban's prevailing preoccupation with the *zafra* and his attitude toward the United States be understood without a bit of sugar history.

Sugar and Cuba's other basic crop, tobacco, have been brilliantly presented by Fernando Ortiz in *Contrapunteo Cubano, Cuban Counterpoint*. The book's form is extraordinary and beautiful, for it is an essay, compactly scholarly and highly readable; it compliments the reader by assuming great erudition on his part and quietly supplies him the facts in an encyclopedic appendix. It should be read first studiously with the notes and then with full delight and to the accompaniment of well-sugared coffee and Cuba's best tobacco.

Sugar came to the Indies from the East; the Crusaders brought it to Europe and Velázquez to Cuba. Its name comes from San-skrit; the Arabs called it *alçucar* and in Spain they said: *"Con açucar o miel todo sabe bien."* ("With sugar or honey everything tastes good.") Dr. Ortiz finds tobacco proud, distinguished, aris-tocratic, dignified. It may be good or bad; it always goes alone and seeks individuality. Sugar, its counterpoint, is common, in-distinct, undistinguished. An unformed mass, from cane to cake, it always needs a companion, a chaperone. Tobacco is the de-light of primates and princes; sugar is the solace of the common run. Obviously, tobacco is masculine (as obviously as our author is) and sugar is feminine.

Tobacco is cultivated not only plant by plant, but leaf by leaf. It demands expert and individual handling. Sugar, conversely, requires many workers, cheap, untrained, and easily disposable. African slaves cultivated sugar, which Indians, never easily dis-posed of, refused to do. Sugar, according to Dr. Ortiz, is the root of all evil in Cuba, not slavery. Under slavery, making sugar was a gentleman's business and honorably conducted. But when it got into the machine age and the world market, corruption be-gan. Sugarmills require specialists, but never as individuals; they are always controlled by business, and that means crooked dealing. Sugar's only graces are brandy and rum, and they are no longer sugar. Sugar, as we know it, is of the machine age. It is a huge operation, and everything about it must be rapid, speeded by the machine, timed by the whistle. Clearly sugar and the Yankee were made for each other.

Even the Yankee's machine mind has not changed or solved the basic human problem created by sugar. A tough crop, which cares for itself during most of the year, at harvest time the cane requires many workers and intense activity, as spoilage is pos-sible at any point from cutting to bagging. But bright workers are not necessary. Skill is needed only in the mills and in a few top jobs. Yet three quarter of a million Cubans work sugar, de-pend upon sugar, live lives molded by the demands of sugar. In a country of four million people, nobody is really free of sugar. If his job seems free, his state of mind never is.

First, the *guajiro* on the plantation. Sometimes he has been recently imported from Haiti or Jamaica. Sometimes his forebears include one or more of those Chinese coolies. He generally has some white blood. Altogether he is an illiterate, living in a dirt-floored *hobío*, breeding children with no restraint, nominally Catholic but ridden by fear of witches and demons, taking his fun at cockfights and fiestas, often orgiastically African, knowing there is no security ahead and so gambling his few coins away. Gambler's luck is really his only chance to beat the cycle in which he is caught. For he earns only during the three months of the *zafra*. Then he is laid off. Tens of thousands of him with no work anywhere. Tens of thousands of families sliding down the dietary scale into undernourishment on a handful of beans and a bit of *yuca* or *malanga*. This system breeds new evils at every downward step. Men grow lazier and lazier, women more and more slatternly. At worst they turn to crime or vice, perhaps to African superstitions not yet washed out by education. And children? Any teacher or social worker can plot the curve by which they slide from eagerness to listlessness and finally into sheer stupidity.

Because sugar requires few special skills, and because it is, on the whole, easier to handle illiterate and unquestioning people, Cuba has not felt the urge toward education that diversification and industrialization bring. The school program has lagged. Because uneducated people did not develop small farms there was no demand for roads, and there are few roads. Because wealthy Cubans could invest along with the Yankees, upper-class intelligence was not turned sooner upon betterment of the *guajiro*. So he remains largely an illiterate, futureless plantation worker. Whatever sugar's price on the world market, the price the little Cuban has paid has been consistently too high.

Almost equally affected, though in another way, are the Cuban politician and the thinker. A leftist leader, who would have called himself a Communist a few years ago, said: "Policy? We have no policy. We Cubans can do nothing without reference to the United States. Your country holds us in a death-grip. The price you pay us for sugar determines everything in our little country." Such frustration is not uncommon. I made a point of asking; politicians of all persuasions gave me similar answers. Not many leaders are considering their country's potentialities outside the field of sugar. This hangover of colonialism is one depressing item in the price Cuba pays for sugar. The fearsome shadow of Uncle Sam falls across all Cuban life and thought.

The United States had interests in Cuban sugar long before the occupation. The first machinery for sugar mills was imported by a Yankee in 1830. After that Cuba became the richest colony in the world with a high level of culture among the upper classes and sugar as the dominant crop, forcing out coffee. In the 1880's hard granulated sugar began to replace the soft brownish sweetenin' our grandmothers knew, and northern business men began to combine. In 1888 Henry O. Havemeyer united seventeen companies and the Sugar Trust was on its way. Cuba was then supplying the United States with from seventy to ninety per cent of its sugar. The need to extract more sugar from the cane, and faster, forced inventions such as the vacuum pan and a centrifugal process.

Small operators could not compete, and the *central* system developed. Many old mills, which had been operated by oxen, gave up, and their owners hauled their cane to the nearest big *central* for grinding. This cut the number of sugar mills in half and made *colonos* of their owners. The *colono* may own his own land or lease from the big company. In either case he hires labor, plants and harvests the crop, and assumes all the risk of hurricane or drought. He is every type of Cuban from the gentleman who owns large estates to the *guajiro* raising a patch of cane with his sons.

248

By the turn of the century Cuba was the world's sugarbowl, and all Cuba was involved in its culture. But sugar's rivals were coming into political power. The French had begun to extract sugar from beets as early as the middle of the nineteenth century, and were soon exporting instead of importing. The Germans followed, and by 1900 the United States was experimenting with beets and soon had enough sugarbeet senators, headed by Reed Smoot of Utah, to provide a powerful opposition to Cuba's favored position in the sugar market. As early as 1899, Cuban sugar, through a reciprocity treaty, was allowed to enter United States ports at lowered duty. During the first twenty years of the new century a fair balance was maintained between beet and cane, supply and demand, though Cubans could not understand then, as they cannot now, why they should yield to areas where sugar production is more costly and uncertain than in their favored land. All this made politics in the United States, as New York capital controlled beets, Louisiana cane, and Cuban plantations. But Yankee capital was seeing many opportunities in Cuba other than sugar.

Cuba had come into the orbit of the United States when nineteenth-century thinking prevailed, with its faith in business and no restraints on its exploitation of resources or of people. Cuba seemed just another West waiting to be opened up. As Cubans — those with power or voice — stood to profit by the developments, they might have borne the impact of northern business if they had not also had to stand United States moralizing. Alberto Arredondo expressed it thus. "The ideological vanguard of imperialistic stamp . . . adorned it with all the ingenious splendor of moral objectives. Thus they spoke of 'manifest destiny,' of the civilizing role of North America, and of the need to make friends with Latin America."

The Foraker Amendment of 1899 had stipulated that during the occupation "no franchises or concessions of any kind shall be granted by the United States." But that was easily interpreted to exclude certain harbor works, street railways, and other attractive undertakings. Frank Steinhart, General Wood's knowing aide, managed to get a financial start during those years. He it was who proposed to General Wood that the Church be paid rent for the use of church property for profane purposes. The old San Francisco Convent is still the national postoffice and a most impressive one. So the new Cuban government paid $3,000,000 to the Church, and Mr. Steinhart, the financial genius who had handled the negotiations, was fee'd generously and promptly invested his earnings in the street railway for Havana. Under Governor Magoon this sort of thing went merrily on. Contractors from New York, who knew Tammany ways, undertook to build roads, railway and streetcar systems, dredge harbors. Under President José Miguel Gómez, elected in a fair election, even more elaborate schemes appeared for the development of all Cuba's waste lands and their colonization with North Americans who were privately assured that Cuba would soon belong to the United States.

Many Cubans believe that annexationist North Americans fomented a Negro revolt in 1912. By that time the Bethlehem Steel Company had acquired nearly one billion tons of iron reserves in Oriente, Cuba's greatest mineral deposit. The Cobre and Juragua coppermines were American owned, as were large sugar plantations. The Negroes, according to Jenks, were attacking only property, not people; they were protesting against a law that forbade political parties along racial lines. But they scared the North Americans out of their wits, and such a hullaballoo reached Washington that battleships appeared off Havana and Cienfuegos and Marines were landed in Oriente to take over mines and sugar mills.

President Gómez was more vigorous than Estrada Palma had been when Gómez himself was in revolt in 1906. He informed Washington, by message and emissary, that he was quite able to handle his own revolt. Cuba's Secretary of State Sanguily wrote:

"It is a notorious fact that no American property had been destroyed nor had the life of any American citizen been endangered before the landing of the Marines." Our minister Beaupré, in Havana, saw beyond the immediate revolt (which was quite easily subdued). He cabled Washington in 1912: "The floating of a new loan would offer us an extremely good opportunity to be of real assistance to the Cuban people . . ." and "This might readily be made to entail some more or less active fiscal control which would protect the Cuban treasury against wholesale looting."

Mr. Beaupré's chief was Secretary of State Philander C. Knox who called his Cuban policy "preventative." The United States would take a hand in Cuban affairs early in order to prevent the need for intervention. This might also be called the Meddlesome Mattie method, whose total effect on Cuba — especially upon the forever forgotten little man — was probably much worse than anything Cuba could have done for herself. It brought a specious stability. Cubans knew that intervention was possible, and were emboldened to take long chances with each other. Capital knew that it would be protected. And United States capital, because the Platt Amendment gave the United States the right to scrutinize all loans, had a virtual monopoly. Every Cuban government found it delightfully easy to borrow money. And many Cuban politicians partook of the largesse. Even Roig de Leuchsenring admits that much of Cuba's difficulty was due to "the fault of governors and politicians, lack of patriotism and of any idea of the public good in our moneyed and powerful classes and to the fatalistic apathy and civic laziness of the people in general."

In Washington, "manifest destiny" had been succeeded by "dollar diplomacy." We were out now to show Cubans how to govern themselves for the benefit of business from which all blessings flow. Loans to Cuba would be a good way to keep the blessings flowing, and with certain reciprocity features. It is worthy of note how often our ministers and special advisers in

Cuba were also gentlemen prominent in the corporations and banks that were doing business with the Cuban government.

Cuban governments found many good reasons for borrowing. Veterans perennially wanted more money. Sanitation, paving, public utilities were all needed and all good causes. Each administration, going in on an economy platform, found it necessary to borrow in order to refinance and recoup the losses and errors of the preceding administration. Politics swung back and forth between Liberals and Conservatives. General Gómez, a Liberal, was succeeded in 1913 by Mario Menocal, the darling of both business and State Department. He was a Cornell graduate, had been a manager of great sugar plantations; Wall Street considered him "a sound man." Washington sent him Enoch H. Crowder, now a general, as special adviser. General Crowder carried over into the next administration, and supplied President Zayas with fifteen memoranda offering him guidance in every detail of his adminstration. This president, nonetheless, goes down in Cuban history as the one who got more relatives on the payroll and countenanced more graft than any other. Cubans deplore that, but they gloat a bit because Zayas took advantage of Ambassador Crowder's diplomatic status to decline further surveillance. He finally dismissed his "Crowder Cabinet" and set out on his own for re-election. But he was defeated in 1924 by a young Liberal, Gerardo Machado y Morales, who promised economy and honesty in office, no re-election, and Cuba for the Cubans. His anti-Platt plank was probably his most effective. President Machado was to serve until 1933. By that time, New York bankers had lent Cuba over $200,000,000, Americans owned or controlled three quarters of the island's sugar output, dominated the tobacco business, owned one of the two railroads, and either dominated or largely controlled much lesser business.

With the war of 1914, Cuba had become again the world's sugarbowl, the United States bought all the planters could raise, and planters, foreseeing nothing, sacrificed everything to sugar.

These were the years of the "Dance of the Millions," when Cuba's great mahogany forests were cut down and, as Delgado Montejo expresses it, "the new tropical El Dorado was overcome with reckless well-being . . . while *hacendados* and *colonos* traveled with their families through old ruined Europe, exhibiting all the vulgarity of the new rich." Elías Entralgo offers an interesting explanation of the lack of protest among Cubans: "The highest moral value for the Cuban people is charm. Among us the charming man is entitled to everything, even including crime. . . ." Charming Cubans were everywhere. Brilliant intellectual Cubans were making themselves heard in international deliberations, in their writings, in growing protests. But they had not yet allied themselves with the strength that comes from the people. Labor was only beginning to organize and to stir, though Machado's administration was bedeviled from the beginning with strikes and the rising demands of labor.

One would like to understand Gerardo Machado y Morales. He came to the presidency under such good auspices. A wealthy cattleman of Santa Clara, he was caricatured as a butcher. But his friends were American business men, he was socially acceptable, attractive, and generally liked and trusted. He had good ideas. His favorite project was a highway the length of the island, which would open up the country, stimulate diversification of crops, and employ many people. Money was of course required, but the Chase National Bank stood ready. It advanced $10,000,000 on contractors' certificates for roadwork to be done, taking a first lien on ninety per cent of the revenue for the public works fund. The president also erected to his glorification a new capitol, costing some $18,000,000 and set with the famous diamond in the rotunda, from which all roads were measured. This was a fantastic extravagance in a country in dire need of education, agricultural development, and public health. Machado had soon added some $86,000,000 to the national debt, and had proportionately increased the power of the New York banks. Ill-advised as these acts were, they were not incompatible with good government; they do not explain what turned this charming man with good, if grandiloquent ideas, into one of the most vicious and ruthless of modern dictators.

Machado's career advanced along classic lines. He was soon boasting, in the United States, that no strike in Cuba lasted longer than twenty-four hours. He jailed leaders, often without trial, terrorized simple workers. For he was using his borrowed millions to build up a well-trained army and a tough secret police loyal only to him. He united several political parties and rewarded his adherents well with a variety of *botellas*, including sinecures in the sale of lotteries, which enriched the favored middlemen and gave the President a generous squeeze.

In 1928 Machado was powerful enough to demand and get a new constitution providing for a six-year presidential term with no re-election and no vice-president. This act disregarded the constitution of 1901 and called forth strong opposition on the part of Cuban lawyers and constitutionalists. The press protested, and was put under stringent regulation. University students, always politically alert, protested in their publications, in printed posters and defiant scrawls in public places, in parades and meetings. Machado countered as dictators do. He suppressed the newspapers, and all publications that protested against his methods. He closed the University and even the secondary schools. He arrested numberless young people, girls as well as youths. He attempted to break up their processions by sending out the city's lowest elements. A girl of good family, aflame to make Cuba free and decent, might find herself forced into a brawl with a prostitute and so railroaded to jail. From the jails few returned. Youths in their teens were set free to run while police shot them down, invoking the ancient Spanish *ley de fuga*, which allowed the shooting of an escaping prisoner. The secret police, *la porra*, the Bludgeon, lived up to its name. Machado also could count on his army, which was well-armed and sup-

plied by United States dealers with the machineguns and air-
planes that made old-fashioned fighting in the *manigua* impossible.

There was nothing for it but to go underground. The ABC, a
cellular organization whose members knew only their immediate
superiors and next in line, enlisted professional men, thinkers,
Cuba's best. Middle-aged men and women recall with pride how
they published handbills in the cellar, smuggled arms with a
wink from sympathetic policemen, stood guard on important
meetings, went into exile or to jail. Machado's henchmen followed them even to other countries. One of Cuba's heroes is Julio
Antonio Mella, a student who was shot in Mexico at Machado's
order.

It was a time of terror and revolt that spread the length of the
island and enlisted sympathy and support in other countries. It
was, according to some Cuban students, the first real revolution
Cuba had known, for this was not an insurrection of outs against
ins, but of the Cuban people against an intolerable dictatorship.

Cuban historians generally blame Ambassador Guggenheim
for not openly favoring the insurgents. But Russell H. Fitzgib-
bon, generally impartial, holds that the fault lay in Washington.
The Hoover administration, having neglected prevention, hesitated before any action which might lead to intervention. Representative Hamilton Fish, Jr., aware of the relations between the
National City Bank and the Chase National Bank and Machado,
said in Congress: "It is characteristic of the American 'dollar
diplomacy' at its worst — anything to protect property invest-
ments, regardless of human rights and the liberties of the Cuban
people."

In 1933, Franklin Delano Roosevelt opened his administration by announcing the New Deal at home and the Good Neighbor
Policy in the Americas. In line with this approach, President
Roosevelt sent Sumner Welles as his personal representative to
try to assist Cuba in bringing order out of what amounted to

chaos. When Mr. Welles reached Cuba in May, the opposition had grown and split. The students and the professors did not agree. Machado was afraid. He was living behind closed iron shutters guarded by his faithful *porra;* he drove out only in armored cars with shatter-proof glass. Nobody was safe, not even the dictator.

The sauve and adroit Mr. Welles managed to get leaders of all factions to call upon him at the Hotel Nacional; he even got some of them to confer together. Only the students and certain even more leftish groups refused this mediation. President Machado then proposed — and his proposals suggested that Mr. Welles had had a hand in them — that the office of vice-president should be restored, and that the President should resign in favor of a new vice-president. This would save the dictator's face and allow for forming a new government with a show of legality. Word got out that an agreement had been reached and that Machado had resigned. Students of all ages, factory workers, clerks, shoppers, passersby heard it and started marching through the streets shouting the old cry "Cuba Libre!" But the *porra* still functioned. They turned machineguns on the jubilant crowd, killing, wounding, and rousing a spirit of resentment that would be hard to curb. This was the Revolt of August 7th, which brought out the people's most potent weapon. A strike of bus and streetcar operators soon involved taxi-drivers and spread and grew into a general strike. Not only was all labor paralyzed, but business and professional people also stopped work. Havana was a functionless city. The August air was torrid; the human atmosphere tense with menace.

Then Machado's officers turned against him. This was the Revolt of the Colonels, who realized that disaster could be averted only by getting rid of the dictator. On August 12 Machado left by plane for Nassau, and the people, when that news was confirmed, burst out into an orgy of reprisals. They sacked and burned many fine homes of Machado's officials and profiteers; some were killed. But order was soon restored, and, by a series of pseudo-constitutional moves, Carlos Manuel de Céspedes, son of the patriot of 1868, was declared Provisional President.

Sumner Welles was, by many, given credit for this neat transfer of authority. Hubert Herring, who was there reporting the happenings for the *Nation* and *Current History,* wrote of Welles: "There was an unpleasant job to be done, and he did it with the maximum of good taste and the minimum of affront to the pride of Cuba." But too many Cubans refused to accept Mr. Welles's solution. There was strong opposition to Provisional President Céspedes precisely because he was considered Welles's man.

Roig de Leuchsenring, naming the Machado regime one of the most abominable ever known in Spanish-America, continues: "This tyranny was created, maintained, and exploited by . . . North American government and business. . . . And when . . . this tyranny, far from benefiting those interests, only caused them all sorts of conflicts and upsets . . . the Washington government intervened to eliminate the disturbing dictator. And he was snatched from power and replaced by another government pleasing to North America. As in the Spanish-Cuban war, now too the United States intervened . . . when Cubans themselves could have uprooted the despotism that oppressed . . . them. . . . But, one morning, the Cubans threw off the guardianship, pulled down the president named by Washington and put into power men who undertook to govern and administer Cuba, in spite of Washington, for the Cubans."

These men were a *junta* of five, raised to power by a revolt of sergeants against the colonels whom they distrusted as Machado men. The leader was Sergeant Fulgencio Batista, making his bow on the Cuban scene. For ten years he would be Cuba's strong man, as sergeant, as colonel, finally as president. In 1934 he was content to keep order while the five resigned in favor of Dr. Ramón Grau San Martín. A practicing physician and professor of medicine at the University of Havana, Dr. Grau had suffered exile under Machado. He was a man of highest integrity and intelligence and progressive in his political thinking. He was, according to the most disinterested thinkers, Cuba's first chance to see the establishment of a government truly dedicated to the Cuban people.

President Grau made immediate plans for a constitutional convention. Meanwhile he governed by decree, establishing an eight-hour day and a minimum wage for sugar-cutters, creating a Department of Labor, giving autonomy to the University, undertaking agrarian reform, instituting many other measures designed to correct the basic evils in Cuban life. This was government for Cuba's little man, and it aroused much opposition. Lily-white aristocrats complained that too many of the President's visitors were dark or uncouth. Mr. Welles did not support him.

Roig de Leuchsenring again: "North America put in movement at once all its powerful resources, diplomatic, military, naval and economic, to hinder the free decision of the Cuban people. And once again North America triumphed."

Dr. Grau, surrounded by enemies, lacking a well-built political machine, an idealist among very practical gentlemen who knew exactly what they wanted, and lacking the recognition of the United States, could only resign. His term lasted three months. After a brief interim, Carlos Mendieta, another colonel, was placed in power by a coup engineered by Batista. Within four days, Washington recognized Mendieta as president.

Not only Cubans condemn Washington's attitude toward President Grau. The Foreign Policy Association, whose report, *Problems of the New Cuba*, is accepted both in Cuba and the United States as scholarly and objective, concludes: "Had Washington followed a policy of neutrality toward the Grau regime, this regime could either have succeeded in gaining the support of the more stable elements in the country or left office without involving in any manner the responsibility of the United States. As a result of the course actually followed, however, the American government is regarded in many circles as responsible for its overthrow — a belief which has caused considerable bitterness."

This bitterness was so deep and so widespread that not even the abrogation of the hated Platt Amendment could lessen it. Not even the official pronouncements of the great Good Neighbor could make it seem sweet to Cuba. Delgado Montejo, economic historian, expresses this distrust: "The determining cause of this change . . . is founded in the necessity of the United States that Cuba should return to the position of important market for North American articles. . . . Although in a general sense it can be said that this new Reciprocity Treaty resulted in benefits for Cuba . . . it has halted the development of ₄ . . . national industry . . . now that the United States can congest our markets . . . without any possible competition from us."

These questions may be, and are, argued interminably. The incontrovertible fact is that such opinions are widely held and such distrust is widely felt throughout the Americas. In building good will for the new world this too must be figured in as part of the price of sugar.

# VII

# TWO CUBAS

A LOVELY LADY TOOK ME TO DRIVE SO THAT I SHOULD know the real Havana; she feared, I think, that my tastes had been leading me off among people who did not matter. Our objective was lunch at the Country Club, and we took in the Yacht Club and the Tennis Club on the way. We passed miles of stately homes representing every architectural period — from Pepito Martí's verandaed home set in gardens, through the iron and marble mansions reminiscent of Chicago or Buenos Aires, to the broadly glassed apartment houses designed originally for cold gray climates.

We passed a church. "That," said she, "is the work of Padre Spiralli. He is a wonderful Italian priest who has inspired us all. Everybody goes to his church, and he has made us raise enough money to build three magnificent structures. For a long time there has not been such a religious outburst in Havana."

We were driving on the edge of a deep arroyo within which were rows of sad-looking shacks, built of old boards and palm slabs, windowless, gardenless. The lady was pointing the other way. "Those new apartment houses have every convenience of

the best American houses; they are wonderful for young couples
or for women living alone. Of course," sweeping a delicate hand
toward the arroyo, "we'll have to get all that out. But that will be
attended to. We have such a dreadful time with those people.
You will see, out by the Yacht Club, how they are encroaching
with their hideous shacks. We've had to buy land repeatedly to
keep them away."

"Those people" are Cuba's fogotten men and women who have
begun to pull themselves up out of the lowest sloughs of despond.
They have somehow built shacks where they can earn a living.
They have dared to approach the Yacht Club and the road to the
Casino to offer food and drink at lower prices, good dancing in
rough spots, and such related arts as fortune-telling, potion-
vending, and prostitution.

The Yacht Club is a veritable palace by the sea, with sea
breezes sweeping in from the jeweled Gulf of Mexico across
sparkling white sand to cool tiled and scrubbed floors. On the
beaches strong bronzed bodies display the smartest bathing togs
and the best swimming and diving techniques. Children with
Negro maids are beginning a social career that will take them
to every such club in the world. *Las pepillas*, girls not yet out,
gather in giggling groups with soft drinks under striped um-
brellas. Their clothes are straight out of *Vogue*. Older women
lunch before bridge in the exquisitely appointed ladies' rooms,
and men meet in the bar cleverly frescoed with political carica-
tures. The Country Club is much the same, except that a fine golf
course curls around among little hills and dales, and serried
ranks of tennis courts ring to the calls of a tournament's referee.
Cuba's society is up-to-date, cosmopolitan and seemingly carefree, but even these *pepillas* are not unaware of the derelicts
under the hill. Cuban women as a whole accept responsibility
and take some action toward the unfortunate.

This I saw when two social service visitors, both young women
of society families, took me one day to visit those forlorn huddles

under the hill. They have been named — for Cuba's *choteo* never fails — *La Cueva de Humo*, the Smoke Cave, *Llega y Pon*, Squatters, *Isla de Pinos* (who knows why?), and *El Barrio de Las Llaguas*, for the palm slabs of which they are built. As old as the depression, these slums still baffle everybody. Some complain of them as the beginnings of communism, for the people pay no rent. Owners of the land have tried many tricks to force them out, including the collecting of rents in pitiful pittance. In 1944, the newly elected Grau San Martín administration tried moving all these derelicts into military barracks. It was well-intentioned, but the people fought fiercely against a move that would have disrupted families and subjected them to the ignominy of military control and institutionalism. They won, and government seems to do little for them since. One Cuban said: "Grau is just pretending they are not there to see if they will go away."

They have not gone away. Houses in *Isla de Pinos* were numbered up to 500. Most of them were smoky hovels with slatternly women and gaunt children. A few showed efforts at betterment with porchlike shelters, plants in tins, and swept doorsteps. The streets were clean, and the few water spigots were surrounded by patient people with buckets and tubs. *Isla de Pinos* has its own city government. In a shelter-like store the "Mayor" showed us his census. A boy who had recently gone to Matanzas to work was entered with his father's name, that of his employer, his age and wage.

Later a bright thirteen-year-old boy conducted us to the school. Only kindergarten in the morning, he explained. "We adults go in the afternoon." The school was a barnlike structure, built for chapel as well as school: the gift of a Catholic organization. The three teachers were employed by the state. The eldest, a woman with a strong sweet face, had chosen this post. At the sight of us, several children burst into terrified screams. They were afraid, she explained, that we were doctors come to vaccinate them; too many mothers threaten their children with the doctor. But in time they calmed down and sang a song or two. Generally they looked clean and bright.

At *Las Llaguas* we met the "Mayor in charge of sanitation." A very black man, he courteously conducted us through many streets, all well-swept. The population is 6,000. There are four water spigots. Several little grocery stores and barber shops. No beauty shops. Do men take to beautification before women do? One house was labeled *Escuela*. Not really a school, our guide explained, but a kindergarten run by a Mexican woman. She was also the guiding spirit of the patch and served as midwife, nurse, adviser, and comforter of all. She was out; I was sorry not to meet her.

The "Mayor,"seated at home, showed himself an angry man. Government, he complained, did nothing but haul away rubbish and keep policemen on the beat. No light, water, or streetcleaning. No doctor and no nurse. No help in getting work or a decent place to live. He confessed that most of the people had occasional work; perhaps enough to earn $15 a month. Most of the people, he said, were from the interior, not *habaneros*. The policeman, who dropped in just then, confirmed these facts and added that little crime and vice come out of these *barrios*. He smiled as he summed it up: "Here there is no prostitution, only in neighboring Havana."

For schooling, the children of *Las Llaguas* have a choice. There is a nearby public school and the nuns of Jesus y Los Pobres maintain a day and night school helped by Acción Católica, which provides medical aid. The "Mayor" spoke gratefully of these things and of the work of FEU, the Federation of University Students, who send teachers for the night school. But he rose to oratory when he spoke of how FEU had prevented the eviction of these families. "Those young men we adore."

So Cuba lives on two levels with a vast vacuum between. A report of the United States Federal Loan Agency for 1939 states that among one hundred wage-earning Cubans, the average family of five was living on a caloric intake considered adequate for one single worker. This average was 915 calories below that accepted as "desperate malnutrition" by the League of Nations' scale. Hansen in his *New World Guides to the Latin-American Republics* describes the Caribbean people as two thirds undernourished, one half suffering from infectious or deficiency diseases, with no social security, working under semi-feudal conditions, and outside the economic, social, and cultural pale of their country. The consuming power of such people is nil. Latest figures from Cuba do not vary much from this. The sugar industry still dooms some three quarters of a million people to from seven to nine months unemployment a vear. Lack of land and lack of agricultural training, or even of education to the point of literacy, prevent their feeding themselves. In a land fertile enough to produce anything, the development of pay crops other than sugar and tobacco still lags. All these conditions produce problems that all Cubans recognize and that many Cubans are struggling valiantly to solve.

One sees proof of such conditions on all sides. The male chambermaid in my hotel was an unusually intelligent man, of complete honesty and devotion to duty. He could neither read nor write; he had worked since he was ten years old and had never been inside a school. On the Prado, sitting on the step of one of the most elegant and ornate of gentlemen's clubs, I passed every day a beggar, an old man with a child in his arms. A boy of perhaps ten, dressed in rags, pale yellow with dull eyes, and so listless that he just lay, hour after hour, in the arms of grandfather, who was whining for alms. Farther along I was daily accosted by a coal-black Jamaican, brought over doubtless to work on a plantation and unable to get home. "Mistress," he would whine in that amusing Caribbean English, "Mistress, help me to a cup of coffee, please. I British object." Begging is against the law. Havana is well patroled by courteous, well-set-up, well-groomed police. But these things they do not see. However, when I reported the old man and the fading boy to the School for Social Service it sent an investigator, and that pair disappeared from Havana's streets.

But there is more to the problem than the removal of eyesores, as most thoughtful Cubans recognize. Wealthy and sophisticated Cuba presents a charming and highly articulate front to the world. But it rests precariously on an underpinning that is too far under to give the country real security. Cuba, like all countries originally founded on feudalism or slavery, is having a struggle to break that pattern and emerge as a modern democracy. Its new middle class is growing apace, especially in the towns. But so many Cubans still live in primitive conditions and in a primitive culture that they must be taken into account in any general picture of the country.

## PRIMITIVE CUBA

PRIMITIVE Cuba is everywhere. Strongest, of course, on the lower levels, but sending curious shoots of superstition up into the higher culture. Any street in Havana may harbor a room wherein ancient African ceremonies are practiced in ignorant confusion with Catholic observances. Witch doctors advertise to cure disease or relieve a breaking heart; they write prescriptions or stage mystic rites; they are consulted by ladies from the best society and by leaders of business or politics. They are also in close touch with the police, for too often their practices are openly immoral, look so, or lead indirectly to vice or crime. Folkways that may have been harmless or even good in their native place have degenerated when cut off from their roots. Many cases of witchcraft reveal on investigation that their basis was well intentioned. Witch doctors tried forty years ago for the murder of a white child explained that they were trying to help a sterile woman. Only the fresh blood of a white child could cure her.

Such cases grow rarer as education slowly washes superstition out. But in Cuba, as in our southern states, the African influence is still strong. Whites as well as Negroes are affected by it; its serious study makes it possible to understand much that otherwise would be only amusing, disgusting, or frightening.

Cuba is fortunate in having scholarly studies of her African background. Dr. Fernando Ortiz, as a young Cuban student in Madrid, made a survey of that city's underworld. On his return to Cuba he took a look at his native city. Vice and crime, he found, were not only the results of poverty and ignorance; they were involved too with ancient African tribal beliefs and customs. For Havana's underworld, composed of the underprivileged and uneducated, was largely of Negro or mixed blood. As a serious student seeking the springs of the behavior he found in Cuba, Dr. Ortiz was soon deep in African lore. To understand what these people thought they were doing when they sacrificed a cock, what their naked and apparently obscene orgies really meant, he learned much lore their practitioners knew nothing about. These studies resulted in his books.

They also made him the recognized best friend of the colored people of Havana, and later of all Cuba. Who wishes to know something of primitive Afro-Cuban rites must propitiate Dr. Ortiz. Otherwise one sees only pseudo-voodoo cooked up for tourists, marked by African rhythm but drained of all deeper significance.

Dr. Ortiz's most useful book on Afro-Cuban rites is *Hampa Cubana, Los Negros Brujos* (*Cuban Underworld, Negro Witch Doctors*), which describes rites practiced today in the light of ancient African religious beliefs. He studied the various African peoples who were caught or bought by slave traders and shipped to Cuba. All this is a bit vague; slave traders paid no attention to the cultural background of their merchandise. Still Dr. Ortiz has named more than a score of African nations who left cultural traces on Cuba. The most influential, he states, was the Yorubá, which has marked so much modern *brujería,* witching. *Ñañi-guismo,* from Calabar, is a cult so highly developed that Dr. Ortiz names it the Masonry of Cuba.

That the ancient faiths have retained any purity is remarkable, because, as Dr. Ortiz says, for the Negroes "slavery was their enforced novitiate to civilization." Forced into exhausting work, herded and bred like animals with no regard for family or group preferences, denied any education except church attendance, they lost the dignity of tribal ways and the grace of native worship they had known in Africa. There must have been priests among the wretches in the stinking slave ships, but they certainly had no way of preventing deterioration of their beliefs into the most degraded superstition.

The gap between the Negro in the guarded barracks and the white man in the mansion was widened by disdain of the slave, by language, dress, and standards. The immorality of the Negro, so often insisted upon, grew naturally from breaking his ancient pattern of living without giving him a new one. Once baptized, the slave was left to his own devices. Few *fincas* had resident priests; marriages were sanctified once a year or so. And white masters gave a poor example of sexual morality. In Cuba, as in the United States, white men produced the mulatto race, which has almost displaced the black. Vice and crime were the inevitable products of such a system. It is amazing that so much beauty grew out of that slime, especially in the music and the dance that the Negro brought from Africa and has presented to modern white civilization.

Dr. Ortiz writes: "The Negro dance shows us the first steps in the evolution of the dance: sensual, exciting, simulating the pursuit and conquest of the woman, it rises to a lively representational finale when sweating bodies, nerves aroused by violent exercise, drink, semi-nakedness, and contact with the opposite sex, end the dance in unrestrained bacchanal. The dexterity of the woman consists in moving the hips voluptuously and harmo-

niously while keeping the rest of the body almost immobile except for short steps in time with the drum beat or a light vibration
in the arched arms whose hands hold the corners of a handkerchief or raise the skirt in accordance with the erotic excitement
of the dance. This partial movement is the principal characteristic of the tango. The play of the hips depends upon abdominal
contractions which approximate the *danse du ventre,* and the total
effect is erotic stimulation."

All this is traceable to Africa. The other end of its trajectory
is, of course, discernible in the gyrations of our own youth. In
Cuba it is interesting to see how this dance is modified by the
company it keeps. At the Casino it is heavily Hollywood, and the
dancers, lush with African blood, are ivory-toned, slimmed down
to the white man's taste, and studiedly aware. Along the beach
of Marianao where they still dance for tourists, they are less expensive, darker in tone, more violent in gesture. They even smile
as though they wanted to, or sulk or rage. But these are selected
girls, dressed in their long ruffled trains cut high on the thigh
and low on the bosom, decked with beads, and dancing for tourists. One may drop in on dances in Negro quarters where people
are dancing for their own amusement, not expecting white visitors, where they do not know anything about "typical Cuban
costumes," and where old folks generally dance with more fun
and more abandon than the young.

To see dances done ceremonially as they originally were in
Africa is very difficult. Cubans, both blacks and whites, fear that
the United States will get the impression that their country is all
Negro and altogether dominated by black magic. But it is fairly
easy to see some of the modern manifestations of the ancient
African beliefs. Young Cuban intellectuals, all devoted disciples
of Dr. Ortiz, know certain shrines, certain *brujos.*

I was taken one night across the star-spangled bay to Regla,
said to be a center of witchcraft. In a quiet street we knocked on
a door in a house-high wall. A long wait, and then, away inside, a

voice and footsteps. The door was opened by a man of clear brown color, very clean, and of light smooth movement. He led us across a patio damp and springy underfoot, rustling with night sounds, and smelling of unseen flowers. A flashlight revealed how moss covered brick copings and ran up the heavy trunk of a ceiba tree. In its crotch perched a small crude statue of Jesus, and at its foot lay a collection of cock-feathers, which have to do with an African cult much older than the worship of Jesus.

The house was dark inside, but our host soon had it garishly lit with an unshaded electric bulb. It was a clean room furnished only with shrines like Catholic altars set in wall niches or built up on plain wooden tables. Each one held a Catholic saint who was also an African deity. Our host pointed out that each one was dressed in a different color and adorned with flowers and candles to match. Santa Bárbara, with her sword, was in red. The Virgin del Cobre's niche was white. That of San Lázaro, no special color. Each, he explained, was invoked for special needs and worshiped at different seasons. He kept insisting that it was all Catholic, though small crude images appeared alongside the saints, as did cock-feathers and shells. The visit was pleasant, but meaningless. Later I found many explanations in Dr. Ortiz's book.

The Virgin del Cobre, as also several other virgins, seems to enjoy a privileged cult as did Obatalá, the superior Yorubá *orisha*, deity. As the Africans believed in an overall deity who was almost never directly invoked, but was approached through lesser *orishas*, the transition from Yorubá to Catholic beliefs was easy. Ignorant slaves, offered the visible symbols of Catholicism, found many things they were used to. They understood that saints had their specialities, and *cofradías*, societies, of the faithful to attend them. They wore fetiches as Catholics wear scapularies. They, like Catholics, recognized and struggled against ill-disposed spirits. But Dr. Ortiz has found nothing to indicate that Africans dealt with the Devil as Europeans did in witchcraft, riding off on broomsticks to meet him or selling out as Faust did. In African witchcraft the spirit is invoked for both good and bad ends; often the evil done is incidental, as when a pain is transferred from a friend to an enemy.

Santa Bárbara is identified with Shangó, an African god of thunder and lightning, who inhabits a palace with bronze doors and showers the earth with meteors. As Santa Bárbara is also invoked against thunder and lightning, bears a sword, and is often shown in a palace like Shangó's, the identification of African god with Catholic saint was easy. The difference in sex is lightly disposed of by the *brujos;* Shangó is Santa Bárbara *macho,* male. In Africa Shangó was hermaphroditic.

I had a personal experience with Santa Bárbara-Shangó, who is working for me right now. The *bruja,* whom I am not permitted to name or locate, took me into a back room where there were altars to San Lázaro (Babalú Ayé), the Merced (Obatalá), and Santa Bárbara. In front of Santa Bárbara was laid a square of red satin, badly worn, and two candles were stuck to the floor. A glass of water stood in front of one candle. The altar itself, built in steps, was bedecked with white and red flowers, many candles, and the image of the saint robed in red.

The *bruja* squatted on the floor. Crossing herself, kissing her thumb, and muttering prayers, she cast a handful of shells on the red satin square. Among them were several that showed carving and one worn coin, *"antiquísimo, Africano."* Over and over she cast them, asking me questions meanwhile. I proved difficult. I could think of no enemies who wished me ill and no diseases that threatened me. No fears assailed me. But at last she got it. I was planning to leave on Sunday. Dreadful! Again she scooped up and cast the little shells muttering with greater urgency, thrusting out her thick lips, wiping her face with her hands in dire despair.

*"Ay! Vieja,"* she wailed, "not Sunday! For the love of God, not Sunday!" Then, turning from me to the saint, she muttered

appeals, crying aloud, "San-ta Bár-bara, San-ta Bár-bara," in a tone to break your heart. Now she was wringing her hands, trying the shells over and over again, rolling her eyes, going rigid, saying words not Spanish. Every time the shells fell into the pattern of a road blocked by danger. She pointed that out; it was unmistakable.

Then, as I remained obdurate about not trying to change plane reservations as she advised, the *bruja* changed her tactics. Now she was casting her shells feverishly, mumbling strange words, scooping and casting, finding always the pattern of that blocked and dangerous road. She fell then into a cataleptic pose, arms and legs rigid, head thrown back, eyes rolled inward, mouth half open. She seemed to be listening intently. I felt altogether forgotten.

The *bruja* came back finally from her trance and reported that Santa Bárbara said that with the sacrifice of a red cock, the passing of more money, the gift to me of a real amber necklace from Africa, all might yet be well.

The *bruja* then summoned her daughter, requisitioned three dollars from me, and sent the girl off to buy the cock. Then she took off her shoes and really got to work. The altar's base was now revealed as a cupboard from which she took a calabash. Muttering the while, she filled the gourd with water, added a dash of perfume, and floated in it a rose and a lily taken from the altar. She also set out a flat dish and laid in it the amber necklace, the shells and coin, and a black wet rock. The daughter returned to report no red cocks available. This added a complication, but the child was sent forth again and the *bruja* visited the other two altars invoking their aid. From San Lázaro's cupboard she extracted a flat dish filled with sand or ashes and set it there.

By this time the room was so filled with magic vibrations that my sponsor, summoned for consultation, was not allowed to enter until a string of ancient African beads had been wound around his arm as a protection. But the daughter entered freely bringing a cock of mottled plumage.

We were now ready for the great final effort. Grabbing the cock by the legs and wings, the *bruja* flourished him before the saint and applied him to my body. Praying unceasingly, she rubbed my head with the bird, then my back and front, arms and legs to the feet. All the time she was crying "Santa Bár-bara! Santa Bár-bara!" beseeching the saint. Then suddenly she would drop her voice an octave into a tone of harsh command and thunder: "Shangó!" It seemed that one could call on the African deity to end all this nonsense and come across, though the Christian saint required supplication. "Shangó! Shangó!" waving the cock on high before the image.

When she was well worked up, she snatched out his breast feathers in big handfuls and piled them on the amber necklace in the dish and around it. The cock let out a couple of squawks, his last. For as deftly as a barman drawing a cork, the *bruja* was quietly twisting off his head. Like one decanting a bottle, and without losing a drop, she poured the thick warm blood over the beads and shells in the dish. She laid the dead head alongside and quickly transferred the cock's body to that ready dish in front of San Lázaro. This mottled cock was the cock of San Lázaro, not of Santa Bárbara. It had been a complicated rite indeed and justifiable only because my determination to leave on Sunday had demanded the utmost speed.

I returned the amber, suggesting that it remain there to keep me under the protection of the saint and the perhaps more powerful Shangó. The coin I kept. It turned out to be a United States dime minted in 1879. Nice of the Catholic Santa Bárbara and the African Shangó to honor it. Obviously they do; my journey, so portentous in anticipation, was easy and smooth.

Dr. Ortiz offers an explanation for the persistence of these pagan customs in a Catholic country. "Masters of slaves," he writes, "preferred the voodoo to the doctrines of Jesus with their talk of equality and redemption, which might rouse a social ferment they preferred to avoid." Even the clergy, he implies, were content with superficial efforts — baptism and the teaching of a few prayers which the Negro promptly turned to the uses of his magic. "Enough to calm the consciences of the slave-owners; no more." The situation has not changed much today, according to Dr. Ortiz. Unlike the United States, Cuba has no Negro churches and only one Negro priest, whose ordination was postponed for ten years while he was sent to study in Rome and in France. Finally ordained in 1942, he was given a small country parish where presumably he serves his people well.

Dr. Ortiz finds Cuba irreligious on the whole, with no "general, popular, or official creed." This is understandable in view of the Church's allegiance to the crown of Spain during the wars of independence.

Most Cubans of whatever color remember the family *mambí*; there is much seeking for spiritual sustenance along unorthodox lines. An editor who talked Theosophy told me I looked like Annie Besant. In Bayamo a lady invited me to attend a *spiritista* meeting.

We boarded a bus loaded to capacity and my *señora* pointed out two men of indeterminate color as mediums. But this was not Negro paganism; it was similar to many such cults as California knows. During the long ride to Monte Oscuro I had time to learn the story of that shrine's founding by an ordinary, bibulous and profane muleteer. My *señora* had known him then and she had heard him tell how he was moved to prayer at the bedside of a sick daughter. When she got well he saw the light and began to preach. He adopted no cult, joined no church; he just preached that keeping the soul pure would bring all good, physical and material as well as spiritual.

Monte Oscuro was a collection of whitewashed thatched huts with one large wall-less one for the meeting place. Inside, a hundred people were weaving back and forth in a half dance, chanting. Among them certain men and women were working cures, running their hands along the outlines of a body without touching it and jerking away the evil with a loud grunt. The patients sometimes shook and cried out in primitive ecstasy. They were people of all classes. One business man (later I learned that he was a member of the Lions Club) stood among seven young women all working hard on the air around him. His son, a tall fine-looking lad, came to ask me if I believed in immortality; it seemed a matter of great importance to him. A woman nicely dressed in a green sport suit had come from Santiago to seek sanity for her son, a fifteen-year-old too ill to come himself.

At one end of the shelter sat the leader, a muscular graying mulatto in clean white. Every worshiper came to him to take his hand, to spin round under it three times, to mutter some words, and retire. The leader, carrying on a conversation with me, would rise, absently spin his parishioner around, reply in a mumble, and reseat himself without losing the current of his talk. Several other leaders sat behind tables passing out those spins and mumbles. There was a more or less formal ceremony finally, and a school-teacherish woman made a long talk.

In the leader's house he told his story. When his prayer for his daughter was answered, he began to cure. He has cured many cases of insanity, rickets, malaria, rheumatism, and women's special ills. He lives now in a nice *bohío*, where thousands of people come to pray and be cured. The man is quietly sincere, he makes no claim to special powers; even his gift for magnetizing water so it can be taken to other places to make cures is, he says, nothing any believer cannot do.

It was a strange group to find in the midst of a Catholic country, performing the sort of miracles that Catholic shrines perform — a group of seekers whom the Catholic church and all the Protestant missionaries had missed. An old *ñañigo* complained that these *spiritistas* are aping old African rites and corrupting them.

274

Dr. Ortiz cites many similar instances, and also proof that Africa has more directly influenced modern Christian Cuba. Many whites turn to African *brujos* for services their own religion does not provide. Buyers of love potions and potions to harm a hated rival seek the *brujo*. He is also the fortune-teller and the prognosticator. Dr. Ortiz believes that whites as much as Negroes keep the ancient superstitions alive, and are as responsible for the alleged connection between crime and *brujería*. All the badness in Cuba's underworld was not African any more than all the immigration was. Criminal elements came from Spain and all of Europe, even from Asia. The Spanish army, "always anti-social," contributed to Cuba's vice, especially in the cities. Indeed it seems likely that actual crime resulted from witch doctoring only incidentally, as clever and wicked men used the ancient beliefs to hide their nefarious deeds or as *brujos* were betrayed into crime for purposes they considered good.

The *brujo* in his more primitive guise is both priest and doctor. The suppliant or patient visits him, provides a feast for the spirits, and generally pays a fee. Dr. Ortiz has not found these charges excessive. Only food known in Africa is suitable; white man's food would not please the spirits or help to drive away the "doubles," ghosts who haunt the living and who may do harm. All sorts of oddities are used: shells, hair, ashes, teeth or bones, excrement, seeds, leaves, feathers, snakes, scorpions, and articles belonging to the patient or the suspected cause of the disturbance. And the ceremony takes place in the presence of the suitable Catholic saint.

Such a ceremony starts with the cleansing of the patient. This may demand nakedness, and as the patient is often a woman, the authorities do not look upon such practices with the clear eye of the anthropologist. It is necessary to determine what spirit is involved and to invoke him directly. Sometimes he can be lured to leave marks in scattered ashes, to move strategically placed articles, or to influence the movement of a pendulum in the *bru-*

*jo*'s hand. Driving him out generally requires noise, which the African drums and rattles provide, often accompanying the voices. Such a ceremony in time works itself up into an orgy. The patient or another may *dar el santo,* which in our country is called getting religion. In that case she throws herself into wild contortions, speaks with tongues, foams at the mouth, draws others in after her until the whole group is wildly stamping, shouting, singing, seeking release. Altogether very like certain Protestant revivals or Holy Roller ceremonies.

Such affairs are apt to be stopped by the police, as a whole neighborhood may well complain of drums all night with wild outbursts of screaming now and then. The police also keep an eye out for sacrifices. The cock, such as won Santa Bárbara-Shangó for me, is the most usual victim, but animals are sometimes used — goats, pigs, or lambs. The warm fresh blood from a living being is the desideratum. Naturally melodramatic tales are common. The making of charms and fetiches is also suspect, as graves have been violated to secure bones and as queer bundles of this and that can be used to frighten simple people out of their wits. The police have picked up so many that they have the best collection of fetiches and the most hair-raising tales.

Fetiches and charms are found in all sorts of places. Under trees thought to have powers for good or ill. On the banks of ponds or streams. Beside the path to the *bohío* of a *brujo* suspected of bewitching children. Under the palm thatch to protect a house. Ignorant Cubans live lives filled with fear; evil spirits haunt their dreams, threaten health, wealth, life itself; and they spend much in both cash and peace of mind to fend off these dangers. Nicolás Guillén, the poet who has best expressed the primitive Negro mind in the modern world, has written a poem that Eusebia Cosme reads with drama to make you shiver. It deals with the pitiful effort of a Negro mother to save her child from a water demon. I quote some of its stanzas from the translation of Ben Frederic Carruthers.

The Rape of the Mulatas, *by Carlos Enríquez*

The Farm, by Rafael Moreno

Ñeque, away with the ñeque!
Demon, away with the demon!

Beneath the cry of stars above,
Beneath a reddish moon afire,
The river growls among the rocks;
Its unseen claws inquire
And shake the archéd span
And strangle careless man.

Ah, my child of pure black skin,
They will devour you,
They'll drink your blood,
Suck dry your veins too,
And close your bright eyes,
Those eyes that shine like pearls!
Fly, for the monster will kill you!
Fly, for he lurks in the swirls!
My darling little baby boy,
May his neck-charm save my boy . . . !
Ñeque, away with the ñeque!
Demon, away with the demon!
But Shangó would not have it so. . . .
A claw from depths stretched out
To seize him . . . a Demon
Smashed the helpless skull about,
Plucked out the shining eyes,
Tore white teeth from bleeding jaws.
The knotted limbs and twisted arms
Were works of these same iron claws.

Any day's newspaper may carry the story of a man who
thought his wife was bewitched and so killed the *brujo*. Or of a

whole family thrown into hysterical panic and even insanity because a neighbor, coveting their property, is paralyzing their will to such a point that they do not milk their cow, feed their chickens or pigs, gather their crops, or prepare food. Or of a young woman, faithfully following the *brujo*'s directions, who is slowly poisoning a rival in love, or poisoning herself with herb messes prescribed to bring the faithless lover back. Such cases often reach the courts, which are hard put to it to find suitably dignified legal language to describe the violations or suitable punishment for the criminals.

African customs pleasanter than witchcraft survive in *las comparsas*. *Comparsas* are groups of masked merrymakers, suggestive of carnival. But unlike carnival, Havana's spring festival does not occur on Shrove Tuesday, Mardi Gras, but on five successive Saturday nights beginning just before Lent. It is unique in that the *comparsas* are composed entirely of colored people who show up brilliantly as designers, costumers, directors, dancers, and pantomimics. The custom goes back to slavery days when slaves were allowed one day of release a year, *día de los reyes* (Kings' Day), our Twelfth Night, and perhaps the Roman Saturnalia. Negro groups dressed and masked as though in Africa went through the streets of the town, dancing their traditional measures, singing their ancestral songs to the accompaniment of drums and rattles. At the *ayuntamiento* the Governor himself appeared to throw them coins from the palace balcony. The custom continued after Cuba won her independence, but in time it became almost a menace. The *comparsas*, neighborhood gangs, developed a rivalry that sometimes resulted in gory clashes.

Meanwhile white Cubans, aping Nice and New Orleans, were making the Saturday processions affairs of high society and crowding the Negroes back into the poor districts. The Prado and the Malecón were gay, then, with processions of *volantas*, carriages, and four-horse coaches, and later with cars and floats, flower-decked and filled with gorgeously costumed "best people." Havana was proving herself white and European, but she was losing irreplaceable primitive ceremonies such as our Southwest has found well worth preserving not only as anthropological data but as tourist attractions.

Happily in 1946, after the war's recess, Havana's *comparsas* appeared again sponsored by such diverse godparents as Dr. Ortiz, wishing to preserve old customs, the Tourist Commission, and certain merchants, who had heard that tourists liked such things. Unhappily, several commercial houses had been able to force themselves onto the scene with huge puppets, advertising Coca Cola, Hatuey ices, milk, and general merchandise. They spoiled the effect, and should be forgotten. It is to be hoped that they will be omitted later.

Long before the scheduled hour of nine, the Prado, the Parque Central, and the bleachers in front of the Capitol were massed with people and patrolled by police. Police on foot, pushing. Police on motorcycles swooping in curves and scooting up and down. Police issuing orders and quietly admitting friends inside the lines. The people were pleasant, munching sweets, tipping pop bottles, rising from curb to wall to window to roof in a mosaic of dark and light with splotches of colors. Street lamps glowed among the trees. Then, far up the Prado, came moving constellations of colored lights. *Las Comparsas!*

Every group was beautiful or otherwise effective, showing good direction and long training. Every *comparsa* of from fifty to a hundred people came along in two files, stepping in the conga rhythm to African drums and modern brass. Ahead of each group danced a banner giving its name and the date of its founding; some of them are as much as a hundred years old. Other men bore two *farolas,* elaborate candelabra on tall poles, glowing with colored lights; these were the constellations we had seen far up the Prado. An occasional bearer was so skillful that he could balance his long pole in its pouch without touching it, dancing the step, now right, now left. Next came the featured dancers, soloists or couples, more striking in costume than the chorus, freer in step and form, but never losing the beat. Even the director, also in costume, dancing from point to point, keeping everybody in line, calling the changes, never lost step. Nor did the comics who aroused gusts of laughter along the march. The *comparsas* came well spaced to give each group time and room for its evolutions and to show off the varied costumes. The entire procession was given unity by that continuing thread of the conga beat, sung and danced as well as played on drum and cornet. The groups came in no apparent orderly sequence, but it was easy to recognize certain types.

*El Alacrán* (the scorpion) and *El Majá* (Cuba's boa) suggest that these symbols were originally African clan totems. The dancers were dressed like slaves, women in looped-up calico skirts and straw hats, men in rolled-up trousers, all with tin cups and plates tied to their belts. The *Majá* group had their snake and made much sport of it, pantomiming fear and worship. Several other *comparsas* showed amazing willingness to portray the Negro's most tragic experience as slaves. *Las Lavanderas* (the washerwomen), with little wooden tubs filled with suds of cotton on their heads, and *Los Macheteros*, wielding *machetes* as in the canefields. Almost too painful were the slave-driver, who danced in among these groups cracking a long vicious whip, the other white man with a gun, and especially *el cimarrón* (the wild runaway slave). More amusing was *el sereno* (the night watchman) with his lantern and dog. Taking off the forever stupid *gallego*, he won laughter and applause when he removed his shoes to ease his aching feet, and when he chased an equally dull Chinaman with flat baskets of vegetables. All this seemed spontaneous, but was part of the dance.

A prouder picture of Cuba's past came along in *Los Mambises*, dressed as their own ancestors may have been, in unfinished straw hats fringed out, ragged trousers, open shirts or none, with a few guns and many *machetes*, swinging. Their *farola* was

Cuba's single star; they carried the flag of the revolution and sang *La Bayamesa*, miraculously accommodated to the conga rhythm. With them came their women as they followed in the war, keeping step, supporting their men.

The other *comparsas*, more expensively and elaborately costumed, but perhaps less interesting, were patent copies of what white folks had done. *Las Jardineras* (the gardeners) flouncing short flowered skirts, bearing baskets of flowers, and squired by men in dark velvet with sleeves and headkerchiefs of dull gold. Their featured dancers wore diaphanous white embroidered with bouquets. *Los Turcos* were Turks indeed in long bloomers, fezzes, and veils. Their color scheme was built on white with accents of pastel shades, most effective against the colored skins. It is always a marvel to see how many shades of dark skin there are. Pale flower tones, softer, deeper beige, warm chocolate, and finally dull black. Some dancers were in shiny artificial black face; perhaps white people. One man with *Las Jardineras* was clearly white: a *gallego*, so a Cuban said. But these were rare. *Las Comparsas* present an all-colored show. Now and then I suspected a burlesque of whites, as when *Los Marqueses* came along in velvet coats and powdered wigs, with ladies in pink and blue hooped skirts. They moved in the figures of the minuet quite as elegantly as Cuba's old marquis might have done, but always in that old African beat.

*Las Sultanas*, most costly and gorgeous and a favorite for the first prize, came singing: "Good-bye, Mamá, Good-bye, Papá, I'm off to the harem, and I'll not be home until morning!" Men in scarlet and white, women in pale blue and pink, they presented the most elaborate and almost too long ballet. Among their soloists was a pale brown girl with midriff showing between silver bra and white trousers, and a huge silver headdress as intricate as a snowflake. She danced alone or with a tall statuesquely draped man, equally good. Untiring, graceful, swirling like mist, leaping into high comedy, chasing each other, disappearing and reappearing among the others, they won repeated applause as they would have won it from any audience in the world.

The second night I saw the *comparsas,* eighteen groups appeared. Cubans said there would be more before the last Saturday. Perhaps Rio de Janeiro's carnival may equal this in beauty. As the creation of a special group and the persistence of an ancient observance with roots in Africa as well as in colonial and revolutionary Cuba, Havana's *comparsas* are unrivaled. One can only hope that the city authorities will realize what a priceless asset they have and keep it as clear and distinguished as it now is.

## SOPHISTICATED CUBA

SOPHISTICATED Cuba is where you find it.

It is a smart cosmopolitan society composed of diplomats from all the world and Cubans who have known them at home. It is also people careless of society but interested in the intellectual, political, and artistic currents of as wide a sphere. And it is the growing group of Cubans, mostly young, who are making significant contributions to a changing world in various fields. These groups overlap, interplay, meet in many places and for various purposes, or bypass each other in ignorance or disdain as such groups always do.

Society is to be met at the Yacht Club by day and the Casino by night. During working hours the men are in offices or banks. Cuban men, who, under Spain, could not soil their aristocratic hands with trade, are now ardent supporters of a Chamber of Commerce, members of Rotary and Lions clubs, and active in many businesses. They also support the clubs whose imposing stone edifices line the best streets. The older ones sit there most of the day discussing politics, business, and scandal. In the late afternoon the younger, busier members drop in for the before-dinner apéritif, which often fills the gap between golf, tennis, or swimming, and the eight o'clock dinner.

A smart matron said to me: "We like the American women, but their hours are so odd that we prefer to play bridge without them. They always want to stop at six o'clock. And we have nothing to do between six and eight, while our men are at the clubs."

Havana's social season is in the winter. As that is tourist season too, visitors have the benefit of the best music, theater, and entertaining. In the summer, society moves northward. Cubans know all the resorts from Maine to North Carolina and they pause on the way for shopping in New York. Those who do not go so far afield retire to the family plantation and enjoy inter-*finca* visiting much as in the old days. Or they visit El Varadero, that splendid sweep of gently shelving beach along the peninsula that encloses the Bahía de Cárdenas. The DuPonts have a home there, as do many wealthy Cubans, and the hotels are all "clubs" to which many unintroduced visitors have access, but which graciously refuse guests of too-pronounced pigmentation. Varadero is warm enough for any northerner in the winter. Cubans find its caressing breezes too chill until Holy Week opens the correct season. Then the seventy-five mile road from Havana out through Matanzas hums with fine cars, the beach blossoms with striped parasols, and the sea comes alive with the white sails of yachts.

Cuban hostesses, in town or country, carry on the old house-keeping tradition. Husbands' careers are advanced, distinguished visitors entertained, children's interests kept paramount. Every matron, complaining of how servants have degenerated, keeps several, preferably Jamaicans or *gallegos*. Even family meals are on a lavish scale and every *cubana* cherishes her special recipes. Food is forever important, as it must be in a land so providentially endowed with every good thing to eat.

The sea is dragged and plumbed daily by fishing, crabbing,

and lobstering fleets whose take goes into the pan or the pot still sparkling with brine. Served with sliced limes or in complicated sauces flavored with herbs or wines, they are luscious beyond belief. Cuba's beef lacks the glory of a steak in Buenos Aires, perhaps; but as in every country the native stew is superlative. In Cuba it is *ajiaco*. Based on pork and jerky, *ajiaco* includes all Cuba's natives: *yuca, malanga,* yams, bananas, squash, corn on the cob, and pepper. But it is the hidden herbs and spices and the long slow simmering that make *ajiaco* a noble dish in any setting.

Naturally tropical fruits abound. Oriente claims to produce the best mangoes in the world. Hawaii or Guatemala would have an argument on pineapples. Texas's delta region extols its grapefruit as "almost as good as those from the Isle of Pines." Homegrown coffee is still preferred by gourmets, and Cuban rum appears in many guises besides the Bacardí cocktail.

Señora Blanche de Baralt, who has written the essential book, *Cuban Cookery (Including Cuban Drinks)*, says that drinking fresh fruit juices was a custom in the island long before the United States had discovered how refreshing they could be. Crushed pineapple, *guanábana,* orange, mango, papaya, cocoanut milk, with plenty of sugar, singly or in combination are sold everywhere from pushcarts to the best refreshment parlors. And many a tall cooling and exciting drink is compounded of fruit juices with judicious splashes of native rum or imported liquors.

Obviously, eating and drinking in Havana are one of the world's most sophisticated pleasures. Ladies take one to El Patio on the Prado, which, like the best hotels, serves a cautious menu sure to please tourists, or to El Paris, which features *pargo*, redsnapper, with a delicate lime and almond sauce. Men are more likely to suggest La Florida or La Zaragonzana, both famous for shell fish. La Zaragonzana will produce a marvelous turtle soup for one who knows. El Templete offers a most savory *arroz con mariscos,* rice with shell fish, and *paella,* an all-inclusive stew based on chicken. Tourists must sit at El Dorado's sidewalk tables where three female orchestras vie for attention, and drive out to Río Cristal on the road to the airport. There is no river there, but plenty of tiling and synthetic atmosphere. Its pride is *arroz con pollo,* and rice with black beans, amusingly called *moros y cristianos.* Where the Malecón crosses the Prado, is El Club Vasco, where Basque food is expertly cooked and simply served. It is a club, but gaining admission is a trick every Cuban knows. Farther out the Malecón, on the Plaza Maceo, is Vista Alegre, a happy view indeed of the blue Gulf.

*Los intelectuales,* wishing to show you the real Havana, make for Los Dos Hermanos, where the liquor is good, the food superlative, and the entertainment in watching the people. There are many such places along the waterfront and out in Marianao. And, as if Cuban food could ever pall, there are numberless French, Spanish, and Italian restaurants, and back of the capitol in the Chinese quarters, places where real Chinese food is served. All in all, Cuba's gift for living and enjoying it is nowhere more apparent than in the way her people eat, with leisure and good taste, her delicate and subtle dishes.

Cuban society women, despite the ornamental effect they achieve, are not only concerned with food and entertaining. Nor are they the cloistered, homekeeping Latin women of tradition. Much of the breath of freedom that blows through Cuba seems to be stirred by women. They are so easily busy, so unfettered compared with women in other Latin lands. This may be due to the numbers of them who have been educated in the States. But in one regard at least feminism is farther advanced in Cuba than among the Anglo-Saxons. A *cubana* is known all her life by her own name. It is old Spanish custom for a married woman to retain her father's name, adding her husband's surname. She then is Señora Leida Zarabia de González. She does not use her husband's given name. A *cubana,* referred to in New York as Señora Pedro Montoya, cried: "I am Carmela Ortiz de Montoya. I am never, never Mrs. Pedro!" In Cuba the husband's name is often quite neglected. Ask for the architect Señora de Baralt and there may be some doubt; but Lillian Mederos is known at once as herself.

The Spanish and Catholic tradition also produced the solicitous mistress and the charitable lady. Cuban women work through sodalities, carry the real work of the *patronatos*, conduct drives for every good cause, and are ready any day to join a new association.

The Lyceum and Lawn Tennis Club, a union of two older organizations, best exemplifies how Cuba's fashionable women are turning from traditional charity to more modern social service. The club is housed in a spacious building that is the work of Doctora Lillian Mederos. It is a busy place, day and evening. Classes in everything from equitation to woodcarving, and including Russian, cookery, dietetics and bridge. Exhibts of paintings by Cuban and foreign artists and lectures on art. Concerts and lectures on music. Library and night school for all people in the neighborhood attracts many poor folks. These busy women were instrumental in getting the University to establish the School for Social Service, which still depends upon support from the Lyceum and the co-operation of professors who receive no pay for their lectures. Much of this socially conscious activity is due to the efforts of Elena Mederos de Gonzáles, who spends hours a day at the Lyceum and consistently refuses any office.

The same women who support the Lyceum and Tennis Club, support also La Sociedad Pro-Arte Musical, which conducts monthly concerts and a ballet and presents opera and concerts. Most notable European and North American musicians have appeared in the handsome auditorium, also designed by Lillian Mederos. The women are proud that their financial reputation is so good that every bank in Havana bid for the loan. Men may be members, but never directors of SPAM. One of them suggested that those initials might stand of *Sin Pantalones Andamos Mejor;* without trousers we get along better.

The most ambitious musical venture is El Patronato Pro-Musica Sinfónica, government sponsored, which maintains ninety musicians and brings in foreign conductors. Erich Kleiber, conductor for several years, inaugurated Sunday morning concerts at lowered prices. The contrast with the Monday evening social function is delightful. On Sunday morning one sits among quietly dressed people, many young, many of color, many following the score. On Monday evening the auditorium offers a brilliant clothes show with imported models, diamonds and emeralds, silver fox and chinchilla. A lady said: "Americans think we are silly to wear furs, but we like outdoor entertaining — the smartest New Year's party is outdoors at the Country Club — and of course we *need* furs."

Frequently the orchestra presents the work of Cuban composers. Cuba has a long musical history beginning in the colonial era when music, like all culture, followed Europe closely. Only lately have Cuban composers discovered the riches of their African rhythms, themes, and instruments. Alone in the Americas, Cuba has no Indian coloration: her primitive culture is Negro. Dr. Ortiz has noted that slaves in Cuba did not compose religious songs comparable to our spirituals. This he attributes to the fact that the Protestant congregation sings while the Catholic does not. The Cuban Negro's life was apart from the church; his songs, *sones*, were folksongs with the accompaniment of barbaric instruments. A variety of drums and rattles of seed-filled gourds, the *maracas* that every tourist buys, and notched sticks rubbed together. In Negro rites only the players sing, though all may join and new stanzas are added endlessly.

The appearances of these Negro themes and tonal patterns in serious music is very modern. Amadeo Roldán and Alejandro García Caturla, the first to dare them, were both born in the twentieth century. Roldán has used Negro percussion instruments in symphonies that recreate much of the counter rhythmic effects of the *son*. Caturla, perhaps more original, uses dissonances as violent as tropical hurricanes, as savage as the African terrors they recount. Unlike Roldán, he depends upon conventional instruments for his effects. His *Rumba y Yamba-O, Mito Manué* and various chorals have been presented with success both in the United States and in Europe. Considered queer at the beginning, these men have given even Europeanized Cubans a pride in their native art and won acclaim for it abroad. Caturla was all-Caucasian of a type that might have been Scandinavian; yet he was all Cuban in that his truest expression partook of both Cuba's cultures. Perhaps the Cuban best known in the United States is Ernesto Lecuona, whose *Malagueña, Siboney*, and *Say Si Si* are so hummable. Accepted also as a serious artist, Señor Lecuona considers Afro-Cuban music the true expression of the Cuban soul as gypsy music is of the soul of Spain or of Hungary.

Lecuona, like Gilberto Valdez and other Cubans, has consciously crossed that invisible line between popular and classical music; like our own Gershwin his works are acceptable on serious programs and irresistible in night clubs. When Xavier Cugat, a Spaniard, heard the Casino's orchestra he took it bodily to New York — eleven men with infectious grins, ruffled sleeves, and African instruments. After that the rumba and the conga were part of our culture too, and Cuban musicians were names one knew. Henry Cowell, writing in the *New York Times*, calls Cuban music one of the freshest, most vigorous, and most important musical influences of the Americas.

Cuba also has a school of music that holds out against this rising tide of African influence, preferring the Spanish folk songs. Ignacio Cervantes, a master of classical forms, was the first to cultivate native themes. He wrote many *puntos cubanos* with rhythm based on the *punteo*, plunk, of the *guajiro's* three-stringed guitar. Cervantes's daughter sings them with nostalgic *cubanismo* in the Sevilla Biltmore's night club.

Today's most energetic exponents of this school are the Spaniards, Antonio Quevedo, editor of *Musicalia*, and his wife,

María Muñoz de Quevedo. Musicians of sound training, endless enthusiasm, and tireless in working for music in Cuba, these two conduct a school in addition to the magazine. Señora de Quevedo also goes out weekly to the Escuela Cívico-Militár to teach wriggling youngsters musical facts by rote and to train them in very good choral singing. Every Good Friday she conducts a chorus of over a hundred voices in the Cathedral. It is a lovely sacred concert with beautiful women in lacy mantillas against the organ pipes and the best of sacred music.

Composers who, like the Quevedos, prefer European to African tradition, are led by José Ardévol, a Spaniard, who tends toward neoclassicism rather than toward any native Cuban expression. He founded the Society of Chamber Music Concerts, which has presented may of his concertos, and he is followed by a school of younger men.

Theater shows less awareness than music of Cuba's background or her future. José Antonio Portuondo, a student of the social content of Cuban literature, names several dramatists who treat of the *guajiro* and the imperialist menace, but does not give them first importance. Oddly the predicament of the Negro in a white civilization has reached the New York theater before that of Havana. El Patronato del Teatro, in one season at least, presented more translations than Cuban plays. The two offered were *Suicidio* by Luis Amado Blanco and a historical theme in *El Camino del Cementerio* by Rafael Suárez Solís. Both writing and acting are a bit lush for the northern taste. Havana's little theater, however, presents an interesting season and is kept fresh and experimental by Dr. Luis A. Baralt of the University faculty.

At the other end of the dramatic arc is El Teatro Martí, fount of political burlesque and today's *choteo*. It is always crowded, but beginning perhaps to be threatened by the radio. Havana's air vibrates day and night to the unremitting screams of twenty stations, sixty per cent of whose output is commercial. Only by attentive listening can one disentangle the program from the soaps and soups, the furs and furniture that support them. As in our country, radio runs the scale from such topical skits as those of the *gallego* and the Negro to serious political comment, by way of sobbing serials as mournful as ours, to high-grade cultural programs often sponsored by the Department of Education. Notable among the political programs is that of Edith García Buchaga, a Communist leader, who appears on Mil Diez, 1,010, which offers the best, and very good, musical programs, both Cuban and foreign.

Newspapers and magazines reflect as catholic a taste. *Diario de la Marina* ranks with the best edited papers in the Americas. It is faithfully read by all the best people, who enjoy its sly digs at Uncle Sam and take comfort in its constant reiteration that every liberal proposal is Communist at heart. *El Mundo*, not as old but equally good journalistically, represents Cuba's democratic thinking and carries editorials and signed articles by Cubans who seem least afraid of the future. *Hoy*, the labor's daily, is frankly biased, and well worth reading. *El País*, the evening paper with all the scandals, is considered dangerous by some, amusing by others, and "just a political sheet" by the scholarly. They all read it.

All newspapers carry society pages, which charge for the mention of one's luncheon, cocktail, wedding, or baptismal party. Until recently Havana society had an arbiter, Enrique Fontanills of *Diario de la Marina*. Meticulous in the use of ancient Spanish titles, in the hyphenated name that connected one with the revolutionary hero or the erstwhile president, adroit with the phrase to make the scandal clear or to expose the climber, and free to mention commercial firms, Señor Fontanills made a fortune out of his column, *Las Habaneras*. The $10,000 trousseau came from such a *modista*, the creation the *condesa* wore from another, flowers or jewels were the work of Fulano de Tal. And Señor Fontanills was the recipient of unmentioned favors and unsolicited checks. An indispensable guest, he could always appear dressed by the best tailors, compliment favored ladies with the most expensive flowers, fans, or jewels, and he lived and died in a mansion designed by society's favorite architect. Those happy days passed with Señor Fontanills; commercial firms may no longer be named in the society columns.

Havana newspapers feature also the doings of women interested in politics, social movements, international affairs. Women writers present interviews with visitors, stories of Cuban women, both living and dead, and informed and critical political comment. Berta Arocena interviews all notable women and writes a thoughtful column in *El Mundo*. The far left is represented by Mariblanca Sabas Alomá, a social worker, whose social conscience leads her to write political articles, always trenchant and usually influential, wherever they appear.

Many newspaper writers also appear in magazines, which range from highly specialized scientific, philosophical, and international publications, like *Ultra, La Revista de Habana,* and *La Revista Bimestre,* to gay weeklies that are snatched from the stands as soon as they bloom forth. More tender plants are little magazines put out by young poets who have wearied in the struggle for political purity and social justice and taken refuge in "pure poetry." Still in the battle and first rate as a magazine is labor's *CTC,* biased, of course, but edited, written, printed, and illustrated well.

The magazine everybody reads is *Bohemia,* a lurid-looking weekly with lurid features, which carries also thoughtful articles by such liberal Cubans as Herminio Portell-Vilá, Emilio Roig de Leuchsenring, and Jorge Mañach. It reports honestly on labor, national and international, and it is generally anti-United States. Or rather pro-Cuban.

That Cubans read books as well as periodicals is plain to see in a stroll down Obispo and up O'Reilly streets. Here are book-stores, fresh with glass and paint, bright with color, well-stocked, and attended by well-informed salesmen. At night they roll down iron shutters and by day the streets are like a bazaar with open stalls and counters and shelves piled with books. The Cuban buys his books in paper backs and has them bound if he finds them worth keeping. Books go out of print fast. A work published two or three years ago may have disappeared entirely, but current works from all American countries, including our own, and many from Europe, are available. There are few lending libraries outside of clubs, but if one has the privilege of the University he can find almost anything there including the advice of the charming librarian, Dr. Jorge Aguayó, notable throughout the Americas.

Cuba's serious literature indicates that Cubans are interested in ideas: they write essays, psychological, philosophical, historical, political, and critical; and especially ever new and ever thicker volumes to add to the "hagiography of Martí." This is the phrase of José Antonio Portuondo, whose *El Contenido Social de la Literatura Cubana, The Social Content of Cuban Literature,* is very helpful. He dates the modern school from the revolt against Machado, which stirred all Cubans to their depths and made writers aware of the three unfortunate groups — the Negro, the *guajiro,* and the proletarian.

*Ecue Yamba-O,* by Alejo Carpentier, proves its author's sympathetic understanding of African lore; and *Pedro Blanco, el Negrero, The Slave Trader,* by Lino Novás Calvo, suggests Faulkner's influence in its harsh treatment of an ugly subject. Carlos Montenegro's *Hombres Sin Mujer, Men Without Woman,* Portuondo calls "the strongest Cuban novel of any period." Carlos Enríquez, the painter, has given "a fresh picture of country life, full of color and sensuality," in *Tilín García;* and Enrique Serpa's *Contrabando* is named as worthy for its detailed descriptions in spite of its Joycean monologues.

These novelists and others have also written short stories. Excellent tales appear constantly in magazines, but not many outstanding collections have yet been made. Portuondo lists one woman as of first rank in this form. Aurora Villar Buceta, he says, has caught "the silent sorrow of countrymen and city workers . . . in unforgettable short stories."

As the lyrical beauty of the Spanish must in every land, it has in Cuba produced modern poets concerned with their own emotions and the most musical expression of them. These are the untranslatables in any satisfying form; English and Spanish are too far apart. Among the artists of the classical forms, Portuondo mentions Eugenio Florit. But the Cuban poets who have aroused most admiration abroad are those who have written of *negrismo,* the cult of the Negro, which Portuondo compares with the *indianismo,* the cult of the Indian, of the other Americas.

These poets began with the picturesque, fascinated by the rhythm of Afro-Cuban chants and with the lawless charm of their half-hidden life. Portuondo lists several of this school, including Nicolás Guillén, whose *Motivos de Son,* published in 1930, first presented the *son* as literary material. Many of these men soon deepened their understanding and widened their scope to give voice to the Negro, whose position, even in tolerant Cuba, remains equivocal and trying. Among these may be listed Agustín Acosta, a white man whose poem *La Zafra* etches sharply the hopelessness of the cane cutter. Juan Marinello is a singularly Cuban figure. A tall distinguished gentleman of wealthy and conservative forebears, he carries out that tradition by being a poet and a senator. But he violates it rudely and shocks his society friends by being the outspoken leader of the Communist Party in Cuba. Happily Senator Marinello's gifts include a quiet sense of humor.

Regino Pedroso's poems of protest arose from his experiences as a factory worker in Havana, but took in the whole Cuban scene, with Soviet overtones.

*Vendremos de los campos, de las ciudades, de los talleres:*
*cada instrumento de trabajo será como un arma;*
*una sierra, una llave, un martillo, una hoz —*
*y ocuparemos la tierra como un ejército en marcha,*
*saludando a la vida con nuestro canto unánime!*

We shall come from the fields, from the towns, from the shops:
each working tool shall be a weapon;
a saw, a winch, a hammer, a scythe —
and we shall occupy the land like an army on the march,
saluting life with our unified song!

Young Cubans, like bright young people the world over, have
been deeply stirred by happenings in Europe. Havana filled up
with refugees, the Loyalists bound for Mexico, the Franco adherents for Argentina. Many of both faiths stayed in Cuba and
acquired followers. Many Cuban writers traveled and learned at
first hand what was going on. Among these was Nicolás Guillén,
who in his maturity left the picturesque aspects of the dark half
of his heritage to write with deep feeling of injustice, social as
well as racial.

Spanish as well as American critics rate Guillén the best Cuban poet of today, one of the best writing in Spanish. The titles
of his poems show his preoccupations. After a visit to Spain he
wrote: *España, Poema en Cuatro Angústias y Una Esperanza;*
*Spain, Poem in Four Anguishes and One Hope.* There are several with African names, written in the syncopated rhythm of the
African dance; many of these have been set to music and are
sung wherever Spanish is known. Disdain of senseless wealth
comes out in *Sones para Turistas, Songs for Tourists,* and *Can-
taliso en un Bar, Singing in a Bar.* The pitifulness of life for the
working Negro haunts Guillén, who has written many tender
lyrics on that theme; and the dilemma that all the world faces
has never been so well said as by Guillén in his *Balada de Los*

*Dos Abuelos,* Ballad of Two Grandfathers. I give bits of it in the
translation of Ben Frederic Carruthers who, with Langston
Hughes, is preparing a collection of Guillén's poems in English.

> Shadows which I alone see
> Overcast by my two grandfathers.
> Lance with bone-point,
> Drum of skin and wood;
> My black one.
> Wide-armored collar,
> Grey coat of mail:
> My white one.
> Bare of foot, hard of torso,
> Is my black one;
> Pupils of Antarctic glass,
> Have the eyes of my white one. . . .
>
> In me they meet.
>
> The two, same size,
> Beneath the high stars;
> The two, same size,
> Black anguish and white anguish,
> The two, same size,
> Shout, dream, weep and sing,
> Sing . . . Sing . . . Sing. . . .

The plastic arts, like poetry, venture to embody the African
content of Cuban life; perhaps because so many of the leading
artists have Negro blood. Sculptors have generally stuck closer
than painters to the conventional training of San Alejandro
Academy. Most of the statues which celebrate Cuba's leaders in
both war and peace are the sort one finds the world over. Juan

José Sicre y Vélez has felt ahead of that tradition in a thoughtful statue of Martí. José Núñez Booth, Juan Esnard, and Alfredo Lozano show the influence of the modern French more than of Cuba of any age. Teodoro Ramos Blanco, a mulatto quite unconventional in manner, besides making several large occasional pieces, has produced penetrating studies of his people as they struggle for a foothold in a white world.

Among the painters, some cling to the belief that Cuba is a Spanish land without mixture and paint heroes, *guajiros,* and historical scenes in that conviction. Notable among them is Esteban Valderrama, who has produced vigorous paintings of Cuba's hard earth.

It is the younger painters, both colored and white, who have expressed Cuba in a more general sense. They have painted a land terrorized by hurricanes and outlaws, dominated by the sea, by palms stirred or tormented by winds, by spreading ceibas and mangroves with contorted roots. They have dared to show Cubans living in dire poverty or in tasteless middle-class homes. Most of these young painters have studied abroad — in Madrid or Paris or as exiles in Mexico, where one learns respect for one's own backyard. In New York many have won critical approval that has helped to give them standing at home. There are almost as many styles of painting as there are painters, and they are all marked by vigor, vivid or strange color, and excitement of theme.

Artists are rated according to personal taste, but several may be mentioned. Amelia Paláez de Casal, the outstanding woman, shows that she has studied with Picasso and Braque, but she seems Cuban for all that in her use of daring color.

Fidelio Ponce de León, who seldom shows his face by day, is a character almost as weird as his paintings of string bean figures, wispy, wind-blown, but with an almost hypnotic fascination. His palette is strangely muted for a Cuban, off-color yellows, yellow-greens, grays, and mauves, but with it he produces

striking effects. A mysterious unknown person, Ponce has won
prizes, been acclaimed by critics, and sold well. He continues to
live as a poverty-stricken waif.

The Museum of Modern Art, at the time of its first showing of
Cuban painters in 1943, nominated Mario Carreño "the most
versatile, learned, and courageous of the new generation." An
all-white of the privileged group, Carreño worked in Europe and
in Mexico and returned to Cuba with the fresh eye of the foreigner and the knowledge of the native. Scorning conventional
paint, he used Duco, which he splashed on freely and with fine
African abandon and rhythm. All his work shows this ability to
break with tradition, though sometimes one feels a sense of stri-
dency in his convoluted figures and crowded canvases.

Another who paints the terrors of Cuban life and history is
Carlos Enríquez, whose shadowy figures of men and wild horses
caught in swirling mists are like evocations of the *mambí* in the
*manigua.*

A gentler side of Cuban life is painted by René Portocarrero,
who knows well the proper home and the church and who paints
with sensuousness of color and design not lacking in humor.
Portocarrero has never left Cuba.

Felipe Orlando and Mariano Rodríguez, who paint also the
Cuban scene, have been instrumental in promoting open air
shows, and a free school of painting and sculpture. Rodríguez,
who signs his name as Mariano, is notable for the vigor with
which he has painted men and cocks, but mostly cocks. One, *El
Gallo Pintado* (*The Painted Cock*), is also the very apotheosis of
masculine pride and vigor — and a little funny.

Funny too are Cundo Bermúdez's pictures of middle-class Cubans. *El Balcón* shows a couple rocking in bentwood chairs, un-
concerned with the lovely scene outside their shutters and grilled
balcony. And his *Barber Shop,* lush in color as a Venetian scene,
is full of humor.

These are by no means the lot; they are merely representative of the painting being done in Cuba. Trained in good schools, influenced by the greatest painters of France or of Mexico, these men paint the Cuban scene. The one who seems to use best his discipline and creative skill not to paint Cuba, but as a Cuban painting, is Wilfredo Lam.

I saw him first at a meeting of a newly-formed Cuban-Soviet Cultural Association. The company included the same intellectuals who form other similar groups in Havana, met again to dedicate yet another society to the proposition that through culture may come mutual understanding and global amity. As in all such groups in Cuba, these well-dressed and intelligent people were of all colors from ruddy white to dark Negro. What they said was not half so interesting as the speakers, who talked as fast as the fizzing of soda from a bottle, gesticulated wildly, tripped each other up on minor points, joking and advancing each his pet project — music, painting, education, or schools for the illiterate. Then one rose who was different.

Tall, dark and slim, he moved with the grace of leashed strength, and what he said was clear, brief, and to the point. Perhaps his terseness stemmed from the same experience that gave his Spanish a French ripple and a Castilian lisp. He gesticulated little, his manner was of Europe, not Cuba. I watched him frankly then and made a point of meeting him, later. He was like a poet's creation with his interracial features — a long head covered with thick black hair like a casque, high cheek bones, delicately modeled nose and lips, but especially for the eyes' awareness. He was alive to every tip of his body and fully conscious of everyone who spoke to him.

In a moment's interchange at meeting I felt even more strongly the man's restrained force; not physical or even nervous force, but the power of an intelligent spirit shining through remarkable eyes. He was Wilfredo Lam, one of Cuba's best-known artists.

Wilfredo Lam was born in 1902 in the little town of Sagua la Grande. His parents were a cultivated Chinese of seventy years and a young *mulata*. With the aid of a scholarship, the boy went abroad to study. In Spain he became deeply incensed by the political scene; in Paris he attracted Picasso, who had been studying African influence in art and who saw in the young Cuban the embodiment of modern expression based on ancient concepts. But the young Cuban was too much an individual to follow any master far; on his return to Cuba in 1941, Lam was mature and free enough to evolve his own manner. Painting the Cuban scene, he has invented a sub-species of his own to express the evils that hamper the human being everywhere. His *Jungle,* which aroused a furor of critical approval in New York, is a conglomeration of human and plant forms; but highly disciplined in form, neither forced nor frantic. So much one could gather from looking at Lam's pictures but one would wish to know the man too.

Later I met him at a cocktail party in a penthouse on the Malecón. He came in with his wife, a very fair Alsatian woman, speaking fluent English and Spanish with a French accent. My first impression of the man was strengthened. He was actively interested in everyone, a part of talk if he did not speak; when he spoke it was without emphasis, easily and well.

We stood before a painting that glowed with jewel colors — ruby, amber, emerald — one of those pictures that seem so lopsided at first glance and which, looked at steadily, gain proportion and stability as their very distortions give truth.

"Yes," he said, reluctant to give an opinion but speaking with complete honesty when he spoke at all, "it is a good painting, expertly done; but it has nothing to say. The painter was experimenting. He is a craftsman in love with his medium. But true art must have intelligence, not just emotion. Human emotions are the same everywhere: love for a woman, a child. The most primitive man can look at a sunset like this and be stirred emotionally by its beauty. But who could reproduce it? No, painting must be infused with intelligence."

Later I stood with his wife, looking out across the seawall at the shining sea, striped with blue and blue green, jeweled by the sunset with amethyst and sapphire. She liked best to talk about her husband.

"He is not as young as he looks," she said. "He is past forty, he has lived and suffered much. . . . I have been married with him now for seven years and he is still the most intelligent and sensitive person I have ever met; I love him more than ever."

She was feeling her way, I knew. She spoke of new paintings now in process at the studio, of how they had left a flaming Europe in 1940 and slowly made their way among the Caribbean islands, studying types, reveling in landscape, making friends. She spoke of an exhibition planned for New York next fall, his second one-man show in the great northern city. "New York is now the center of every art," she said, coming closer to her point. "Every artist must show there; every one should know it. My husband needs now very much to go. He is thirsting for everything he misses in Cuba. Four years without seeing great art!"

She paused, and then it came with a rush.

"Could we go to New York?" she asked. "I have been warned never to risk it. I am afraid. Would we be refused a place in a hotel? Should I have to sit in another part of the theater? Couldn't we eat together, travel together on the train? What do you advise?"

What could one advise? For Wilfredo Lam is a Chinese mulatto — a highly developed representative of the three great races of mankind; a brilliant portent of the future human race. But he looks negroid. Could the great democratic metropolis receive him decently? I answered what I believe to be true: that with the right introductions they could doubtless travel in comfort, live well, and meet the people who would most interest them in New York. They could certainly see all the finest art, hear the best music, and sit in good if not the best theater seats.

Suddenly I realized that I was warning and counseling as one would advise a friend how to comport himself among barbarians, being careful not to run counter to local taboos or to arouse the undisciplined savage just under the surface.

In substance I advised them to go. But warily. I wondered how they would fare. And again I was abashed at how much farther Cubans have traveled than we have along the hard road toward democracy and true sophistication.

## VIII

# DESPEDIDA

HERE IS NO PROPER WAY TO END A BOOK ABOUT A COUNTRY. The country goes on; it seems that the book should too. The only way is to stop short. But in the case of a country as polite and hospitable as Cuba and which one hopes to revisit, it is only courteous to add a few lines of *despedida,* the Spanish farewell.

Revisiting Cuba is highly recommended. A second visit sharpens first impressions and brings out even more clearly the distinctive character of the people, showing how they are going ahead often in spite of themselves. In talking with the returned visitor, most Cubans tend to sound a note of gloom. The government, so they say, is unbelievably stupid, the prey of selfish politicians; graft is rife and no strong leader appears. Business is just as corrupt with the best merchants patronizing the black market in the States. Two alarming menaces are mentioned, depending upon your informant. To some the Catholic Church, tied to Franco's Spain and Cuba's blindest conservatives, is gaining such power that it threatens the very bases of democracy. To others, Labor, dominated by Communism, grows bolder all the time and threatens the sacred institution of private property. Negroes are getting too well educated, outdoing white children in the schools, pushing into the University. On the other hand, illiteracy is widespread and poverty, disease, and hopelessness threaten the very bases of democracy.

Such talk soon takes on the familiar beat of the Litany; it should end: "And there is no health in us." But it does not. Instead the speaker quotes the latest *choteo* to clinch his point, chuckles over his own bout with a crooked politician or the black market. Dr. Fernando Ortiz, a shrewd student of his countrymen, suggests that this is the other face of the *choteo*, which not only guys the pretentious, but excuses the erring. This, he believes, accounts for the Cuban's easy amusement with dishonesty in office. "What of it?" is the prevailing attitude, a pleasant one because tolerance of another's misdemeanors may excuse one's own.

It is refreshing, and just as typical of Cubans, that when you lead your critic away from generalities into his own personal interests, he sounds a different note. Not a note of dreamy hope, but of quick up-and-doing. As individuals, in organizations, in the *patronatos*, in government departments, Cubans are so busy that they have little time for recriminations.

There is general agreement among thoughtful Cubans that their country needs better communications, small scale and diversified agriculture, more education, and better health. Cuba, like all countries, has its quota of citizens who fear expanding democracy, though they do not so word it. The *voluntarios*, of course, left no descendants; they disappeared as completely as collaborationists in Europe, though their unacknowledged spiritual offspring still demand their special privileges, still hesitate to invest their capital in developing their country. But the strongest currents of the country run against them. Cuba is bravely facing a new world, developing her people to take a place in it. They differ only as to what should come first.

Those who put communications first believe that better roads will stimulate the *guajiro* to raise varied crops, that markets will develop, that education will be demanded by changing conditions, and that better health will result from more money in hand and more and better food on the table. Every government has made roads; the splendid highway the length of the island, fine roads to watering places and resorts. So far all-weather country roads to help the small producer have not been made, but they are now in the planning stage and promised soon.

Men in the department of agriculture are fully aware of the need for better roads, but they believe that the *guajiro* must also be taught to use his land, shown what to plant, and how to market it. There is an agricultural agent in every province who dispenses advice and seeds and forms clubs of youngsters like our 4–H Clubs. Even now Cuba takes in over $6,000,000 a year from her cucumbers, melons, tomatoes, and other vegetables, which go mostly to the United States. Producers complain that they often lose because of changing tariffs. They hope to build up a steadier and profitable market for these vegetables with the other Caribbean lands as those people learn to eat better. The *guajiro*, even the cane cutter, has plenty of time for truck gardening. The *zafra* is in before the rains begin; much land now lying fallow could produce enough to feed the ordinary Cuban better than he has ever been fed and to make a good export trade too.

Educators naturally believe that all advance must begin in the schools. They claim over 5,000 schools serving some 500,000 children. They are slowly breaking down the *guajiro's* feeling that learning is of no value, they are working toward a school within walking distance of every child or toward buses to take him there. Most of the schools are primary, though there are many kindergartens and a growing number of secondary schools devoted to preparing the student for agricultural or vocational training. Cuba, working toward democracy, is leaving the old-fashioned gentleman's education in law and the arts, to educate artisans and farmers. All teachers are professionally trained and all receive the same starting salary of $92 monthly. There is no discrimination between the sexes or as to color or race. Critics complain that only one per cent of government expenses goes for education and thirty per cent for the army. "And we don't need an army," said the critic, "we've got a neighbor with a bomb." The administration points to detailed plans for great educational improvement.

To give people the health necessary for education, better work, or wider expansion, the health department co-operates with all the others. Parasitic diseases and malaria, which are Cuba's scourges, can be combatted only by sanitation, and that depends upon people who know enough to clean out the pest holes and put shoes on the children. Nothing in Cuba is more exciting than to hear Doctora Hilda Peraza, director of La Defensa del Niño, Defense of the Child, tell how much is being done through the schools and various *patronatos*. Cuba has also many public hospitals — for soldiers and their families, for maternity cases, for children. There are not enough, never enough, but those in operation are well managed and staffed by fine public-spirited men and women.

All these things are good. An even better augury for the future, perhaps, is the growth of individual responsibility that one sees on every hand. More than forty cities and towns now have associations like the civic unions or *Miles*, organizations of a thousand citizens, which are doing for their own towns and at much less expense many things which the central government used to do. They have not yet begun to go out into the provinces with their better roads, water supplies, and marketing facilities. But they have set their feet in a path from which there is no turning back.

All workers, both government and private, find good response wherever they go. Bootblacks contribute to the civic association. Country children eagerly spade up a patch of land and raise vegetables to improve the family diet. The most forlorn illiterate mother comes back to a clinic where she has been given advice about her baby. She may even try a few vegetables to vary the starch and find them really good to eat. The American Embassy has found its mail weighted with requests for cultural and informative material of any kind. Inquiries come from schools, clubs, and labor unions, of course. They also come from hundreds of individuals who range from the student preparing to go to the United States to the humble citizen who has obviously just learned to write. The man in the Embassy who handles this mail compares Cuba's hunger for learning with the smalltown thirst for culture in our Chautauqua era. Cubans show a similar conviction that it is never too late to learn. Nightschools for adults spring up on every hand, sometimes government sponsored and with paid teachers, often on a volunteer basis. In the ports are Centros Especiales de Inglés, centers specializing in English. Cubans need our language, either to visit us or to trade with us. And an important phase of trade is tourists.

No country on earth that can claim anything to look at or to play with will be fairly counting its post-war assets if it does not figure on tourists. Everything — quicker transportation, easier living, and the knowledge of the world that all young men have acquired — points to an insatiable urge to travel far from where one lives, leaving home and its peculiar charms to visitors from the antipodes.

Cuba was one of the first Latin American paradises to be discovered by tourists. In January 1940 the Tourist Commission welcomed 12,000 tourists to Havana. They dropped off during the war; but in January, 1946, the number was back to 8,000. They all arrived by plane; forty planes a day land in Havana. With steamers back in service and a ferry from Key West to Havana carrying cars as well as passengers, Cuba can count on seeing most of us every year. Unfortunately Havana was first discovered as a handy wet spot during the prohibition era; Cuba as a whole was quite unknown to people seeking liquor, sexy entertainment, and gambling. But the Tourist Commission, with affiliates throughout the island, is beginning to advertise Cuba's remoter beauties and to attract travelers who seek to know a country's real quality, and to enjoy quieter vacations.

Good motor roads lead to most well-known places, planes touch others. For the adventurous, Cuba offers mountains to explore on horseback, the hundred bays to lure a navigator into following Columbus or Cortés, and every sport except those requiring deep snow. Hotels are in the planning stage; meanwhile steamship companies offer tours that allow one to stay aboard at night and visit beautiful or historical spots by day. Cuba has no Indian crafts, but one should never forget that it was Negro slaves who worked the stone that makes Cuba's cities so lovely, carved the hard wood into beams, lintels, and furniture, beat brass and silver into altar and table services, wrought iron lace, and fashioned elegance from tortoise-shell. Cuba has skills that will doubtless be turned to good account. Tourists want to buy. People need small industries.

The visitor who looks about him cannot miss the implications of all this. Cuba has suffered greatly from all the evils that marked the nineteenth century; first colonialism, then imperialism, both political and economic, and blind exploitation and even destruction of natural resources, including the human. Cubans are complaining less of these things; certainly those who see farthest, and are consequently most important for the future, have forgotten their woes and are realistically grappling with their problems. They have many assets, and the greatest of these is in the realm of human relations.

Now that the world is striving for a unity that will consider the good of all people everywhere — and what else can we do and survive? — Cuba stands ready to take her place with dignity in such a union. We recognize, at last, that safety is impossible for any of us without safety for all, regardless of race, color, or creed. For the first time in history there is no evading the dilemma this situation presents. Somehow human beings have got to learn to live together in peace and fairness. Cuba, seeming so powerless among the mighty, is farther than most countries along the road toward a sensible and workable solution of this universal problem. Some Cubans worry lest we think of their country as a "Negro republic." They should instead be proud that they have so well avoided the crippling clumsiness in human dealing and the demeaning hypocrisy that afflicts those who cherish race prejudice. With few exceptions, the Cuban has the grace to retain his right to choose his friends and associates without denying any human right or dignity to another. Cuba again holds a key, this time to a much wider area than the Caribbean.

# INDEX

was born in Albuquerque, New Mexico, in 1888. Her maternal grandfather had reached Santa Fe by wagon train in 1848; her father, from Alabama by way of Virginia, had gone west in stage-coach days. She herself was graduated from the University of New Mexico, after which she took a master's degree at Columbia University. During the First World War she came, as representative of the Red Cross, to know every county and almost every town of her state by intimate experience. Later she started a tourist bureau there, and became known as the first woman dude-wrangler. In 1930 she began to write her first book, *Dancing Gods,* putting into it what she had learned of Indians and their ceremonies in New Mexico and Arizona. Since that date she has traveled extensively, the results of her travels being a series of books whose titles describe her interests: *Fiesta in Mexico, Guatemala, Venezuela, Our Southwest, Our Hawaii, Chile,* and now *Cuba.* When not traveling, she still lives in Albuquerque and takes an active interest in its affairs and those of New Mexico.

This book was set on the Linotype in *Bodoni Book,* printed, and bound by The Plimpton Press, Norwood, Mass. The binding is based on designs by W. A. Dwiggins.